# Voices of the Civil War

# Voices of the Civil War · The Wilderness

*By the Editors of Time-Life Books, Alexandria, Virginia*

# Contents

# THE FIELD OF THE WILDERNESS CAMPAIGN

*The great Battles of the Wilderness and Spotsylvania Court House were fought in the central Virginia counties of Spotsylvania and Orange, south of the Rappahannock River. This artist's rendition shows the cutover woodlands and scattered farm fields that were the scene of fierce fighting in the spring of 1864.*

Rappahannock River

Chancellorsville

Fredericksburg

Piney Branch Church

Massaponax Creek

McCoull
House

Alsop
Farm

Spindle
House

Harrison House

Ny River

Laurel Hill

Black House Bridge

Block
House

Spotsylvania Court House

Snell's
Bridge

# Grant Takes the Reins

Early in March 1864, as the Civil War dragged on toward its fourth year, Ulysses S. Grant was summoned to Washington, promoted to lieutenant general, and given command of all Federal armed forces as general in chief. President Abraham Lincoln, desperate for a decisive victory in the East, was placing the hopes of the Union squarely on the shoulders of this slight and unassuming man from Illinois.

Grant scarcely looked the part of the warrior who could save the Union. One observer who encountered him for the first time in a Washington hotel described him as an "ordinary, scrubby looking man with a slightly seedy look, as if he were out of office on half pay; he had no gait, no station, no manner." A journalist attending a White House reception for the new commander labeled him a "little, scared-looking man."

But as President Lincoln well knew, appearances in this case were deceiving. Grant had waged an impressive campaign in the western theater. In July 1863 he had captured the key Mississippi River bastion of Vicksburg and thereby secured the river for the Union. The following November, he broke the Confederate siege of Chattanooga and sent the Rebel Army of Tennessee retreating into Georgia.

In Grant, Lincoln saw a general who was aggressive and resolute, a relentless fighter who would make up for the army's leadership shortcomings of the past. In the East a succession of promising field commanders—Major Generals George McClellan, John Pope, Ambrose Burnside, Joseph Hooker, and now George Meade—had failed to score the victory that would bring the Confederacy to its knees. Even after Meade turned Robert E. Lee back at Gettysburg, the Union commander had allowed the battered Confederates to slip away across the Potomac into Virginia. And in eight months of maneuvering since then Meade had failed to deliver a telling blow.

Meade half-expected to be fired as commander of the Army of the Potomac for his failure to bring Lee to bay. But when Grant visited Meade's headquarters near Brandy Station on March 10, the two men warmed

*During the long winter break from active campaigning, Federal staff officers of Major General John Sedgwick's VI Corps relax beside their comfortable log hut constructed in the yard of the Welford family mansion, "Farley," near Brandy Station, Virginia.*

to each other. And when Meade proposed to step down, Grant declined the offer. Meade would continue to lead the fight against Lee, but Grant would map the strategy—not from Washington but in the field, with the commanders of his armies.

After his cordial meeting with Meade, Grant took a train west to meet with his friend and most trusted subordinate, Major General William Tecumseh Sherman, whom Grant had named as his replacement in command of the Union's western armies. Poring over maps in a Cincinnati hotel, the two men devised a new, coordinated strategy to cripple the Confederacy and win the war.

At Grant's disposal were some 662,000 soldiers in 22 corps, of whom perhaps 533,000 were combat ready. He intended to put all his armies, east and west, on the move that spring in simultaneous offensives that would exhaust the Rebel forces and destroy the Confederacy's capacity to wage war.

Grant's primary objective was not to win and occupy territory, but to conquer the two powerful Confederate armies in the field: Lee's Army of Northern Virginia and the consolidated western army under the command of General Joseph E. Johnston. Sherman, with his force of 100,000 men based in northwestern Georgia, would attack Johnston while Grant assailed Lee in Virginia.

When Grant returned to the East, he issued succinct orders to Meade: "Lee's army will be your objective point. Wherever Lee goes, there you will go also." Grant also planned to put two other Federal armies into action in Virginia. A force of 26,000 men under Major General Franz Sigel was to advance southward through the Shenandoah Valley, disrupting Lee's food sources and rail communications and menacing his left flank. And a third

Federal army, commanded by Major General Benjamin Butler, would advance across Virginia's Peninsula, between the York and James Rivers, pushing toward Richmond and seeking an opportunity to join Meade's Army of the Potomac in a giant pincers movement.

Grant's enemy, Robert E. Lee, had endured a long season of frustration. The Gettysburg campaign, the previous July, had been costly; Lee had lost more than one-third of the 75,000 Confederates engaged. After the battle, as the Rebel army retreated slowly up the Shenandoah Valley, a rash of desertions further sapped its strength—losses that the South could not replace.

The setbacks continued after the Army of Northern Virginia settled into earthworks on the south bank of the Rapidan River in central Virginia. In early October Lee made an attempt to outflank the Yankee army facing him across the Rapidan, swinging his forces around Cedar Mountain and marching northeast. Meade responded smoothly, however, and succeeded in blocking Lee's thrust just south of Manassas.

Lee pulled back south of the Rapidan again, and his men began building huts for shelter against the oncoming winter. But the fighting was not over for the year. Meade, stung by criticism from Washington, launched his own attack on Thanksgiving Day, crossing the Rapidan downstream of Lee's position in an attempt to roll up the Rebel right flank. Lee got wind of the Federal movement and had time to reposition his forces and dig in along a small stream called Mine Run.

So formidable were the Rebel earthworks that the Federals called off their attack and retreated. But Lee, far from being pleased at having stopped the Yankees again, was again disappointed. He was heard to mutter, "I am too old to command this army; we

should never have permitted these people to get away." Lee had perfected the art of repelling Federal offensives, but he was galled at never being able to achieve more.

The Rebel troops spent a miserable winter along the Rapidan. Shortages were acute. Lee spent the early months of 1864 petitioning Richmond for food, shoes, and clothing for his men. In one dispatch he deplored "the wretched condition of the men, thousands of whom are barefooted, a great number partially shod and nearly all without overcoats, blankets or warm clothing."

But Richmond, in the war's third winter, had little to offer. Commodities were scarce and inflation was rampant in the Confederate capital. Coffee cost $10 a pound, beans $60 a bushel. Citizens were reduced to pooling their resources and holding "starvation parties" in an air of desperate gaiety. There was little extra for Lee's troops.

As spring budded through the Virginia countryside in late March, General Grant commandeered a plain brick house in Culpeper, just down the road from Meade's headquarters at Brandy Station and—as newspapers pointed out—six miles closer to the front.

Grant's reputation had preceded him. In Northern households his initials were said to stand for "Unconditional Surrender." But many in the Army of the Potomac were not impressed. After Grant reviewed the army's V Corps on March 29, an officer wrote of the new commander: "He rode along the line in a slouchy unobservant way, with his coat unbuttoned and setting anything but an example of military bearing to the troops."

Many of the Army of the Potomac's veterans were already in a dark humor, because Meade had disbanded the understrength I and III Corps and redistributed the men among the II and V Corps to streamline the army's organization. But even though angry at the high command, some soldiers seemed disposed to give Grant a chance. One man wrote in his diary: "He cannot be weaker or more inefficient than the generals who have wasted the lives of our comrades during the past three years."

Grant, aware that numbers could be the key to a Union victory, did all within his power to build up the strength of the Army of the Potomac. He instructed the Union's far-flung departmental commanders to pare their garrisons and send the extra men to Virginia. Closer to home, he evicted thousands of troops from their comfortable quarters within Washington's fortifications and transferred them to the field armies. He also converted the excess cavalrymen stationed in and around the nation's capital into infantry. He even reduced the number of wagons allotted to a headquarters, freeing hundreds of teamsters and mule skinners for service in the ranks.

In another move aimed at sustaining the Union's numerical superiority, Grant abolished prisoner exchange. For three years, the Union and the Confederacy had routinely swapped prisoners of war. Now Grant put an end to the practice, knowing that the North could replace such losses from its larger population but the South could not.

Despite such measures, the Union confronted a potentially disastrous manpower problem, for 1864 was the year of discharges. Those men who had enlisted for a term of three years after Fort Sumter would soon be entitled to go home. Nearly half the Union's fighting force was eligible, including many of the crack regiments in the Army of the Potomac.

The Federal government waged an intense campaign to inspire reenlistments. It offered each man who signed up again a

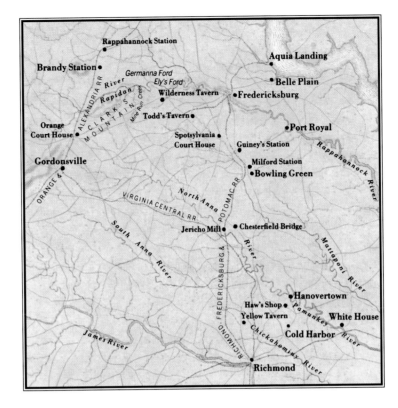

*In early May 1864 Ulysses S. Grant ordered the Army of the Potomac to cross the Rapidan River and begin a march toward the Confederate capital at Richmond for the purpose of confronting and destroying Robert E. Lee's Army of Northern Virginia. The Confederates blocked Grant in a bloody series of engagements in the tangled scrub of the Wilderness, but the Federal commander persisted, forcing Lee to fight again at Spotsylvania Court House.*

30-day furlough and $400 in cash, to be supplemented by bounties from individual states.

Pride and peer pressure also played a role. A man who reenlisted could wear a special stripe indicating that he had been in the fight from the start and was now serving of his own free will. If at least three-fourths of a regiment reenlisted, the regiment would remain intact, retaining its name and colors. Regimental officers, afraid of losing their commands, politicked furiously among their men. In the end, more than half of those eligible for a discharge chose to fight on. And those who reenlisted were joined by fresh volunteers, draftees, and hired substitutes.

Across the river, Robert E. Lee watched the ominous swelling of the Federal camps. Lee had all but despaired of receiving additional provisions. What he concentrated

on most urgently now was getting more men. Lee implored President Jefferson Davis to send him soldiers—a brigade that had been detached for coastal duty in North Carolina, a division posted south of Richmond. "We shall have to glean troops from every quarter," Lee wrote in mid-April, "to oppose the apparent combination of the enemy."

But Davis was unswayed. Long committed for political reasons to defending Southern territory, Davis was loath to leave too much of it unguarded, even if that policy meant spreading troops thinly. He would rearrange the Confederacy's military dispositions only when he believed the situation compelled him to.

At the end of April Lee had only 65,000 men on hand to confront Grant's 120,000, and the Rebel commander realized that time was growing short. Lee knew from intelligence sources that Grant was preparing to attack. On March 26, the wives of Federal officers had begun to leave camp. On April 7, the Yankee army had started sending the sutlers away.

On May 2 Lee mounted his horse, Traveller, and rode with his officers up Clark's Mountain, the highest lookout point available. Hugging the foot of the mountain was the flat, brown Rapidan. Across the river lay the tents of the Union army. Lee doubted that Grant would launch a frontal assault across the river against the formidable Rebel fortifications. More likely, he would move by either flank.

Due east, about 13 miles downstream, was Germanna Ford; a few miles farther was Ely's Ford. South of the fords lay a gray-green expanse called the Wilderness, 12 miles wide and six miles deep. If Grant could pass his troops through this tangle of briars, stunted pines, and dense undergrowth, he would emerge into open country where he could use his superior numbers to smash Lee's army. Moreover, a line of advance that stayed closer to navigable rivers would maximize the flow of supplies available to Grant's army as it pushed southward.

An alternative for the Union commander was a move by his right flank, west of where Lee stood on Clark's Mountain. Going that way, Grant would be following the line of the Orange & Alexandria Railroad, toward Gordonsville. A westward move would give Grant favorable terrain, but it would expose the Union line of communications and uncover Washington itself.

Lee studied the terrain through his telescope and pondered his opponent's options. Then he raised a gloved hand and pointed eastward, to the two fords across the Rapidan. "Grant will cross by one of those fords," he told his officers.

# CHRONOLOGY

1864

| | |
|---|---|
| May 4 | *Army of the Potomac crosses the Rapidan River; Lee moves up to confront Grant* |
| May 5-6 | *Battle of the Wilderness* |
| May 7 | *Cavalry actions around Todd's Tavern; Grant and Lee shift southward* |
| May 8 | *Engagement at Laurel Hill; Confederates win the race to Spotsylvania Court House* |
| May 9-24 | *Sheridan's raid to the James River (May 11: Battle of Yellow Tavern)* |
| May 9 | *Actions along the Po River and the Fredericksburg road* |
| May 10-18 | *Battle of Spotsylvania (main Federal assaults on May 10, 12, and 18)* |
| May 19 | *Engagement at Harris Farm* |
| May 20-21 | *Grant disengages and heads south* |
| May 22 | *Lee beats the Federals to the North Anna River* |
| May 23 | *Actions along the North Anna* |

## ORDER OF BATTLE (to May 12)

### ARMY OF NORTHERN VIRGINIA (Confederate)

Lee 65,000 men

| First Corps Longstreet/R. H. Anderson | Second Corps Ewell | Third Corps Hill/Early | Cavalry Corps Stuart |
|---|---|---|---|
| Kershaw's Division | Early's/Gordon's Division | R. H. Anderson's/Mahone's Division | Hampton's Division |
| *Henagan's Brigade* | *Hays'/Monaghan's Brigade* | *Perrin's Brigade* | *Young's Brigade* |
| *Humphreys' Brigade* | *Johnston's Brigade* | *Mahone's/Weisiger's Brigade* | *Rosser's Brigade* |
| *Wofford's Brigade* | *Pegram's/Hoffman's Brigade* | *Harris' Brigade* | |
| *Bryan's Brigade* | *Gordon's/Evans' Brigade* | *Wright's Brigade* | F. Lee's Division |
| | | *Perry's Brigade* | *Lomax's Brigade* |
| Field's Division | Johnson's Division | | *Wickham's Brigade* |
| *Jenkins'/Bratton's Brigade* | *J. A. Walker's Brigade* | Heth's Division | |
| *G. T. Anderson's Brigade* | *Steuart's Brigade* | *Davis' Brigade* | W. H. F. Lee's Division |
| *Law's/Perry's Brigade* | *Jones'/Witcher's Brigade* | *Kirkland's Brigade* | *Chambliss' Brigade* |
| *Benning's/DuBose's Brigade* | *Stafford's/York's Brigade* | *Cooke's Brigade* | *Gordon's Brigade* |
| | | *H. H. Walker's/Mayo's Brigade* | |
| | Rodes' Division | | |
| | *Daniel's Brigade* | Wilcox's Division | |
| | *Ramseur's Brigade* | *Lane's Brigade* | |
| | *Doles' Brigade* | *McGowan's Brigade* | |
| | *Battle's Brigade* | *Scales' Brigade* | |
| | | *Thomas' Brigade* | |

### ARMY OF THE POTOMAC (Federal)

Meade 120,000 men

| II Corps Hancock | V Corps Warren | VI Corps Sedgwick/Wright | IX Corps Burnside |
|---|---|---|---|
| 1st Division Barlow | 1st Division C. Griffin | 1st Division Wright/Russell | 1st Division Stevenson/Crittenden |
| *Miles' Brigade* | *Ayres' Brigade* | *Brown's Brigade* | *Carruth's/Weld's Brigade* |
| *Smyth's Brigade* | *Sweitzer's Brigade* | *Upton's Brigade* | *Leasure's Brigade* |
| *Frank's/Brown's Brigade* | *Bartlett's Brigade* | *Russell's/Eustis' Brigade* | |
| *Brooke's Brigade* | | *Shaler's/Cross' Brigade* | 2d Division Potter |
| | 2d Division Robinson | | *Bliss'/Curtin's Brigade* |
| 2d Division Gibbon | (disbanded on May 9) | 2d Division Getty/Neill | *S. G. Griffin's Brigade* |
| *Webb's Brigade* | *Leonard's/Lyle's Brigade* | *Wheaton's Brigade* | |
| *Owen's Brigade* | *Baxter's/Coulter's Brigade* | *Grant's Brigade* | 3d Division Willcox |
| *Carroll's Brigade* | *Denison's/Bowerman's Brigade* | *Neill's/Bidwell's Brigade* | *Hartranft's Brigade* |
| | | *Eustis'/Edwards' Brigade* | *Christ's/Humphrey's Brigade* |
| 3d Division Birney | 3d Division Crawford | | |
| *Ward's Brigade* | *McCandless'/Ent's Brigade* | 3d Division Ricketts | 4th Division Ferrero |
| *Hays'/Crocker's Brigade* | *Fisher's Brigade* | *Morris'/Schall's Brigade* | *Sigfried's Brigade* |
| | | *Seymour's/Smith's Brigade* | *Thomas' Brigade* |
| 4th Division Mott | 4th Division Wadsworth/Cutler | | |
| *McAllister's Brigade* | *Cutler's/Robinson's Brigade* | | |
| *Brewster's Brigade* | *Rice's/Fowler's Brigade* | | |
| | *Stone's/Bragg's Brigade* | | |

Cavalry Corps Sheridan

| 1st Division Torbert/Merritt | 2d Division D. M. Gregg | 3d Division Wilson |
|---|---|---|
| *Custer's Brigade* | *Davies' Brigade* | *McIntosh's Brigade* |
| *Devin's Brigade* | *J. I. Gregg's Brigade* | *Chapman's Brigade* |
| *Merritt's/Gibbs' Brigade* | | |

# "I should hate very much to fall now after so many battles have been fought but perhaps it may be as well now as any time."

## CAPTAIN EDWARD H. ARMSTRONG
### 3D NORTH CAROLINA INFANTRY, STEUART'S BRIGADE

*As spring approached and the fields and roads of central Virginia began to dry, soldiers on both sides readied themselves for the coming campaign. Armstrong had left the University of North Carolina in February 1862 to enlist in the 3d and was promoted to captain after the Battle of Antietam. He wrote this letter to his father in New Hanover County, confiding his feelings about the upcoming fight. Armstrong was mortally wounded on May 12 at Spotsylvania Court House.*

Camp 3 N.C. Troops
April 8th 1864
Dear Pa

Yours of the 31st is in hand. Since I last wrote we have been having very bad weather. We had snow again last week and on Monday we had a sleet which lasted until Wednesday morning changing occasionally into rain. We came on Picket Monday and yesterday (Thursday) was the first pretty day we have had. This morning (Friday) we had a sermon from our chaplain the Revd Mr Patterson. We have fine weather today and the woods are drying very fast. I should not be surprised if the Yankees cross in a few days if the weather continues so good. I have been managing to get rations for Mose by allowing him to wash for 21 men and unless they prevent me from doing so I shall keep him. I know of no chance to get the provisions you offered me and shall consequently have to do without them. I get along very well on the small rations allowed us, so far, but I don't know how I shall hold out when we get to marching. . . .

Unless your next letter reaches me very soon our first big fight will be over before it comes. All seem to be of the opinion that the Campaign will open about the 28th. Some think that Gen Grant will cross near our present position—by Morton's Ford but others think he will by Hooker's route via Chancellorsville. All seem to dread the approaching struggle, though they feel hopeful of success. We all feel that though Grant may be driven back beyond the Rapidan yet our lives may be lost in the struggle. Such feelings of course make us wish the day deferred as long as possible. I should hate very much to fall now after so many battles have been fought but perhaps it may be as well now as any time. We cannot live over 40 or 50 years more any way, and we would probably hate to die as much then as now.

I haven't been able yet to draw a cent from the Govt and have consequently had to borrow about $100. If any thing should happen to me you will see that it is paid of course.

Excuse my writting as it is done in soldier style sitting flat on the ground and using my knee as a desk.

Give my love to all
Your Affectionate Son
Edward H. Armstrong

*My 9 × 11 house, roof a wagon cover —*
*Bealton Va. Jan. 20th 1864*
*John M. Bancroft*
*1st Lt Co H. 4th Mich Inf. 2nd Brig.*
*1st Div. 9th A.C. Army of the Potomac.*

*Lieutenant John M. Bancroft of the 4th Michigan made this sketch showing the interior of his 9-by-11-foot winter quarters at Bealton Station, Virginia, in January 1864. The log structure, roofed with a canvas wagon cover, featured a stone fireplace and a plank floor. Faced with the expiration of three-year enlistments during the upcoming summer, many officers, including Bancroft, spent considerable time trying to persuade the veterans in their regiments to reenlist.*

## SERGEANT WILLIAM TODD
### 79TH NEW YORK INFANTRY, CHRIST'S BRIGADE

*Following service in Tennessee, Todd's regiment and the rest of the IX Corps returned to Annapolis, Maryland, in March 1864. Todd, having campaigned for almost three years, shared his comrades' dismay at the prospect of fighting in Virginia again, which seemed certain after a visit from Lieutenant General Ulysses S. Grant.*

On Saturday, the 9th (April), General Burnside rode through our camps, and received a cordial greeting from the Highlanders. We found that all the regiments of the corps who had reënlisted had returned from their vacation, and also that a large number of new regiments had been added, and the work of organizing into brigades and divisions was being rapidly pushed. The old regiments were distributed in such a manner as to leave at least one in each of the new brigades, and we were sorry to see some who had served with us assigned to other divisions.

On the 11th "A" tents were furnished us, and for the first time in about a year we enjoyed the luxury of occupying tents in which we could stand upright. On the 13th Lieutenant-General Grant, accompanied by Generals Burnside and Meade, reviewed the corps. This was the first time that many of us had seen General Grant, and his appearance in connection with General Meade looked very much as though we were to spend the last few days of our term of service with the old Army of the Potomac. We had fondly hoped we would not see Virginia again during the war, but if such was to be our fate we would do our

best and close our term with flying colors. Annapolis had been the rendezvous of several expeditions, and it was generally understood that Burnside was to lead another army somewhere down the Atlantic coast. Burnside himself was ignorant of the destination of his command until a day or two before we started. General Grant kept his own counsel, and not even the President or Secretary of War knew, "up to the last moment," what purpose Grant had in view respecting the Ninth corps. On Thursday, the 21st, we received orders to be ready to move on Saturday. Our "A" tents were at once struck and carted off and our "shelters" put up in their places, and on Friday evening we were warned to be ready to march at seven o'clock on the following morning.

## PRIVATE MARCUS B. TONEY
### 44TH VIRGINIA INFANTRY, JONES' BRIGADE

*A native Virginian, Toney had moved with his family to Nashville, Tennessee, in 1852. At the outbreak of the war he joined a Tennessee regiment and served until after the fall of Chattanooga, transferring to the 44th Virginia in February 1864. Toney was captured at Spotsylvania and spent the rest of the war as a prisoner.*

One day I was on picket duty near the Rapidan River, which is a stream a little larger than Duck River; just opposite us were the Yankee pickets. One of them yelled out: "Hello, Johnny Reb! how is sassafras tea to-day?" I told him the tea was all right, but we had no sugar. I asked him how he was fixed for tobacco, and he said, "Very short"; so we arranged on the morrow to get on duty again. I was to bring a plug of tobacco, and he a shot pouch of coffee. The Federals had their coffee parched, ground, and sugar mixed with it, so on the morrow we made the exchange and I don't think that I ever enjoyed

coffee as much as I did that, having been months without a taste of pure coffee. After making the exchange, he asked me how I would like to have a New York *Herald*. He said that it was not contraband, for it was several weeks old. I told him that I would like very much to see it, as we did not get any papers now, and the ones received were printed on the reverse side of wall paper and were so flimsy that they would not stand the mails. So he tied the *Herald* to a stick and threw it across to me. When I opened it up, I read as follows: "*The Rebel Capital Must be Captured at All Hazards; General Grant Has Been Appointed to the Task.*" He afterwards uttered what became a memorable saying: "I will fight it out on this line if it takes all summer."

## MAJOR HENRY L. ABBOTT
### 20TH MASSACHUSETTS INFANTRY, WEBB'S BRIGADE

*In a letter to his mother, Abbott, a veteran of most of the battles of the Army of the Potomac, spoke with considerable pride of his regiment's precision on the review field. On May 6, 1864, the 22-year-old officer was mortally wounded in the abdomen leading his regiment into action in the Wilderness.*

Near Stevensburg, Virginia, April 15, 1864
My Dear Mamma,
I have received yours of the eleventh. I believe I have answered every one at home since they have written, except you. It is again raining, though we have had an intermission of a couple of days in which we managed to have the greatest review of the corps. Our divis[ion] was reviewed by Hancock; Meade, Sedgwick & a host of inferior lights were over to see it.

We knocked all the other 3 divisions of the corps into pie. This regiment led the column, & with glittering brass, polished belts, shining faces, white gloves & trefoils to contrast, well set up, hair & beard close

# "Uncle Abe was very tender hearted about shooting a deserter, but . . . he was perfectly willing to sacrifice a thousand brave men in a useless fight."

cut & clothes clean, but above all marching in lines absolutely perfect, the rear rank moving snug on the front rank and like Siamese twins, it could not be surpassed. All the generals were in raptures over the regiment & in fact their marching fairly surprised me. But they were on their taps, because I told them before starting that there was one other regiment which could march better than they. They all admired it so much that they had the regiment up to drill at Gibbon's [headquarters] before them all, after the review, when we showed them something none of them had ever seen before, breaking ranks to go through each tactical change, every man on his own hook. . . .

Well, the regiment behaved so finely that it reflected its glory on me as its commander, & Gibbon sent for me into his tent, where [there] were nothing but general officers, & I was presented to Meade & 7 or 8 others, who all spoke in the most flattering manner of the 20th. At the corps review, I believe they are going to trot us out for Grant, who has just got back. I had quite a talk with Meade, who said among other things that Uncle Abe was very tender hearted about shooting a deserter, but that he was perfectly willing to sacrifice a thousand brave men in a useless fight. . . .

I find I have written more about regimental & personal matters than I can hope you will read with interest, & left myself very little room to speak of family matters, on which I had considerable to say. Much obliged for those photographs. Can't you send me one of those earliest with blouse & bunch of cigars. . . . Are you all well yet? Nearly every body here is a little under the weather. . . .

There is a rumour that all letters *from* the army are to be stopped after Monday. Won't Fletch hunt up that brown round hat of mine & send it on by *mail* (the express will be stopped.) I have got to have one for the campaign.

*Accompanied by VI Corps commander John Sedgwick (second from right), Major General George G. Meade (fourth from right), commander of the Army of the Potomac, visits the staff of Captain James M. Robertson's brigade of horse artillery in their camp near Brandy Station. The round of official visits, reviews, and inspections increased as the army prepared for the spring campaign.*

# "Every one, officers & men, felt a keen personal delight in the re-union with our old comrades, & in the command of Gen. Lee."

## BRIGADIER GENERAL E. PORTER ALEXANDER
### COMMANDER, FIRST CORPS ARTILLERY

*In early March 1864 Alexander, a 28-year-old Georgian, was promoted to briga-*
*dier general and given command of three battalions of artillery. Alexander's first*
*appearance in his new position was at a review held shortly after General James*
*Longstreet's corps returned from Tennessee. During the march-past, Alexander*
*marveled at the affection the soldiers felt for their commander, Robert E. Lee.*

On Friday, April 22nd, we marched down to a locality called Me-
chanicsville (though I never saw any ville out there) five miles
S.W. of Gordonsville & encamped in some light open woods. . . .
We were now at last reunited with the beloved old Army of Northern
Virginia, for Gen. Lee's headquarters were only 14 miles away—two

miles beyond Orange C.H., & Ewell's corps & Hill's were in their winter quarters holding the line of the Rapidan. We had been absent seven
months, but it seemed a year & every one, officers & men, felt a keen
personal delight in the re-union with our old comrades, & in the command of Gen. Lee. We all knew of the tremendous preparations of the
enemy, & enormous odds we would have to face, under their new general, who had beaten all our people in the West, & we knew that rivers
of blood must be poured out in the struggle. But we were only anxious
for it to begin. We wanted to see Grant introduced to Gen. Lee & the
Army of Northern Virginia, & to let him have a smell of our powder. For
we knew that we simply could never be driven off a battle field, & that
whatever force Grant brought, his luck would have to accommodate
itself to that fact. . . .

Lee honored our return to his command with a review. It was the first
review held since the Shenandoah Valley after Sharpsburg in '62. Gen.
Lee was not given to parades merely for show. Now, I am sure, he felt &
reciprocated the stirrings of that deep affection in the hearts of his men
inseparable from our return upon the eve of what all felt must be the
struggle to a finish. It was the last review he ever held, and no one who
was present could ever forget the occasion. It took place in a cleared valley, with extensive pastures, in which two divisions of infantry, & our
guns, could be massed.

It is over 40 years but I can see now the large square gate posts, without gate or fence, marking where a broad country road lead out of a tall
oak wood upon an open knoll, in front of the centre of our long grey lines.
And as the well-remembered figure of Lee upon Traveller—at the head
of his staff, rides between the posts, & comes out upon the knoll, my bugle sounds a signal, & my old battalion thunders out a salute, & the general reins up his horse, & bares his good gray head, & looks at us & we

shout & cry & wave our battleflags & look at him again. For sudden as a wind, a wave of sentiment, such as can only come to large crowds in full sympathy, something alike what came a year later at Appomattox, seemed to sweep over the field. Each man seemed to feel the bond which held us all to Lee. There was no speaking, but the effect was that of a military sacrament, in which we pledged anew our lives. Dr. Boggs, a chaplain in Jenkins's brigade, said to Col. Venable, Lee['s] aid, "Does it not make the general proud to see how these men love him?" Venable answered, "Not proud, it awes him." He rode along our lines, close enough to look in our faces. And then we marched in review & went back to our camps.

## LIEUTENANT COLONEL CHARLES H. WEYGANT
### 124TH NEW YORK INFANTRY, WARD'S BRIGADE

*In his 1877 regimental history Weygant recalled the preparations for the campaign and the morale of his men. He was wounded in the right leg at Spotsylvania Court House on May 12 and shot in the chest at Burgess' Mill near Petersburg. Weygant ended the war with a colonel's brevet.*

*Every inch the great captain, General Robert E. Lee posed for this full-length portrait in the Richmond studio of photographer Julian Vannerson in early 1864. So formidable was Lee's reputation on the battlefield that a Federal officer wrote, "he was like a ghost to children . . . something that haunted us so long."*

As the month of April wore away, the fact that our long period of comparative repose was drawing rapidly to a close became daily more and more apparent. On the 12th an order was received directing that all surplus clothing, blankets, and the like, be packed in cracker boxes and sent to Washington, where it was said, they would be stored until needed again, or the owners should call for them. On the 16th all sutlers were ordered to leave the army. On the 21st regimental hospitals were broken up, and the entire ambulance force was kept busy for several days carting the sick, first to division hospitals, and then from the division hospitals to the depot at Culpepper, where they were packed in cars and started for government hospitals in and about Washington. On the 22d there was a grand review by Generals Grant and Meade, accompanied by the corps commanders; and on the 26th the entire army vacated its winter camps and moved out and pitched its canvas and muslin shelters in the open fields—our brigade encamping in a ravine, from which the men had to go half a mile for water, and a mile and a half for wood. To this last movement there was but one accepted interpretation, which was given by the soldiers, one to the other, in such figurative but very plain terms, as "Stand from under"— "Time is up"—"Look out for breakers"—or, "I want to go home."

*Flanked by its regimental band, the 17th Maine poses near Brandy Station just hours before its march to the Rapidan. Within days the 17th, part of General Alexander Hays' brigade of General David B. Birney's division of the II Corps, would suffer massive casualties in the Wilderness—192 men, including its commander, Colonel George W. West. In fighting at Spotsylvania the regiment would lose 69 more men, ending the campaign with only 246 effectives of its original 507. With most of the senior officers killed or wounded, command of the regiment fell to Captain John C. Perry of Company D. By the time the 17th returned home in 1865, it had suffered the most casualties of any Maine regiment in the war.*

# "We were all ready to pick up and go; we were on the eve of battle and everybody was on the 'qui vive' for decisive orders. They quickly came!"

## PRIVATE WILLIAM M. DAME

### 1ST COMPANY, RICHMOND HOWITZERS, FIRST CORPS

*Dame was only 18 years old when he left his studies at the Danville Military Academy to enlist in the famed artillery unit in October 1862. In his memoirs, "From the Rapidan to Richmond," Dame recounted the steps taken by the veteran soldiers of his battery when they received the order to quit their winter camp and prepare once again for battle. Paroled at Appomattox at the war's end, Dame became an Episcopal clergyman, rising to the office of bishop before his death in Baltimore in 1923.*

One bright sunny morning, the 2d of May, 1864, a courier rode into the Howitzer Camp. We had been expecting him, and knew at once that "something was up." The soldier instinct and long experience told us that it was about time for something to turn up. The long winter had worn away; the sun and winds, of March and April, had made the roads firm again. Just across the river lay the great army, which was only waiting for this, to make another desperate push for Richmond, and we were there for the particular purpose of making that push vain.

For some days we had seen great volumes of smoke rising, in various directions, across the river, and heard bands playing, and frequent volleys of firearms, over in the Federal Camp. Everybody knew what all this meant, so we had been looking for that courier.

Soon after we reached the Captain's tent, orders were given to pack up whatever we could not carry on the campaign, and in two hours, a wagon would leave, to take all this stuff to Orange Court House; thence it would be taken to Richmond and kept for us, until next winter.

This was quickly done! The packing was not done in "Saratoga trunks," nor were the things piles of furs and winter luxuries. The "things" consisted of whatever, above absolute necessaries, had been accumulated in winter quarters; a fiddle, a chessboard, a set of quoits, an extra blanket, or shirt, or pair of shoes, that any favored child of Fortune had been able to get hold of during the winter. Everything like this must go. It did not take long to roll all the "extras" into bundles, strap them up and pitch them into the wagon. And in less than two hours after the order was given the wagon was gone, and the men left in campaign "trim."

This meant that each man had, left, one blanket, one small haversack, one change of underclothes, a canteen, cup and plate, of tin, a knife and fork, and the clothes in which he stood. When ready to march, the blanket, rolled lengthwise, the ends brought together and strapped, hung from left shoulder across under right arm, the haversack,—furnished with towel, soap, comb, knife and fork in various pockets, a change of underclothes in one main division, and whatever rations we happened to have, in the other,—hung on the left hip; the canteen, cup and plate, tied together, hung on the right; toothbrush, "at will," stuck in two button holes of jacket, or in haversack; tobacco bag hung to a breast button, pipe in pocket. In this rig,—into which a fellow could get in just two minutes from a state of rest,—the Confederate Soldier considered himself all right, and ready for anything; in this he marched, and in this he fought. Like the terrapin—"all he had he carried on his back"—this *all* weighed about seven or eight pounds.

The extra baggage gone, all of us knew that the end of our stay here was very near, and we were all ready to pick up and go; we were on the eve of battle and everybody was on the "qui vive" for decisive orders. They quickly came!

# Stalemate in the Wilderness

The Army of the Potomac moved out just after midnight on May 4 and was soon crossing the Rapidan River fords east of the Confederate position—precisely where Robert E. Lee had predicted. General Grant then intended to swing his troops westward, march swiftly through the tangled Wilderness, flush the Army of Northern Virginia out of its earthworks, and crush it on open ground.

The Federals moved over newly laid pontoon bridges in two long columns. The V Corps, commanded by Major General Gouverneur K. Warren, crossed at Germanna Ford and headed southwest, followed closely by Major General John Sedgwick's VI Corps. A few miles farther east the II Corps, under Major General Winfield Scott Hancock, crossed at Ely's Ford.

Lee learned of the Federal advance and, ever combative, determined to meet it. Although outnumbered 2 to 1, he had the advantage of

*A line of log breastworks near the Orange Turnpike sheltered Confederate soldiers of Richard Ewell's corps as they confronted the Union advance into the Wilderness. Both armies built similar entrenchments during the bloody two-day clash.*

operating on interior lines and in familiar territory. Lee quickly spurred his veteran corps commanders into action. He sent troops of the Second Corps, under Lieutenant General Richard S. Ewell, marching east on the Orange Turnpike. Farther south on a parallel route Lieutenant General A. P. Hill's Third Corps started out on the Orange Plank road. Still farther south, around Gordonsville, Lieutenant General James Longstreet received orders to set out with his First Corps toward the Catharpin road. All three corps were soon converging on the Wilderness and Grant's unsuspecting troops.

The Federal plan depended on swift movement to clear the Wilderness before engaging the enemy. No one wanted to wage war in that jungle of dense thickets and choked undergrowth. Artillery and cavalry would be mostly useless there, and infantry maneuvers all but impossible. "This, viewed as a battle ground, was simply infernal," a Union officer remarked.

Yet the Federals halted in the Wilderness early on May 4, after General Meade recommended stopping to let the wagon trains catch up. This pause meant that the Federal vanguard would have to spend the night there. The Union command, however, was untroubled over this situation, believing that Lee could not reach the Wilderness before the night of the fifth. To compound that miscalculation, Union cavalry failed to post patrols on the Orange Turnpike that would have detected the approach of the enemy.

That night, after cavalry scouts under Major General Jeb Stuart reported that the Federals were stationary in the Wilderness, Lee decided to attack at first light. Ewell and Hill would pin down Grant's army until Longstreet arrived and slammed into the exposed Yankee flank.

Ever the bold strategist, Lee was counting on the miserable terrain of the Wilderness to help neutralize Grant's superior numbers. But it was a risky scheme—Lee would have to immobilize the Federal army for an entire day with fewer than 40,000 men, gambling that Longstreet would reach the field in time to support the attack.

On the morning of May 5, Yankee pickets on the Orange Turnpike reported the approach of enemy troops, and General Meade, assuming that the unexpected intruders were a small party, ordered General Warren to attack. Warren formed up a division astride the turnpike and moved out.

When Warren's troops attempted to advance across a clearing called Saunders' Field, they were rocked by a cyclone of fire from Ewell's brigades on the far side. The blue-clad line shattered, and the survivors broke across the field, many stumbling toward the refuge of a gully.

In the dense woods south of the road, Warren's men made some initial headway against the Rebels, but a vicious counterattack sent the Yankees reeling. The fighting in the deep woods of the Wilderness soon proved a nightmare for Yankee and Rebel alike—described by one participant as a "weird, uncanny contest, a battle of invisibles with invisibles"—as reinforcements from both armies joined in the fight.

The lines swayed back and forth as each side made fierce but inconclusive charges. Fighting continued sporadically throughout the evening, but neither side could claim the advantage. The stalemate meant, however, that Ewell had perfectly executed his assignment. He had kept two Federal corps—for Sedgwick had pitched into the fray by midafternoon—at bay.

Two miles south of Ewell, A. P. Hill's Confederates lost a race for a crucial crossroads that day. Around noon, Hill's lead elements moving along the Orange Plank road approached the Brock road—about the same time as the Yankee troops of Brigadier General George W. Getty's VI Corps division, dispatched by Meade to defend the intersection.

After a collision and a fierce skirmish, Getty forced Hill back a few hundred yards. General Meade, meanwhile, sent urgent word to Hancock, several miles south of the intersection, to hurry to Getty's assistance with his II Corps troops.

About 4:00 p.m. Getty spearheaded an attack that slammed into Major General Henry Heth's Confederate division a few hundred yards west of the Brock road. Heth's troops, dug in on a low ridge, managed to pin the Federals down, but the battle grew in scope and intensity as the newly arrived Hancock fed his divisions into the fray and Hill committed his reserve.

Darkness put an end to the fighting. Hill's Confederates had stopped the Federals, but they had suffered mightily in the effort. Their lines were now in chaos, fronts askew, regiments and brigades scattered all over the forest.

Lee, headquartered a mile to the rear at Widow Tapp's farm, realized that Hill's situation was perilous. He sent couriers to Longstreet urging him to hurry to the battlefield. Hill's survival would depend on the arrival of Longstreet's troops by dawn to absorb the Federal attack that was sure to come.

At 5:00 a.m. the Union attack erupted, and Longstreet was nowhere to be found. Hill's weakened front collapsed before the enemy onslaught, and the Rebels streamed toward the rear. In desperation, Lee formed artillery above the Plank road at Widow Tapp's farm; the Rebel gunners, loading and firing furiously, managed to momentarily stanch the blue tide. But it was clear that the gunners would soon be overwhelmed.

Suddenly Lee saw Confederate troops approaching from the rear. When he asked who they were, an officer replied: "The Texas Brigade." At the last possible moment, Longstreet had arrived.

"Hurrah for Texas," shouted Lee, waving his hat. "Texans always move them." The Rebel commander was so excited that he rode forward, intending to lead the fresh troops into battle. The Texans gathered around their beloved commander, crying out, "Go back, General Lee, go back!" He finally moved to the rear only at the insistence of Longstreet.

Hancock's Federals had become disorganized during their advance, and when Longstreet's fresh troops charged into them, the Yankees fell back in confusion. Within an hour, the Rebels had regained several hundred yards of the Plank road. Lee's chief engineer, in the meantime, had explored an unfinished railroad bed and discovered that it passed by Hancock's left flank. Lee sent several brigades down the rail bed; they attacked the unsuspecting Yankee troops and rolled up Hancock's line.

Then disaster struck: Around noon Longstreet was riding down the Plank road with his staff and other officers in the wake of his advancing forces. Suddenly rifle fire opened up from the woods on the right. A brigade of Virginians had mistaken Longstreet's party for enemy troops.

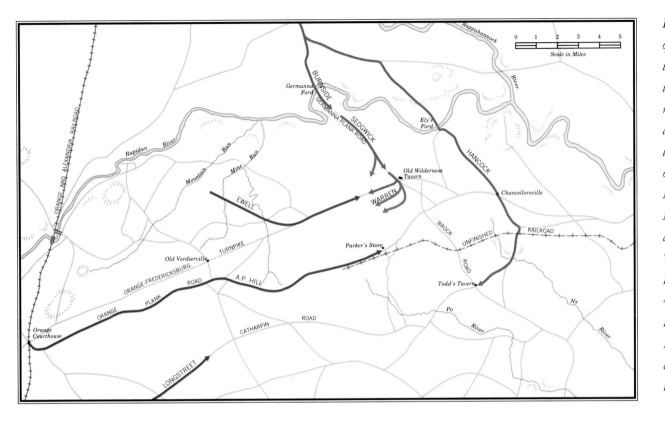

*In the early-morning hours of May 4, Meade's Army of the Potomac began crossing the Rapidan River at Germanna and Ely's Fords in an attempt to envelop Lee's left flank and force him out of his entrenchments along Mine Run. To counter Meade, Lee shifted Ewell's corps east along the Orange Turnpike and ordered A. P. Hill's corps to move eastward from Orange Court House over the Orange Plank road. Longstreet's corps was to follow later on the Catharpin road.*

Before the firing stopped, a courier and a staff captain lay dead. A promising and popular young officer, Brigadier General Micah Jenkins of South Carolina, was mortally wounded by a bullet in the brain. And Longstreet suffered a severe wound in the throat. Almost exactly a year earlier in the same woods and under similar circumstances, Stonewall Jackson had fallen. But unlike Jackson, Lee's "Old War Horse" would recover.

Longstreet's wounding seemed to drain the initiative from the Rebel attack, however, and the Federals were now retiring behind fortified positions. For the next several hours Lee struggled to reorganize his troops. At 5:00 he attacked Hancock's men in their earthworks along the Brock road but was eventually repulsed.

Just about the time these assaults were losing their momentum Ewell was preparing to launch an attack of his own north of the turnpike. Early that morning Brigadier General John B. Gordon, whose Georgians manned the Confederate far left, had scouted the area and discovered that the enemy flank opposite his position was "in the air"—unprotected. Gordon had pleaded with his division commander, Major General Jubal A. Early, to let him make an attack, but Early had deemed it too risky. Finally, near dusk, Ewell overruled Early and gave his consent.

Gordon's assault routed two Federal brigades, and confusion soon enveloped the Federal headquarters. A distressed officer rode up to Grant and advised a retreat, which Grant angrily rejected.

As it happened, darkness and Federal reinforcements put an end to Gordon's attack.

The darkness, however, was anything but complete. The woods along the Plank road had caught fire, and in the hellish light men who were too severely wounded to move were screaming as the flames engulfed them. The Battle of the Wilderness was over.

In two days of fighting, Lee's forces had sustained at least 7,500 casualties. But as badly as the Confederate army had suffered, the Union toll was far worse. The action had cost Grant's Army of the Potomac 17,666 men killed, wounded, or captured.

The Union commander, however, was undeterred. He was sticking with what he had stated the previous night to a correspondent who was headed to Washington. "If you see the president," Grant said, "tell him, from me, that whatever happens, there will be no turning back."

# LIEUTENANT BENJAMIN L. WYNN
## CONFEDERATE SIGNAL CORPS

*Wynn initially served in the 21st Mississippi Infantry, but in November 1862 his captain recommended him for transfer to the Signal Corps in recognition of Wynn's "steady and temperate habits." In early May 1864, while on duty at the signal station on Clark's Mountain—a promontory south of the Rapidan that the Rebels used as a lookout post throughout the war—Wynn became one of the first Confederates to observe Grant's opening movements.*

During the latter part of April, 1864, President Davis, accompanied by Col. Randolph Tucker and General Lee (the latter's headquarters were near Orange C. H.), rode up to Clark's Mountain, where I as sergeant had charge of the signal station. This promontory overlooked much of the country lying between the Rapidan and the Rappahannock Rivers, where Grant's army was encamped.

Having pointed out to General Lee the various encampments of the enemy and the changes they had recently made, General Lee said to Mr. Davis: "I think those people over there are going to make a move soon." Then turning to me, he said: "Sergeant, do you keep a guard on watch at night?" I replied that I did not. "Well," said he, "you must put one on." . . .

About midnight of the 3d the guard called me to the glass. Occasionally I could catch glimpses of troops as they passed between me and their camp fires, but could not make out in which direction they were moving. I signaled to General Lee at once what I saw. He asked me if I could make out whether they were coming toward Germania Ford or Liberty Mills. I replied that I could not. His next message was that I make a report to him as early in the morning as possible.

An hour or so after this the following from General Lee passed over the line or station: "General Ewell, have your command ready to move by daylight."

*From Pony Mountain, southeast of Culpeper, Union Signal Corps officers keep an eye on enemy encampments south of the Rapidan River. Illustrator Edwin Forbes drew this view, labeling several points of interest: 1) The Rebel signal station on Clark's Mountain; 2) the Confederate camps, where, Forbes wrote, "men could be seen and all movements noted" with the use of a telescope; 3) the Rapidan; and 4) the Wilderness.*

Longstreet's Division was encamped near Orange C. H. Ewell's was some four or five miles northeast of Clark's Mountain along the Rapidan, and his headquarters were at the Morton house. On the morning of the 4th I signaled General Lee that the enemy was moving down the river, that clouds of dust were rising from all the roads leading southeast and toward Fredericksburg, and that Germania Ford seemed to be their objective point.

## CHAPLAIN HENRY R. PYNE
### 1ST NEW JERSEY CAVALRY, DAVIES' BRIGADE

*On May 4 Brigadier General David Gregg's cavalry division, which included Pyne's regiment, trekked to Ely's Ford with pontoons and canvas boats. The Federals scattered the small Rebel force guarding the ford and got to work. By 6:00 a.m. infantrymen of Major General Winfield Scott Hancock's II Corps were already marching across the bridge.*

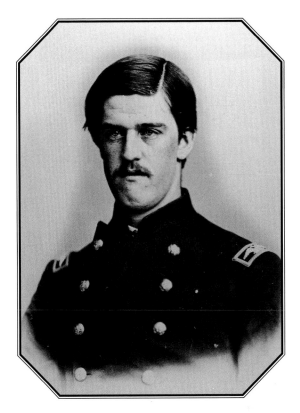

*Major Hugh Janeway, shown after his promotion to colonel in October 1864, directed the 1st New Jersey Cavalry's seizure of Ely's Ford on May 4. Janeway had been wounded in December 1861 and in July 1864. He returned to duty in March 1865 and was killed on April 5—just four days before Lee surrendered at Appomattox.*

At two o'clock on the morning of the fourth of May, after a night of marching and open bivouac, the regiment, leading the column of the division, approached Ely's Ford on the Rapidan. The night was dark, and the air in the hollow near the river very cold and chilly, as Major Janeway, with the advance guard, cautiously drew near the bank without alarming the rebel vidette. Under the guidance of one of our most enterprising scouts, who had just returned from a reconnoissance, Lieutenant Craig, with the men of Company H., stole quietly down to an unguarded point on the river, and waded through the almost freezing water, the men carrying their arms and ammunition above their heads. Creeping up the hill-side, they plunged into the woods, aiming for the rear of the rebel reserve picket fire. In five minutes more the whole party would have been in their power, when, the head of the Second Corps of infantry having closed upon the rear of our

division, General Gregg was compelled to move forward without delay. It was more important to get promptly across the river than to surprise and capture a small party of the enemy. A shot from the vidette on the river gave the alarm, which was at once succeeded by a hurried flight on the part of the enemy, who dashed back towards Fredericksburg, closely followed by Captain Brooks with Company K. Half a dozen men and horses were overtaken, but the rest escaped.

Past the old Chancellorville ground, with its low breastworks and bloody memories, the column proceeded along the plank road towards Fredericksburg, encountering nothing but a few cavalry, who, from a respectful distance, observed its motions. Then, after manœuvering to cover the advance of the Second Corps into the Wilderness, the division picketed for the night the roads leading to Fredericksburg and Todd's Tavern.

*All day long on May 4 seemingly endless columns of troops of the Army of the Potomac crossed the Rapidan heading south toward the scrub forests of the Wilderness. In this drawing by Alfred Waud soldiers of Hancock's corps cross the river on a pontoon bridge at Ely's Ford, heading toward Chancellorsville, their first day's objective. In the foreground, a supply wagon splashes across the ford, while cavalrymen patrol the river's banks.*

## LIEUTENANT MCHENRY HOWARD

STAFF, BRIGADIER GENERAL
GEORGE H. STEUART

*To counter Grant's advance, Steu-
art's brigade and the rest of Lieutenant General Richard S. Ewell's
corps hustled east on the Orange
Turnpike and encamped on May 4
only two miles from the closest Yankee bivouacs. The next day Lee's
rapid deployment would give Grant
his first surprise of the campaign.*

On the morning of the next day (May 3d) a cloud of dust was seen floating over the woods in front and stretching in a long line parallel with and down the river, and at one exposed point the white covers of wagons and glistening muskets were visible, passing in endless succession, and there was no doubt the Union army was moving to cross one or more of the fords below, Germanna we rightly supposed. We signaled back to our principal observatory on Clark's Mountain, but were answered that they had a full view of the movement from that elevated point.

Clark's Mountain . . . is a short distance in rear of the Rapidan, and commands a far and wide view of all the country in front. General Lee had his headquarters near it. All day long we watched the ominous cloud of dust hanging in the air and stream of wagons and glittering gun metal and knew that a few hours would find the two armies contending once more on a Wilderness battle ground. That evening one or two deserters came over and gave confirmation, if any were needed, that Grant had put his whole army in motion.

The next morning, May 4, showed the same line of march and canopy of dust marking its course down the river. Two more deserters, one a Belgian speaking French only, came across at Morton's Ford, closely pursued and fired on to the edge of the water. In the afternoon we received orders to march, the quartermasters and men in camp being directed to pack up at winter quarters and move down the Orange and Fredericksburg Plank Road to join us. About 3 p.m. we moved out under cover of the woods and took a cross road in a [northerly] direction towards Wilderness, the 37th Virginia being left on the picket line with instructions to withdraw after night and overtake us. At dark we struck the Orange and Fredericksburg [Turnpike], which at this point is a mile or more north of the Plank Road, and went into bivouac.

## SERGEANT AUSTIN C. STEARNS

13TH MASSACHUSETTS
INFANTRY, LEONARD'S
BRIGADE

*Stearns and his comrades were not
long into their march toward the
Wilderness when they set about light-
ening their load. The roads were so
littered with items that Grant marveled: "I saw . . . wagon-loads of
new blankets and overcoats, thrown
away by the troops . . . an improvi-
dence I had never witnessed before."*

Wednesday the 4th "Fair, a pleasant day, routed up at I A.M. to strike tents and prepare for a march. Marched at half past two towards Culpepper, turned off and went to Stevensburg. From there to Germania Ford, crossed and went to Wilderness Tavern. Bivouacked at 4 P.M. Marched about 24 miles. One of our hardest marches." My recollections of this day are very fresh. The day was warm, and we were heavily loaded when we started, but as the day advanced the boys commenced to throw away their things. Over coats and blankets went, knapsacks were over hauled, and extra stockings, drawers, old letters that the boys had treasured up, in fact any thing and every thing that could lighten the load. At Stevensburg we came upon the camps of the other Corps, and such sights of clothing as were there, and all the rest of the way. I commenced by throwing away drawers, stockings, then tearing my blanket in two, cutting off the cape of my over coat, knowing from past experience that I should need them in a few days. Some of the boys threw away every thing but their rations.

*Photographer Timothy O'Sullivan took this exceptional view from the south bank of the Rapidan on May 4, capturing a portion of Grant's forces moving to the Wilderness over one of two pontoon bridges at Germanna Ford. Both the V and VI Corps crossed here, while the II Corps was crossing downstream at Ely's Ford. The V Corps was the first to reach Germanna Ford and was fully across the river by about 1:00 p.m. The late-afternoon shadows in this image suggest that the troops pictured here belonged to the rear elements of the VI Corps. An infantry regiment can be seen pounding across the bridge, while a caravan of supply wagons waits its turn. The idle pontoon bridge just downstream was dismantled at approximately 6:00 p.m. on the 4th, while the other bridge remained and was used by Major General Ambrose Burnside's IX Corps on May 5.*

## CAPTAIN PORTER FARLEY

140TH NEW YORK
INFANTRY, AYRES' BRIGADE

*The 140th was among the dozens of V Corps regiments that halted on May 4 along the Orange Turnpike near the Wilderness Tavern. Farley and his messmates sat around their campfire wondering what the morrow would bring. Their expectation of a hard fight was realized early the next afternoon when they came up against Ewell's Confederates camped just three miles down the pike.*

The weather on the 4th of May was fine. In the early morning when we reached the bank of the river a beautiful and interesting scene lay before us. Opposite us was a country which had been long settled by a sparse farming population whose former occupancy was now indicated by the great open fields now worn out by long and shiftless cultivation. It was a pleasant landscape, fields dotted with trees, and all fresh and green in the opening spring time. The open spaces on the farther bank and the roads leading off to the east from the ford were filled with the troops which had preceded us. . . . Altogether it was a sight, the equal of which one sees not often in a lifetime.

We filed across the bridge and with more or less delay marched southeasterly. . . . Our division turned to the right into the pike and proceeded about half a mile, bivouacing about the middle of the afternoon on a somewhat elevated ridge about a mile from the tavern. Our march had been exceedingly slow, owing to frequent halts, so that it was well along in the afternoon when we made our final camping place.

. . . The situation that night was portentous. We well knew that the

*This Alfred Waud view follows the path of the Germanna Plank road as it meanders past the buildings of the Spotswood plantation, seen on the rise to the right. Both the V and VI Corps trudged down this road on their way from Germanna Ford into the Wilderness—visible in the distant background—and elements of the VI Corps bivouacked here on May 4. From the vicinity of the Spotswood home, General Horatio Wright's division of the VI Corps entered into the fighting on May 5, rushing down the Spotswood road to reinforce the V Corps' threatened right flank.*

enemy could not be far distant and that the aggressive movement now begun was certain soon to lead to a collision, which all believed would be the most desperate in the history of the army. Two special considerations operated to impress upon the troops this feeling of the serious nature of the work at hand. One was the realization that the whole country and we ourselves were tired of the indecisive results which had thus far attended the operations of the Army of the Potomac; the other was the known fact that General Grant was with us in the field and practically directing the operations. His reputation for tenacity had even then become so well established that it boded to the army the trial of all its endurance and the certainty of terrible losses. We knew too well the temper and the spirit of the army pitted against us, to hope for any success except as heavily paid for by blood and suffering.

## COLONEL ST. CLAIR A. MULHOLLAND

116TH PENNSYLVANIA INFANTRY, SMYTH'S BRIGADE

*This excerpt from Mulholland's 1899 memoirs offers a sentimental view of the scene around Chancellorsville; most of the Yankees there found the place anything but comforting. On May 3, 1863, Mulholland's regiment, reduced to battalion strength after Antietam and Fredericksburg, had formed part of the Federal defensive perimeter around the Chancellorsville clearing.*

*Before the start of the march to the Wilderness, General Meade incorporated the design of the eagle badges that were worn by his aides into this rather grandiose banner for use as his headquarters flag. General Grant first saw it just after crossing the Rapidan on the morning of May 4. According to Alfred Waud, Grant gazed upon the standard flying in front of Meade's headquarters tent and, in a rare display of wit, remarked, "What's this—Is Imperial Caesar anywhere about here?"*

At noon on May 4th, halted on the open ground around the ruins of the Chancellorsville House where the Second Corps was massed. Pickets were thrown out, a battery placed in position covering the plank road that led to Fredericksburg, arms stacked, the roll called in each company. . . .

And then another quiet evening of peace and rest. Hancock, surrounded by his staff, lay under the apple trees in the orchard, on the ground where Leppine's guns stood firing just a year before that very day. The general, tapping his boot with his whip, chatted of the year gone by. Memories, reminiscences, jokes and merry laughter passed the hours away. A gay and happy group it was, full of life, hope and sans souci, as though it were an excursion of pleasure, instead of the most awful and fierce campaign of the war on which they were starting. The Chancellorsville House still lay a mass of unsightly ruins. The debris of the battery still remained scattered over the ground. Broken wheels, shattered poles, pieces of ammunition chests, bursted shells, bones of horses, remnants of blankets, canteens, bits of leather, rotting harness,

*Most of Hancock's troops ended their 20-plus-mile march of May 4 around the burned-out remains of the Chancellor house, at the intersection of the Ely's Ford road and the turnpike. The house's charred walls conjured unpleasant memories among the Yankees who had suffered through the Battle of Chancellorsville. "Is Grant to repeat [Hooker's] stupendous folly?" one apprehensive veteran mused in his journal.*

etc., mingled in dire confusion. In the evening, after resting, when the rations had been distributed, officers and men strolled around examining the ground on which they had been fighting that day a year ago. The apple trees and lilies bloomed again. Pink and white roses struggled to life in the trampled garden of the old homestead and the fragrance of May filled the air. The old members of the regiment took great pleasure in imparting to the new men the particulars of the battle and showing them how the battery was saved. The boys fresh from home, who had not yet heard the sound of a hostile gun were full of curiosity, and took great interest in everything. The evidence of the fight was so strongly visible that the scene impressed them deeply. The burnt and crumbling buildings, trees torn and rent, the ground strewn with debris, told in mute but terribly strong language of the carnage and storm. The shallow graves of the men of the brigade were discovered and, much to the delight of men, were found overgrown with wild flowers and forget-me-nots.

## PRIVATE FRANK WILKESON
### 11TH BATTERY, NEW YORK LIGHT ARTILLERY

*Wilkeson, an 18-year-old farmer from Buffalo, was one of Meade's many greenhorns, having enlisted on March 29, 1864. He quickly found campaigning with the Army of the Potomac's hard-bitten veterans to be a sobering experience. Before his battery broke camp for the Rapidan, he wrote, he was warned, "Get hold of food, and hang on to it; you will need it. . . . Cut haversacks from dead men. Steal them . . . if you can. Let your aim be to secure food and food and still more food."*

We walked to and fro over the old battle-field, looking at bullet-scarred and canister-riven trees. The men who had fallen in that fierce fight had apparently been buried where they fell, and buried hastily. Many polished skulls lay on the ground. Leg bones, arm bones, and ribs could be found without trouble. Toes of shoes, and bits of faded, weather-worn uniforms, and occasionally a grinning, bony,

# "The dead were all around us. Their eyeless skulls seemed to stare steadily at us."

fleshless face peered through the low mound that had been hastily thrown over these brave warriors. As we wandered to and fro over the battle-ground, looking at the gleaming skulls and whitish bones, and examining the exposed clothing of the dead to see if they had been Union or Confederate soldiers, many infantrymen joined us. It grew dark, and we built a fire at which to light our pipes close to where we thought Jackson's men had formed for the charge, as the graves were thickest there, and then we talked of the battle of the preceding year. We sat on long, low mounds. The dead were all around us. Their eyeless skulls seemed to stare steadily at us. The smoke drifted to and fro among us. The trees swayed and sighed gently in the soft wind. One veteran told the story of the burning of some of the Union soldiers who were wounded during Hooker's fight around the Wilderness, as they lay helpless in the woods. It was a ghastly and awe-inspiring tale as he vividly told it to us as we sat among the dead. This man finished his story by saying shudderingly:

"This region," indicating the woods beyond us with a wave of his arm, "is an awful place to fight in. The utmost extent of vision is about one hundred yards. Artillery cannot be used effectively. The wounded are liable to be burned to death. I am willing to take my chances of getting killed, but I dread to have a leg broken and then to be burned slowly; and these woods will surely be burned if we fight here. I hope we will get through this chapparal without fighting," and he took off his cap and meditatively rubbed the dust off of the red clover leaf which indicated the division and corps he belonged to. As we sat silently smoking and listening to the story, an infantry soldier who had, unobserved by us, been prying into the shallow grave he sat on with his bayonet, suddenly rolled a skull on the ground before us, and said in a deep, low voice: "That is what you are all coming to, and some of you will start toward it to-morrow." It was growing late, and this uncanny remark broke up the group, most of the men going to their regimental camps. A few of us still sat by the dying embers and smoked. As we talked we heard picket-firing, not brisk, but at short intervals the faint report of a rifle.

*The talk of death bandied about the campfires of both armies in the lonely expanses of the Wilderness during the evening of May 4 would come true for many soldiers. The bones above were photographed near the Orange Plank road just after the war, when burial parties returned to gather up and inter the remains of those who were left where they fell during the May clashes of both 1863 and 1864.*

# The Wilderness—May 5

As he often did when ranged against superior numbers, Robert E. Lee on the morning of May 5 chose audacity. Rather than wait for Grant to filter his way through the Wilderness, Lee pushed forward Ewell's Second Corps along the Orange Turnpike and two divisions from Lieutenant General Ambrose P. Hill's Third Corps along the Orange Plank road. They were to keep Grant occupied while Longstreet marched his First Corps from its camp near Gordonsville and swung north into Grant's left flank.

But because Longstreet could not be in position to attack before morning on May 6, Ewell's and Hill's Confederates, outnumbered by at least 3 to 1, would have to stall Grant's Federals for more than a day. If Grant discovered that Lee had divided his force, he could concentrate superior numbers against either prong of the Confederate army and destroy it.

Shortly after sunup, Grant began arraying his army to face Lee. Hancock's II Corps marched from Chancellorsville toward Todd's Tavern; Major General Gouverner K. Warren's V Corps started from Wilderness Tavern along a wagon trail leading to Parker's Store; Sedgwick's VI Corps shuffled south along the Germanna Plank road to fill the position vacated by Warren; and Burnside's IX Corps remained north of the Rapidan River to guard the army's rear. Grant hoped by noon to sweep west and flank Lee out of his last reported positions near Mine Run.

By the time most of Warren's corps was on the march toward the Orange Plank road, Ewell's Confederates had appeared on the Orange Turnpike and begun building earthworks across the western edge of a clearing called Saunders' Field, which straddled the road. Meade, confi-dent that any large Rebel formations were still at least a day away, mistook Ewell's troops for a reconnaissance force and directed Warren to attack them. Grant was also feeling bellicose and encouraged Meade to pitch into the Confederates "without giving time for disposition."

Notwithstanding his superiors' zeal for an immediate attack, Warren struggled for several hours to form a line. As Lee had foreseen, difficult terrain frustrated the Yankee commander's efforts. Grant and Meade became increasingly insistent, but still Warren hesitated to turn his troops loose. His right flank ended on the northern edge of Saunders' Field, and yet Ewell's line overlapped it, revealing that Warren faced far more troops than his superiors maintained. Exasperated by Warren's deliberate pace, Meade issued him peremptory orders to attack.

At 1:00 p.m. Warren moved against Ewell's line. Three brigades of Brigadier General Charles Griffin's division marched across Saunders' Field into a blaze of Confederate musketry. Brigadier General Romeyn Ayres' command north of the turnpike was repelled, but Brigadier General Joseph Bartlett's brigade punched a hole in the Rebel line and advanced a quarter of a mile before being driven back. Brigadier General James Wadsworth's division also sent the Rebels into retreat, but his units became isolated in the dense woods and were repulsed piecemeal. A countercharge by a brigade under Brigadier General John Gordon cleared the Federals from in front of Ewell's right. Within an hour, Warren's attack was a shambles.

At 3:00 p.m. Brigadier General Horatio Wright's division of Sedgwick's corps, after fight-ing through a Rebel cavalry screen, attacked Ew-ell's line north of Saunders' Field. Again Ewell exploited the terrain and repulsed the Yankees.

A second battle front developed on the Orange Plank road, where Hill's Confederate Third Corps advanced in tandem with Ewell's men to the north. To halt Hill's progress, Meade, now fully aware that much of Lee's army was in front of him, sent three VI Corps brigades under Brigadier General George W. Getty to the intersection of the Orange Plank road and the Brock road. Getty arrived just in time to stall Hill's advance and hold on to the key crossroads until Hancock's lead elements could come up from the south to reinforce the position.

At 4:30 Getty and two of Hancock's divisions attacked Henry Heth's division of Hill's corps. As pressure mounted against Heth, Hill fed in his other available division, under Major General Cadmus Wilcox, and Hancock countered with the rest of his corps. Near dark, Meade pulled four V Corps brigades from the turnpike front, placed them under Wadsworth, and hurled them toward Hill's left flank. A ferocious coun-terattack stymied Wasdsworth, however, and darkness finally ended the first day's combat.

Thus far, Lee's plan had succeeded. Ewell and Hill had deadlocked Grant's force. It remained to be seen, however, whether Longstreet could arrive in time to execute his part of the scheme.

*The campaign opened on May 5 along two fronts. Just after daylight Ewell's Confederates emerged on the Orange Turnpike, where Warren and Sedgwick could not dislodge them. Hill's Rebels pressed east on the Orange Plank road, opposed by Getty and Hancock. Fighting raged on both fronts until nightfall.*

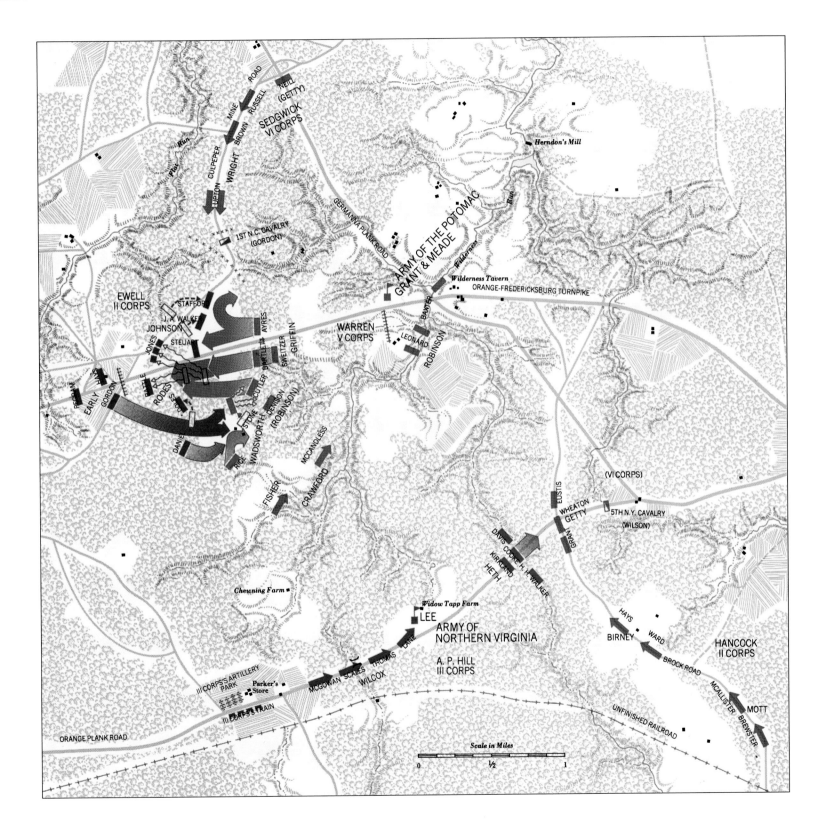

MINE ROAD

BROWN

RUSSELL ROAD

UPTON

CULPEPER

WRIGHT

NEILL (GETTY)

SEDGWICK
VI CORPS

Flat Run

1ST N.C. CAVALRY (GORDON)

GERMANNA PLANK ROAD

Herndon's Mill

ARMY OF THE POTOMAC
GRANT & MEADE

Wilderness Run

Wilderness Tavern

EWELL
II CORPS

STAFFORD

J. A. WALKER

JOHNSON

STEUART

JONES

PEGRAM

EARLY

GORDON

BATTLE

RODES

DANIEL

STONE

CUTLER

BARTLETT

SWEITZER

AYRES

GRIFFIN

BAXTER

LEONARD

ROBINSON

WARREN
V CORPS

ORANGE-FREDERICKSBURG TURNPIKE

DENISON (ROBINSON)

5TH WADSWORTH

RICE

FISHER

CRAWFORD

McCANDLESS

(VI CORPS)

EUSTIS

WHEATON

GETTY

GRANT

5TH N.Y. CAVALRY (WILSON)

DAVIS COOKE H. H. WALKER

KIRKLAND

HETH

Chewning Farm

Widow Tapp Farm

LEE

ARMY OF
NORTHERN VIRGINIA

A. P. HILL
III CORPS

LANE

THOMAS

SCALES

McGOWAN

WILCOX

III CORPS'S ARTILLERY PARK

Parker's Store

III CORPS'S TRAIN

ORANGE PLANK ROAD

UNFINISHED RAILROAD

HAYS

BIRNEY

WARD

BROCK ROAD

HANCOCK
II CORPS

McALLISTER

BREWSTER

MOTT

Scale in Miles

0          ½          1

yet alive. Then another dead, with an ugly bullet hole in his chest, then one wounded in the chest, then one shot in the forehead & about breathing his last; then one shot in the mouth, the ball passing out at the back of his neck, then one poor fellow who had been severely wounded & burnt to death by the burning of the woods. All these & various others were on or near the road: but the fighting extended for some distance on both sides of the road, & we did not see many who groaned in agony or met terrible death all alone in the dense woods. The yankees were all cavalry, sent up the road to delay our advance as much as possible.

## CAPTAIN BENJAMIN W. JUSTICE
### STAFF, BRIGADIER GENERAL WILLIAM A. KIRKLAND

*On May 5 Justice, a 34-year-old farmer from Wake County, North Carolina, who was serving as brigade commissary officer, rode forward along the Orange Plank road with Kirkland's brigade, the advance guard of the Confederate Third Corps. In a letter home he recounted the grim aftermath of the clash at a rural crossroads known as Parker's Store between Yankee soldiers of Lieutenant Colonel John Hammond's 5th New York Cavalry and the 47th North Carolina Infantry.*

Next morning soon after daylight the troops moved forward again, & soon came upon the yankee cavalry on the plank road. Our skirmishers were thrown out, & the 47th Reg'm't of our Brigade was deployed to strengthen the skirmish line. A running fight at once commenced & was kept up for several hours & over 5 or 6 miles of the road. I was with the train in the rear, & when we came on that part of the road, I casually walked out to a little deserted house near the road. Here I found Knox Hunter slightly scratched or bruised on the right shoulder, & another soldier of the 47th shot in the leg. Passing on down the road we soon came to a dead yankee in the road lying flat on his back, his arms thrown out, his head turned back, showing a grey beard, his boots & pants taken off, his features & limbs rigid in death. Soon we came to another, shot through both legs below the knee, &

## PRIVATE JAMES L. McCOWN
### 5TH VIRGINIA INFANTRY, J. A. WALKER'S BRIGADE

*McCown faced his first battle when he and his comrades pressed eastward from their lines behind Mine Run to block the Federal advance through the Wilderness. The 18-year-old from Lexington, Virginia, carefully recorded the events of that morning in his diary. Just over a week later McCown was captured at Spotsylvania and sent to Fort Delaware, where he remained a prisoner for the rest of the war. He returned home to Lexington and began a career as a photographer. He died in 1922.*

Camp in wilderness. At the song of the birds all is life again. Tired limbs are rested. Our rations of corn bread and bacon are soon dispatched. We are awaiting orders to march. Soon they come and slowly we go. Now are halted, then on again. The band is ordered to the rear, this indicates business. After forming in line there is an awful silence. He that a short while ago jested is now grave. Many are seen during this quiet to take out their Bibles and read and silently ask God to spare and shield them in the hour of battle. How awful is this inaction, silence, home flashes up the dear ones and thousands of thoughts crowd in on me. In this state of mind our Captain approaches with a sad but determined face. We are all four together, Charlton, Rhodes, Bumpass and myself. His words are kind but brave, tells us we will, in short time, be engaged in battle and as none having been under fire, he wanted us to stand up like men and do our duty. The skirmish line is advanced. Now we are ordered to fall down. Oh what moments of silence. All nature seems to expect some awful shock.

## LIEUTENANT SARTELL PRENTICE
### 12TH U.S. INFANTRY, AYRES' BRIGADE

*A resident of New York, Prentice obtained a commission in the Regular Army in May 1861. As his regiment marched toward Saunders' Field on the right of Ayres' line, its advance was repeatedly hampered by the heavy undergrowth. Prentice was promoted to captain a week after the fighting in the Wilderness and was awarded a major's brevet the following August for "gallant and meritorious service."*

The jungle through which we now had to struggle was almost impassable. The undergrowth was rank and heavy; the trees, averaging three to five inches in diameter, and reaching up from twenty-five to forty feet, grew abundantly,—in places so thickly that a man must turn sideways to pass between them, and in other places standing eighteen inches or two feet apart; and these trees, thus thickly

At war's end an unknown photographer produced this image looking west over the ruins of Wilderness Tavern, along the Orange Turnpike. On May 5 Meade ordered General Warren to march the men of his V Corps down this stretch of turnpike where, just beyond the distant treeline, they would find Ewell's Confederates waiting.

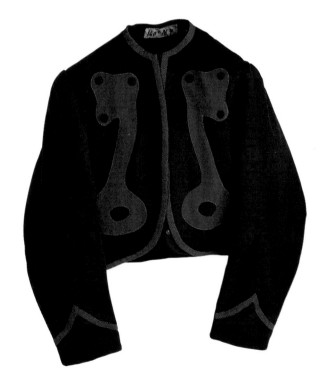

*The 140th New York Infantry, with three other regiments under Brigadier General Romeyn Ayres, wore Zouave uniforms, forming the Army of the Potomac's Zouave Brigade. Jackets like the one above were authorized for the 140th for proficiency in drill.*

"In that dismal Wilderness, in which a bird had scarce heart to peep, there was . . . something oppressive in the dim light and the strange quiet."

*This map by Confederate topographical engineer Jedediah Hotchkiss illustrates the positions held by Ewell's Second Corps during the opening day of the Wilderness. Intended to accompany official reports, the map details the placement of the Rebel brigades deployed to block an advance down the Orange Turnpike.*

massed, were often still further bound together by long creeping vines not larger than one's finger, and running their winding length, at varying heights, through thirty, fifty, or more feet of length.

How far into the jungle we went, I cannot say, but I presume some two hundred yards, before beginning to establish the picket-line. At length the picket-line was established,—the men ten feet apart, and not more than five of them well in view from any spot.

In our front was a rise in the ground, and just beyond it, and perhaps one hundred feet away, was the edge of a clearing,—the east edge of the open field upon the further side of which was massed the enemy. . . .

The morning was still, scarce a sound was heard, as the hours passed, that was not native to the woods; not a sound of hostile encounter. . . . Indeed, in that dismal Wilderness, in which a bird had scarce heart to peep, there was, through all that forenoon, something oppressive in the dim light and the strange quiet.

## LIEUTENANT MCHENRY HOWARD
### Staff, Brigadier General George H. Steuart

*Howard, the youngest son of an old Maryland family and a grandson of Francis Scott Key, left his law studies to volunteer in the Confederate army in 1861. The Princeton-educated Baltimorean joined the staff of Brigadier General George "Maryland" Steuart in September 1862. Captured at Spotsylvania, Howard was exchanged and served until captured a second time at Sayler's Creek in 1865. In his memoirs he recalled the collision between his brigade and the Federals in Saunders' Field.*

Early in the morning, May 5, Johnson's Division being now united . . . we started down the [Turnpike] towards Fredericksburg, but on reaching a point nearly abreast of Germanna Ford and within two miles of Wilderness Run and Tavern, were brought to a halt by the information that the enemy, having crossed the Rapidan at Germanna, were moving out into the country along our front. And a brisk skirmish soon began, probably with J. M. Jones's Brigade which had the advance, and turning down an old woods road which diverged from the [Turnpike] to the left oblique, we presently halted again and formed forward in line of battle. . . .

Some little delay occurred in making a connected line, facing to the direction in which we had been marching, but by midday the men were

*Saunders' Field, a corn patch on the Orange Turnpike, saw a violent clash between Ewell's Confederates and units of the Federal V Corps. Caught in a crossfire from Rebels posted along the treeline in the distance, the men of Ayres' brigade were driven back with heavy losses. Many sought shelter in the swale visible in the foreground.*

lying down in position, our Brigade being nearly at right angles with the [Turnpike], which was perhaps a couple of hundred yards south of our right. The skirmish firing indicated that the enemy were moving diagonally across and towards our front, and it drew closer until stray bullets were cutting through the branches overhead. I was at the right of the brigade line, General Steuart being towards the centre, when Major-General Johnson rode by in some haste and called out to me, that it was not intended to bring on a general engagement that day. When he presently rode up a second time and called out, "Remember, Captain Howard, it is not meant to have a general engagement," I said, "But, General, it is evident that the two lines will come together in a few moments, and whether it is intended to have a general engagement or not, will it not be better for our men to have the impetus of a forward movement in the collision?" "Very well," said he, "let them go ahead a little." I looked down the line towards General Steuart . . . and, raising my sword, I called out "Forward!" The men responded with alacrity and almost immediately a tremendous fire rolled along the line.

woods opposite and a volley of musketry sent its bullets into our ranks. Its effect was serious. Just how many men were struck it is impossible to say, but probably a dozen or more. Lt. John Hume who had been commissary sergeant and who had just received his commission and had never before been under fire, was wounded in the knee by this volley and lost his leg by subsequent amputation. Colonel Ryan's horse was wounded and became so unmanageable that he dismounted and led the regiment on foot. This volley was the signal for a halt. The command was given to lie down. . . .

Excitement and expectancy were now at their highest pitch. The men who for those few minutes lay there and faced the possibilities of the tragedy then inevitable can never forget it. The suspense and

## CAPTAIN PORTER FARLEY

140TH NEW YORK INFANTRY, AYRES' BRIGADE

*By 1864 Farley, a 23-year-old from Rochester, New York, was a seasoned veteran who had risen to command a company of the 140th New York. Marching into Saunders' Field north of the Orange Turnpike in the first line of Ayres' brigade, Farley and his fellow New Yorkers advanced alone into murderous Rebel fire when the U.S. Regulars on their right were slowed by thick brush and uneven terrain.*

We had advanced probably about a mile from our starting place when we reached the edge of a small clearing. It occupied a hollow with a water course now dry running through it. It extended to the right but a few rods beyond the right wing of our regiment, and was, I should judge, cut about through its middle by the pike. Surrounding it the wood and underbrush were of the same general character as those through which we had been advancing. When we reached the edge of this clearing we had before us a gentle downward slope of open field and then a corresponding rising slope to the edge of the woods beyond. The distance across this field was probably six or seven hundred feet. Just before we reached the opening we were halted and the alignment of the troops was corrected. . . . The alignment being completed the order was given to fix bayonets. A few minutes later a staff officer brought word to our colonel to advance. Ryan gave the word of command and at the ordinary pace we moved on towards the clearing. The instant the regiment showed itself and before it was fairly out into the clearing a line of smoke puffed from the edge of the

*Lieutenant James R. Campbell of the 140th New York was wounded while advancing with the regiment across Saunders' Field. The 20-year-old was later awarded a captain's brevet for "gallant and meritorious service" during the engagement.*

# "Each man simply had to brace himself for an effort supreme in all its fearful possibilities."

dread and hope which possess men during such minutes cannot be adequately told in words. But even those who have never experienced it may imagine the tension which men so placed must put upon themselves to screw their courage to the sticking point. Every man knew that the effect of that single volley was but a foretaste of what was sure to follow. That volley had been delivered before we were fairly out of cover, and its volume and results showed that no mere picket line, but a strong force lay in the woods before us. We were to advance against them in the open, and without firing a gun till we reached them. Who and how many would fall before we could even cross the field; and then would it be a fight at close quarters or would the enemy fall back, or would we be checked in our charge and see a repetition of the scenes at Fredericksburg? Each man simply had to brace himself for an effort supreme in all its fearful possibilities. . . .

There were a few minutes of preparation after that first volley, and then word was passed along the line by a staff officer to advance. Our colonel gave the orders "Stand up! Right shoulder arms. Forward double quick. Charge." The last word was hardly out of Ryan's mouth when the regiment started on a run with a yell from the whole line. . . .

. . . the regiment needed no leaders and in the literal sense it had none. The company commanders ran each in the front rank on the right of his company, and the colonel ran in a little interval just to the left of the color guard, so that he was right at my elbow and we exchanged words with each other as we crossed the field. Ryan had no sword with him, for he had left it sticking in his saddle girth when he jumped from his wounded horse; but he carried his soft felt hat in his hand and waved it as he ran. Down the slope we rushed; killed and wounded men plunging face forward to the ground. The yell spent its force when we reached the bottom of the hollow, but the men rushed on up the hill with no perceptible abatement of speed. Relief from the galling fire from which they were suffering could only be expected

*In the aftermath of the fighting in Saunders' Field Colonel David T. Jenkins and several subordinate officers of the 146th New York were reported missing in action. Although the others were eventually accounted for, Jenkins' fate remains a mystery. Witnesses reported last seeing him in the thick of the fight bleeding from at least one wound. He was probably buried in an unmarked field grave.*

when they reached the enemy and could use their weapons upon them. Into the woods we rushed and it seemed as if in the next second we would be upon the rebels with our bayonets, but just as we entered the underbrush they fell back, firing as they went and here our men for the moment stopped and delivered their first fire. . . . The rush of the charge was over but the line loaded and fired and still pressed some rods into the woods. From that time till the remnant of us were driven back, there was kept up a savage fusillade in which we found ourselves fighting with an almost unseen enemy but suffering all the time a continuous loss which attested the strength of the force opposed to us. . . . After getting into the woods the line of our regiment seemed to melt away in a most surprising manner. The situation soon became like that of a strong picket line on the defensive against an enemy of unknown force. Many of our men availed themselves of the shelter of tree trunks and from such positions kept up the bushwhacking fight.

## SERGEANT JOHN H. WORSHAM
### 21ST VIRGINIA INFANTRY, JONES' BRIGADE

*Worsham's regiment, posted near the Orange Turnpike, was unaffected when Brigadier General Joseph J. Bartlett's Federals flanked the right of its brigade. The Virginians joined the 1st North Carolina in a counterattack to oust the remnants of Ayres' brigade from Saunders' Field and claimed partial credit for the capture of two guns of Battery D, 1st New York Light Artillery.*

As the streaks of day were just beginning to show themselves, we were ordered to fall in, and resumed our march. We had gone only a short distance when the stillness in our front was broken by the sound of a drum, and the sweet notes of music from a band. Every man clutched his gun more tightly, as the direction of the music told him that the enemy were in front. There was no need of urging us to hurry, no need to inquire what it meant. All knew now that Grant had crossed the Rapidan, and soon the tumult of battle would begin. The march continued, the command was "Close up," soon the order, "Halt! Load your guns!" then "Shoulder arms! March!" Soon a line of battle was formed by the Second Brigade which was in front, the 21st Va. Regt. on the left of the Stone road, the remainder of the brigade on the right of that road. The order "Forward!" was given,—we moved forward through wood and brush! We were in the wilderness! with a tumult that seemed to come from the infernal regions, we were assailed by the enemy! As soon as the lifting of the smoke enabled us to see, we discovered that the portion of our brigade which was on the right of the road had been swept away; there were no Confederates in sight except our regiment. We broke the enemy's line in our front, and made no halt in our advance,—on we went, shooting as fast as we could load! Suddenly I was confronted by a gun, resting on a big stump, and behind the stump we saw a Yank! We hallooed to him to throw his gun down, several of us took aim at him; he started to rise, but before he could do so, a little boy on my left who had also taken aim at him, pulled the trigger, and at the crack of his gun the Yankee fell dead! . . . We captured many prisoners; behind every tree and stump were several who seemed to remain there in preference to running the gauntlet of our fire. We advanced to a dense pine thicket and halted, every man falling flat on the ground at once for protection!

The pine thicket in our front was so dense that we could not see into it twenty feet, but we heard the enemy talking. My company was near the road and I, wishing to see what was going on in front, ran across the road to the top of the elevation, and to the front. What a sight met my gaze! Obliquely across the road and just behind the pine thicket, the enemy was massed in a small field. I looked down the road and saw two pieces of artillery coming up in a run, and at this time I perceived that I in turn was seen, and guns were leveled at me! . . .

I ran back to my company, and seeing the colonel of the regiment of the Third Brigade who was with us, I informed him of the position of affairs in front. He gave the order at once, "Forward, men!"—the two regiments jumped to their feet and advanced, the whole of the Third Brigade taking part. Through the thicket we went, coming upon the mass of the enemy, the battle raging again more fiercely than before! With a yell we were on them, front and flank! They gave ground and then ran! Such a yell then went up as fairly shook the ground! Hurrah! the cannon are ours, we capturing both pieces. The enemy in their flight had crossed to the right of the road, and we followed through the field about two hundred yards into the woods; here we halted and were ordered back.

## LIEUTENANT HOLMAN S. MELCHER
### 20TH MAINE INFANTRY, BARTLETT'S BRIGADE

*Melcher fought in the 20th Maine at Antietam, Fredericksburg, and Gettysburg. He narrowly avoided capture in the Wilderness, only to be severely wounded four days later at Laurel Hill. He later served as a staff officer, ending the war with a major's brevet for gallantry. After the war he was twice elected mayor of Portland, Maine.*

About twelve o'clock, orders came to "advance and attack in force," and climbing over the line of works we had erected with so much interest and pleasure, we pushed out through the thick woods in our front,—the right of my regiment resting on the pike,— till we came near an open field, where lines were carefully formed, my regiment being in the second line of battle. The bugles sounded the "Charge" and advancing to the edge of the field, we saw the first line of battle about half-way across it, receiving a terribly fatal fire from an enemy in the woods on the farther side.

This field was less than a quarter of a mile across, had been planted with corn the year before, and was now dry and dusty. We could see the spurts of dust started up all over the field by the bullets of the enemy, as they spattered on it like the big drops of a coming shower you have so often seen along a dusty road. But that was not the thing that troubled us. It was the dropping of our comrades from the charging line as they rushed across the fatal field with breasts bared to the terrible storm of leaden hail, and we knew that it would soon be our turn to run this fire.

As we emerged from the woods into this field, General Bartlett, our brigade commander, came galloping down the line from the right, waving his sword and shouting, "Come on, boys, let us go in and help them!" And go we did. Pulling our hats low down over our eyes, we rushed across the field, and overtaking those of our comrades who had

*A graduate of West Point, John Marshall Jones had a fondness for the bottle that kept him in staff positions until he was appointed a Confederate brigadier general in 1863. Wounded at Gettysburg, he returned to duty four months later. When his brigade was routed at Saunders' Field on May 5, a staff officer recalled that "disdaining to fly," Jones "was killed while sitting on his horse gazing at the approaching enemy."*

survived the fearful crossing of the front line, just as they were breaking over the enemy's lines, we joined with them in this deadly encounter, and there in that thicket of bushes and briers, with the groans of the dying, the shrieks of the wounded, the terrible roar of musketry and the shouts of command and cheers of encouragement, we swept them away before us like a whirlwind . . . and pursued them like hunted hares through the thick woods, shooting those we could overtake who would not throw down their arms and go to the rear.

This pursuit with my company and those immediately about me continued for about half a mile, until there were no rebels in our front to be seen or heard; and coming out into a little clearing, I thought it well to reform my line, but found there was no line to form, or to connect with. I could not find my regimental colors or the regiment. There were with me fifteen men of my company with two others of the regiment. I was the only commissioned officer there, but my own brave and trusted first sergeant, Ammi Smith, was at my side as always in time of danger or battle, and with him I conferred as to what it was best to do under the circumstances.

There was nothing in front to fight that we could see or hear, but to go back seemed the way for cowards to move, as we did not know whether our colors were at the rear or farther to the front. . . .

While earnestly considering this question, one of my men came to me and said, "Lieutenant, come this way and let me show you something." Following him, he led me to the Orange Pike, and pointing back down that straight level road he said, "See that!" I looked in the direction he pointed and saw that which froze the blood in my veins and made my heart almost cease beating for a time. Some half a mile down the road from where we had just charged up through in our advance, I could see a strong column of rebel infantry moving directly across the road into our rear, completely cutting us off from the direction we had come. . . .

I called all my men together, stated to them how I understood the situation, and said, "Now, my men, as for myself, I had rather die in the attempt to cut our way out, than be captured to rot in rebel prisons. Will you stand by me in this attempt?" It was a moment that tried men's souls, and boys' too, but the resolution was quickly formed, and every one said, "Yes, Lieutenant, we will and gladly, too." I looked in their faces and I knew there was not one that would fail me. . . .

. . . I said, "Every man load his rifle, fix bayonets and follow me." And with Sergeant Smith at my side we started to cut our way out to "liberty or death."

## SERGEANT JAMES B. STAMP
### 3D ALABAMA INFANTRY, BATTLE'S BRIGADE

*Having served in the army since June 1861, Stamp was captured when Bartlett's Federals advanced into the gap left by Jones' broken brigade and overran his skirmish line. Stamp's account is a mix of wry humor and dispassionate description of what he saw and experienced. He recalled that he was held with the Army of the Potomac for 10 days without rations before being sent to Fort Delaware for transfer to prison in Elmira, New York. He was paroled and exchanged in March 1865.*

Only a skirmish line of the enemy had appeared in our front, and this had been successfully repulsed, and as there was no indication of their return, I with others remained in position, expecting the fleeing brigades to at once recover from their fright, and refrain us. Those of us who remained were deployed at intervals of fifteen or twenty feet, and the first intimation I had of the proximity of the enemy, I was covered by the gun of a soldier who under concealment of the chaparral had approached within ten feet of me. He muttered out something, which I supposed to be a command to surrender. I now discovered that the enemy by a flank movement, occupied our rear, thereby, cutting off all means of escape, and resistance would have simply invited death. I yielded to the command of my captor, whom I found to be a Sergeant, and from his extreme bad English, for a moment, it was a question, as to whether I had surrendered to Germany or the United States. However the quandary was soon removed, by the Sergeant putting me in charge of a private, who was a regular "down eastern" of the "blue belly" stripe. I was now satisfied that I was in the custody of "Uncle Sam," with all the dreaded honors of a prison life, staring me in the face.

The soldier to whom I was assigned,—with orders to convey me to the rear—was evidently quite proud of his possession of a live Confederate, and doubtless elated with the opportunity of getting to the rear; as he approached me in great ecstasy; hailing me as Johnnie—a name the federal soldiers had for Confederates in Common—and seizing me by the lapel of my jacket, endeavored to force me along. I did not see the need of being thus encumbered, and as it had the effect of rendering unpleasant our progress through the thick under-growth, and over the brushwood, I demanded to be released; asserting, that I preferred to do my own piloting. He readily yielded to my demand, but insisted on hurrying up, and claiming that we were in great danger from stray balls. . . .

On our way we passed quite a number of wounded soldiers, who were being conveyed to the hospital, and among them was a Zouave. As soon as he beheld me, he became violently enraged, and swore that he would avenge his wounds by murdering me; but from the loss of blood, he was entirely too feeble for action, so he had to content himself with profane and vulgar abuse.

We finally reached the "Bull Pen," where I was assigned to the custody of the guards for prisoners, and the guard who had accompanied me, was sent back to the front under the escort of a Cavalryman.

The pen was established in an old field, and but a short distance

*With the shout, "Here's our western men!" Brigadier General Lysander Cutler's Iron Brigade advanced to hammer Jones' Confederates. As the fighting dissolved into a melee, Major Albert M. Edwards of the 24th Michigan (left) seized the flag of the 48th Virginia Infantry (below). Tearing the flag from its staff, Edwards sent it to the rear in the knapsack of his wounded colonel, Henry A. Morrow.*

from General Grants head quarters. Wagons, Ambulances and other vehicles were to be seen in every direction. Long lines of troops and artillery were continuously passing, on the way to the front. Besides the guards for prisoners, there was a large number of soldiers on the field, who were serving as guards for head quarters, and various wagon trains.

From General Grant's tent proudly floated the United States flag, while in front a sentinel was seen in his "lonely walk." As a whole the scene was an imposing one, and one in which, were displayed the equipments of a well appointed army. I knew nothing of the fate of my comrades, and evidently was the first prisoner to arrive, although, I observed a man on the opposite side of the pen, talking to one of the guards, who bore the appearance of a Confederate soldier.

I laid down on the ground, using my blanket roll for a pillow, and as I was dreaming of the hardships and cold comforts of prison life, I was suddenly aroused by some one exclaiming "hello! when did they get you?" Looking up, I saw that it was the chap I had observed talking to the guard. I told him I was captured two or three hours ago, and enquired, when and where, did they capture him. "Oh" he replied, "I was not captured, I came to them soon this morning." "What" I asked, "do you really mean to say, that you are a deserter." He answered with rather a triumphant air, "I am." This poor, ignorant and degraded creature, was a member, of a Georgia regiment. My comrades all arrived, together with a large number of others, and the work of enrolling the prisoners was commenced. The enrolling officer, who bore the rank of Major, was to put it mildly, very over-bearing and insulting in his treatment of the prisoners. To give an example of his conduct—while Captain Witherspoon of the Mobile Cadets, was being enrolled, and standing in front of him, he, Witherspoon, inadvertently made a step forward, which the officer interpreted, as an attempt to over-look his writing. With an oath of abuse, he reversed the end of his pencil, and with force thrust it into Captain Witherspoon's mouth, inflicting a severe and painful wound. An explanation from Captain Witherspoon had only the effect of inviting additional abuse.

There was a continuous influx of prisoners, and the number had now increased to more than two hundred.

## BRIGADIER GENERAL JOHN B. GORDON
### BRIGADE COMMANDER, SECOND CORPS

*Riding to the front, Ewell ordered Gordon to support the brigades of George Doles and Cullen Battle in the struggle to stem the Federal onslaught south of the Orange Turnpike. The former Georgia lawyer led his brigade forward in a fierce counterattack that drove the Federals back to their starting point.*

Long before I reached the point of collision, the steady roll of small arms left no doubt as to the character of the conflict in our front. Despatching staff officers to the rear to close up the ranks in compact column, so as to be ready for any emergency, we hurried with quickened step toward the point of the heaviest fighting. Alternate confidence and apprehension were awakened as the shouts of one army or the other reached our ears. So distinct in character were these shouts that they were easily discernible. At one point the weird Confederate "yell" told us plainly that Ewell's men were advancing. At another the huzzas, in mighty concert, of the Union troops warned us that they had repelled the Confederate charge; and as these ominous huzzas grew in volume we knew that Grant's lines were moving forward. Just as the head of my column came within range of the whizzing Miniés, the Confederate yells grew fainter, and at last ceased; and the Union shout rose above the din of battle. I was already prepared by this infallible admonition for the sight of Ewell's shattered forces retreating in disorder. . . . These retreating divisions, like broken and receding waves, rolled back against the head of my column while we were still rapidly advancing along the narrow road. The repulse had been so sudden and the confusion so great that practically no resistance was now being made to the Union advance; and the elated Federals were so near me that little time was left to bring my men from column into line in order to resist the movement or repel it by countercharge. At this

# "The repulse had been so sudden and the confusion so great that practically no resistance was now being made to the Union advance."

moment of dire extremity I saw General Ewell, who was still a superb horseman, notwithstanding the loss of his leg, riding in furious gallop toward me, his thoroughbred charger bounding like a deer through the dense underbrush. With a quick jerk of his bridle-rein just as his wooden leg was about to come into unwelcome collision with my knee, he checked his horse and rapped out his few words with characteristic impetuosity. He did not stop to explain the situation; there was no need of explanation. The disalignment, the confusion, the rapid retreat of our troops, and the raining of Union bullets as they whizzed and rattled thorough the scruboaks and pines, rendered explanations superfluous, even had there been time to make them. The rapid words he did utter were electric and charged with tremendous significance. "General Gordon, the fate of the day depends on you, sir," he said. "These men will save it, sir," I replied, more with the purpose of arousing the enthusiasm of my men than with any well-defined idea as to how we were to save it. Quickly wheeling a single regiment into line, I ordered it forward in a countercharge, while I hurried the other troops into position. . . . Swiftly riding to the centre of my line, I gave in person the order: "Forward!" With a deafening yell which must have been heard miles away, that glorious brigade rushed upon the hitherto advancing enemy, and by the shock of their furious onset shattered into fragments all that portion of the compact Union line which confronted my troops.

*In the aftermath of Gordon's counterattack Sergeant Reuben W. Schell (above, right) and his regiment, the 7th Pennsylvania Reserves, were bluffed into surrender by two companies of the 61st Georgia. Schell, a 20-year-old, was among the first Yankees sent to Georgia's Andersonville prison. He kept his V Corps badge (right) throughout his captivity and was released at the war's end.*

## LIEUTENANT LEMUEL A. ABBOTT
### 10TH VERMONT INFANTRY, MORRIS' BRIGADE

*Abbott, a stonecutter, and the rest of the 10th Vermont had seen little action since the regiment's formation in September 1862. The 10th got its first real taste of combat on May 5 as the VI Corps advanced along the turnpike. In October 1864 Abbott was waiting to take command of a regiment of U.S. Colored Troops when he was wounded at the Battle of Cedar Creek and soon forced to leave the service.*

We pushed on to the front passing many corralled and moving army trains, and through the outskirts of the field hospital near the right of our army's infantry line of battle until we struck the Orange turnpike . . . we turned to the right and followed it some distance until near enough the enemy to draw the fire of its artillery . . . the air was full of solid shot and exploding shells as far each side of the pike as could be seen. The road here ran in a straight line ahead of us almost as far as the eye could reach bordered on either side with a dense forest and underbrush which was also being shelled in places. Shortly after, when within shelling distance, the enemy fired a solid

shot straight along the pike which tore screeching through the air just a little above the heads of the men in column in our regiment till it struck the pike about midway the regiment, providentially where the men had split and were marching on either side of the road, when it viciously rebounded along the pike lengthwise the column to the great consternation of the men all along the extended column in our own and other regiments. This situation was most trying for every moment I

*A photographer's assistant poses amid earthworks constructed by Ewell's corps along the edge of Saunders' Field during the late afternoon of May 5. The stand of pine logs, called a revetment, was used to reinforce the interior wall of the entrenchment.*

dreaded the effect of a better directed shot which would go destructively through our long column lengthwise and do untold damage.

Soon, however, we turned to the left or southerly into the woods and formed line of battle almost as soon as there was room after leaving the road with the enemy close in our front with a field piece of artillery hardly a hundred yards away through the brush which kept each from seeing the other. Before Captain H. R. Steele had hardly finished

dressing his company after forming line a shell from this gun exploded in the ranks of Company K, killing a private and wounding others. The shell had burst actually inside the man completely disemboweling and throwing him high in the air in a rapidly whirling motion above our heads with arms and legs extended until his body fell heavily to the ground with a sickening thud.

I was in the line of file closers hardly two paces away and just behind

*Special artist Edwin Forbes sketched a battle line of the Federal VI Corps firing through pine thickets at an unseen enemy near the Orange Turnpike on the afternoon of May 5. The maze of scrub timber and tangled brush made effective coordination between units nearly impossible. A soldier from Pennsylvania called it the "awfullest brush, briars, grapevine, etc., I was ever in."*

the man killed. We were covered with blood, fine pieces of flesh, entrails, etc., which makes me cringe and shudder whenever I think of it. The concussion badly stunned me. I was whirled about in the air like a feather, thrown to the ground on my hands and knees—or at least was in that position with my head from the enemy when I became fully conscious—face cut with flying gravel or something else, eyes, mouth and ears filled with dirt, and was feeling nauseated from the shake-up. Most of the others affected went to the hospital, and I wanted to but didn't give up. I feared being accused of trying to get out of a fight.

## LIEUTENANT COLONEL THOMAS W. HYDE
### STAFF, MAJOR GENERAL JOHN SEDGWICK

*Hyde began his service as a field officer in the 7th Maine. In 1863 he transferred to the staff of the VI Corps as provost marshal. On May 5 he was busy away from the corps for most of the day. When finally free to return he rode forward along the Orange Turnpike only to find Sedgwick and his fellow staff officers under fire from Confederate artillery. Hyde dodged the shellfire but he was briefly left hors de combat in a gruesome sequence of events.*

After remaining with Meade four or five hours, riding some thirty miles and tiring out two horses, I was released and got back to the general to find the line of the 6th corps busily engaged at close quarters with the unseen enemy. The staff were at a cross-roads. The enemy had two or three guns up, but we had none on account of the dense forest. They seemed to have our range, and several good horses had been knocked out already. Then a shell burst under the horses of two war correspondents,—Jerome D. Stillson of the "World" was one,—and they were advised to go to the rear. The firing redoubled in front, the Jersey brigade was double-quicking by us to reinforce the line, and I had dismounted to fix my horse's bit, when a cannonball took off the head of a Jerseyman; the head struck me, and I was knocked down, covered with brains and blood. Even my mouth, probably gaping in wonder where that shell would strike, was filled, and everybody thought it was all over with me. I looked up and saw the general give me a sorrowful glance, two or three friends dismounted to pick me up, when I found I could get up myself, but I was not much use as a staff officer for fully fifteen minutes.

## CHAPLAIN WARREN H. CUDWORTH
### 1ST MASSACHUSETTS INFANTRY, McALLISTER'S BRIGADE

*As the fighting around the Orange Turnpike sputtered to a halt, Meade, frustrated by poor communications and confusion among his forces, ordered units of the VI and II Corps to attack along the Orange Plank road. Cudworth, a Boston clergyman, described the Yankees' advance through the dense thickets and gulleys that bordered the road and their collision with Heth's Rebels near the Widow Tapp farm.*

The scouts brought in word that the enemy were before us in large numbers, and advancing. Guns were stacked in an instant; and the whole command went to work throwing up a temporary breastwork of logs and rails. Old trees were rolled up and cleared of their branches; new ones cut down as fast as the few axes procurable

*Sergeant Charles Newton of the 4th Vermont was wounded south of the Plank road. "So many were shot down," said a fellow Vermonter, "that it became plain that to advance was . . . destruction." Newton recovered and was later promoted to lieutenant.*

*After a long convalescence from wounds suffered at Gaines' Mill, Henry Harrison Walker was commissioned a brigadier general in July 1863. Walker, a West Pointer, was placed in command of a Virginia brigade, which he handled with skill in the Wilderness on the afternoon of May 5 just south of the Orange Plank road. Another wound near Spotsylvania Court House cost him a foot and his field command.*

could be made to do service; dirt, stones, and rocks thrown up in front and rear; and in an hour's time a passable line of earthworks completed. It was hardly done before an order arrived for the whole line to advance. The woods seemed to be absolutely impenetrable. Trees were so close together, underbrush so thick, and the scrub-oaks so stiff and unyielding, that regular advances were simply impossible. The men went forward, however, in very irregular lines, going round the trees, creeping under the branches, and keeping as closely together as they were able. They had advanced thus only five or six hundred yards from the road, when, directly in front, the enemy, unseen, opened a double volley, which sent thousands of bullets crashing through the woods right into their faces. This fire, so sudden, so unexpected, and so deadly, was returned in but a feeble and scattering manner, because the men were so generally separated from their officers, and so far apart from each other, besides being perplexed by the difficulties they had encountered in forcing their way through the tangled forest, that they were comparatively without organization. The enemy answered with another terrific volley, which told with deadly effect upon the foremost groups struggling along to get into some sort of fighting array, killing and wounding a large number, and straightway forcing the rest to fall back. Along the whole division line, the movement became at once and rapidly retrograde. Branches of trees tore off knapsacks and haversacks, knocked guns out of men's hands, and, in two or three cases, completely stripped them of their accoutrements; but they continued to retire

till they reached the breastwork, and there the majority halted. The enemy then advanced to obtain possession of the road. They met with a fierce and stubborn resistance. Along the front of both corps, the soldiers immediately became engaged, almost entirely with musketry, at short distances. Only four pieces of artillery were got into position. The conflict became extremely bloody. Every shot seemed to tell. Whenever the Union troops moved forward, the rebels appeared to have the advantage. Whenever they advanced, the advantage was transferred to us. So the conflict raged for two hours, hardly a regiment knowing how fared any other regiment, owing to the impenetrable obscurity of the forest.

## PRIVATE WILLIAM C. KENT
### 1ST U.S. SHARPSHOOTERS, HAYS' BRIGADE

*Kent left his job as a bookkeeper to join a company of marksmen being raised near his hometown of Bradford, Vermont. Chronic illness kept him in the hospital for long periods, and except for fighting in the Seven Days' Battles, he saw little action. Kent recovered enough, however, to return to his regiment in March 1864, in time for the Wilderness and Spotsylvania. He was wounded in the head by a shell fragment on June 15 at Petersburg and was discharged on September 13, 1864.*

The firing had all ceased, the noise and movement of the army died away as we advanced and we could see no one but the man on our right and left and hear no noise except what we made ourselves wading through the brush. Next to me on my right was Dick Cross, my bunk mate. I think you remember him, a quiet, steady young fellow. Next, on my left, was Locke, a recruit who had never been in a fight, and next to him, his brother-in-law, Wright.

We advanced about half a mile or less and Locke closed up a little on me and began to ask a lot of questions. "Where are the Rebs?", "How far do we go?", "When shall we run back?"

"I don't know" answered every one of them, but it was a comfort for him to talk and I allow it was for me. At last we came to a gentle slope more open than we had been passing through with a large tree now and then scattered through it. At the base was a dense fringe of willows, indicating a stream which was very welcome in anticipation. As we emerged from the brush we could see our line stretching out right and left to correct the alignment broken by our march through the brush, and we

*An 1844 West Point graduate, Alexander Hays held a brevet for bravery in Mexico. Returning to the Regular Army from civilian life in 1861, Hays earned promotion to brigadier general and three brevets. The red-bearded Pennsylvanian was shot from his horse as he led his men in support of Getty's hard-pressed brigade near the intersection of the Brock and Orange Plank roads.*

advanced slowly in good order down the slope.

Then came from far away on the right the fire of a skirmish line followed by the heavy fire of a line of battle. It rattled down to us and as the crack, crack came on my right, though I could see nothing, I fired into the fringe, then about four rods in front. Locke says, "What is it—what are you firing at?"

I replied, "Fire and you'll see."

By that time our side was firing as fast as we could load. Just as Locke fired the first time, my words being hardly out of my mouth, a Reb line of battle rose up out of the fringe and let us have it full in the face. Talk about astonishment or surprise or dismay. I fired once more because I was almost ready and I could not think quick enough to do anything else, but by the time the bullet was out of the gun, I was in full retreat. As I turned I caught sight of the Rebs taking in the Major who was caught between the two fires. Indeed, he was so near them they could almost have reached out and caught his bridle rein.

. . . The skirmish line, or all that was left, made a stand long enough to fire once or twice in the first 20 rods of retreat. Wright and I both turned and fired, reloading as we ran. Locke was too much demoralized to do aught but run, but we kept together. All this time the Rebs were hard after us, keeping up a smart fire though there were none of the crashes like the first one.

Just as we fired the second time in retreat, as we turned, Wright was

hit in the arm above the elbow. He called out, "I'm hit, don't leave me boys," and that seemed to settle Locke's mind. Though we were running as fast as the nature of the way permitted, Locke promptly supported Wright on one side and I on the other till we found he was all right for a run, though his arm dangling by his side at every step must have given him intense pain.

Just at this time a bullet hit me square in the back with such force I thought it had gone through as I heard the spat and felt the shock. We by this time were nearly back to the reserves and a heavy fire from both infantry and the battery at the plank road crossing showed the Rebs they had run against something stronger than a skirmish line and they fell back leaving our part of the line in peace, while we scrambled over and see how we fared. Our company came out badly.

## LIEUTENANT J. F. J. CALDWELL
### 1st South Carolina Infantry, McGowan's Brigade

*Caldwell returned from law studies in Europe and served briefly in Virginia before illness forced him home in July 1861. He reported again the following spring in time to fight in the Seven Days' Battles. Commissioned a lieutenant in 1863, Caldwell was wounded at Gettysburg. Here he describes a counterattack by General Samuel McGowan's brigade on May 5 to bolster Heth's division. Caldwell was wounded again at Fussell's Mill in August 1864. He ended the war on McGowan's staff.*

About 4 o'clock P.M., when we arrived at Wilderness run, we heard a rambling skirmish fire in front, not far off. We filed to the left and passed through an open field. There were several pieces of artillery here, and near them General Lee and General Stuart, on foot. The battle was evidently not distant, but we flattered ourselves that it was *rather* late in the day for much to be done towards a general engagement. We were carried nearly a mile farther, through a body of woods, and halted on a clear commanding ridge. . . . Rev. Mr. Mullaly, chaplain of Orr's regiment of Rifles, held prayers with his regiment. It was one of the most impressive scenes I ever witnessed. On the left thundered the dull battle; on the right the sharp crack of rifles gradually swelled to equal importance; above was the blue, placid heavens; around us a varied landscape of forest and fields, green with the earliest foliage of spring; and here knelt hirsute and browned veterans shriving for another struggle with death.

In the midst of the prayer, a harsh, rapid fire broke out right on the plank-road we had left; the order was issued to face about and forward; and then we went, sometimes in quick-time, sometimes at the double-quick, towards the constantly increasing battle. The roar of muskets became continuous, augmented occasionally by the report of cannon, and always by the ringing rebel cheer. Heth's division, the only one at this point, was engaged, and we knew that we were going to reinforce them. Just as we reached the plank-road, two or three shell fell among us, but I believe no one was struck in the brigade. The road was crowded with non-combatants, artillery and ordnance wagons. Here and there lay a dead man. The firing in front waxed fiercer, if possible, than ever. . . .

. . . We entered the conflict alone. As soon as the line was formed and dressed, the order to advance was given. Balls fired at Heth's division, in front of us, fell among us at the beginning of our advance. We pressed on, guide left, through the thick undergrowth, until we reached Heth's line, now much thinned and exhausted. We had very imprudently begun to cheer before this. We passed over this line cheering. There was no use of this. We should have charged without uttering a word until within a few yards of the Federal line. As it was, we drew upon ourselves a terrific volley of musketry. The advance was greatly impeded by the matted growth of saplings and bushes, and in the delay a scattering fire commenced along our line. . . .

The pressure was greatest on the right of the brigade; for, in addition to the worst conceivable ground for marching, and the demoralizing spectacle of another division lying down, and, after we had passed

*Lieutenant Vandowh V. Richardson of the 18th North Carolina of James H. Lane's brigade was wounded in the hip when Wilcox's division attacked to slow the advance of the Federal II Corps. The injury ended the 24-year-old's military service.*

*Twisted ramrods from Springfield rifles, possibly fired spontaneously by overheated weapons, testify to the ferocity of the fighting along the Orange Plank road. These were found together beside the road east of the Widow Tapp farm.*

them, firing through our ranks, the enemy's line extended far to the right of ours. . . . All idea of a charge had to be abandoned. . . .

. . . The pressure became fearful on both flanks. Our line . . . miserably short. For a time, we had a front of but a single brigade. I do not judge any one; but I think it was the shortest, most huddled, most ineffective line-of-battle I ever saw. But for the gallantry of our troops, which even surpassed itself, all must have been lost. The balls of the enemy, at one point, crossed the road from each side. Still they pressed on us, filling the air with shouts and the roll of arms, and sweeping the woods with balls. At one time they drove so furiously on the right of the road, that men had to be ranged along the road to keep them back, or rather, to support the meagre line that held them in check. . . . It began to look like every man would have to be his own general.

*Lieutenant Edwin B. Bartlett had been promoted from the ranks and bore the scars of a wound from the Seven Days' Battles. His regiment, the 10th Massachusetts, of Henry Eustis' brigade, attacked on the Federal right flank north of the Orange Plank road. Bartlett survived but was killed by Confederate artillery fire on May 18 at Spotsylvania.*

## LIEUTENANT CHARLES B. BROCKWAY

### BATTERY F, 1ST PENNSYLVANIA LIGHT ARTILLERY, MOTT'S DIVISION

*Artillery was generally of limited use in the tangle of the Wilderness, but along the roadways cannon firing canister could wreak a fearful toll. Here Brockway recalls the part his section of two guns played in halting a determined Rebel assault down the Orange Plank road.*

I never expected to come out of the engagement alive, nor to bring any of my men out. The infantry right and left were to a great extent shielded by the wilderness, but I had to take the open road, and formed a good mark for the enemy. The road was narrow—a ditch on each side—with no chance to limber up and retreat in case of accidents. I had my caissons follow some distance in the rear, and put my guns *en echelon,* to enable me to open with both at once. I took the precaution to have several shells prepared, as I knew the attack would be sudden. Our skirmishers were only fifty yards in front of our first line of battle, the two remaining lines following at close distance. We could not see what was in the woods, but several rebels leisurely paced the road four hundred yards in our front, and we knew "by the pricking of our thumbs, something wicked this way comes."

As the minute of the watch pointed to 4:30 P.M. an advance was made. A few steps forward and the silence changed to a deafening roar of musketry. We advanced about two hundred yards, when the infantry began to waver, and I deemed it proper to perform my share in the tragedy. The guns were unlimbered and a few percussion shells sent into the enemy's ranks, now only a few hundred yards beyond. They immediately placed a section of Napoleon twelve-pounders in the road, and a couple of solid shot whizzed by our ears. Here was a tangible enemy and we all breathed freer in seeing something to fire at. At this time the whole line was engaged; the line of battle advanced and receded, and the yells of either party rose above the rattle of musketry and the roar of artillery. By a fortunate shot we exploded one of the enemy's limber chests, and soon had disabled most of their men and horses. They then threw rounds of double-shotted canister, which bounded like hailstones, tearing up splinters in the plank road, and here and there knocked over men and horses. But our percussion shell was superior and their artillery was soon withdrawn. For a moment there was a lull and then the rebel line charged. Slowly they pressed our men back, yelling like demons incarnate. At first I threw solid shot at the column as it

advanced, until they commenced double-quicking. At this time, an officer of the 93d Penn. hallooed: "Stick to it, Charlie; I've got a thirty days'
furlough," showing me at the same time a gaping wound in his thigh.

The time had now arrived to use canister, and terrible execution
did it do along that narrow plank road. The enemy struggled bravely
against it. If the line broke they steadily reformed; if the colors fell they
were seized by another hand; the wounded crawled into the ditches
and the dead formed a barrier to the second line.

. . . The enemy soon learned that they could not advance down a narrow road in the face of a section of artillery, capable of throwing a peck of
bullets a minute! They then adopted safer tactics by loading their guns
under cover, and taking the road only long enough to fire them. After being under fire over two hours I found only a round of canister remained.

## CAPTAIN
## SAMUEL D. BUCK
### 13TH VIRGINIA INFANTRY, PEGRAM'S BRIGADE

*Darkness finally brought relief to
the outnumbered Rebels of Richard
Ewell's corps, who had fought with
desperate ferocity to keep Grant's
army at bay. Buck, a young dry
goods clerk from Winchester, Virginia, who had recently been promoted to captain, remembered
a tense night in the blood-soaked
thickets bordering the turnpike.*

We wished for night. . . . Work on our right was as heavy almost as in our front and when night did come our line stood
solid, immovable. Shall that terrible night ever be erased from
my memory, the terrible groans of the wounded, the mournful sound of
the owl and the awful shrill shrieks of the whippoorwill; the most hideous
of all noise I ever heard on a battle field after firing had ceased? The
terrible loneliness is of itself sufficient, and these birds seemed to mock
at our grief and laugh at the groans of the dying. Pen and words fail to

General John Pegram fought in western Virginia and led a cavalry brigade in the
Army of Tennessee before commanding an infantry brigade in 1863. He was wounded leading a counterattack against Truman Seymour's VI Corps brigade on May 5.

describe the scene. With these exceptions, all is quiet. When I heard
the familiar voice of Capt. R. N. Wilson, A. A. General, calling and asking along the line for me. As I had just been on duty I felt he could not
want me for regular work so concluded a scout and search for the enemy would be the call and while thus thinking had walked up the line
and met him. Speaking clearly as he always did he informed me that
Col. Hoffman wished me to establish a picket line as close to the enemy as I could. Not being my turn to go on duty and knowing it meant
staying up all night, I told Capt. Wilson that he should send some one
else. Admitting the justice of what I said he repeated the request saying Col. Hoffman desired it and promised to relieve me as soon as I got
the line established. No escape and fully expecting to have another vol-

ley fired into me, I formed my picket line immediately in front and moved forward, stumbling over the dead and dying and they lay thicker than I ever saw them and it was hard to keep off of them in the darkness.

At last I was in speaking distance of the enemy and they seemed disposed to have a truce for the night and we were rid of the usual and useless picket firing. I instructed my men not to fire and it seemed that the officer on the other side did the same as we were so close we could hear them talking plainly.

## LIEUTENANT ABNER R. SMALL
### 16TH MAINE INFANTRY, LEONARD'S BRIGADE

*Nightfall brought no rest to the exhausted soldiers facing each other in the darkened pine thickets and scrub timber of the Wilderness. Nervous pickets and random artillery fire made the retrieval of the wounded a perilous affair. Regimental adjutant Small recalled his foray in search of stragglers in the burning woods just behind the front lines.*

Night was falling when I was ordered to beat the woods behind our line for stragglers. I found a few. They were badly frightened men, going they didn't know where, but anywhere away from that howling acre. I urged them to go back to their companies; told them that they would be safest with their comrades and sure to be more than thankful, later, that they had followed my suggestion. I feel sure that they all went back, as they told me they would, though more than one of them started with shaky knees. I didn't blame them for dreading the return.

Shells were still coming over, and here and there one that burst as it hit the ground would start a blaze in dry leaves. A crash and a flare, a scurry of great leaping shadows, and then the fire would die out and the night would be blacker than before. Once, when the darkness was torn

suddenly away, I saw a dogwood all in flower, standing asleep and still. I groped on, stumbled, fell, and my outflung hands pushed up a smoulder of leaves. The fire sprang into flame, caught in the hair and beard of a dead sergeant, and lighted a ghastly face and wide-open eyes. I rushed away in horror, and felt a great relief when I found our line again and heard the sound of human voices.

We manned our works all night in the edge of the woods. There was no moon to light the clearing, only dim stars, and the air was hazy and pungent with the smoke and smell of fires yet smouldering. We couldn't see the wounded and dying, whose cries we heard all too clearly; nor could our stretcher bearers go out to find them and bring them in; the

*Artist Alfred Waud made this drawing of wounded soldiers fleeing woods set alight by sparks from rifle fire. Many wounded men, unable to move, burned to death.*

# "We couldn't see the wounded and dying, whose cries we heard all too clearly; nor could our stretcher bearers go out to find them."

## MAJOR GENERAL HENRY HETH
### DIVISION COMMANDER, THIRD CORPS

*After a lackluster performance commanding troops in western Virginia Heth was given a command under his old West Point classmate A. P. Hill. He performed well in the Wilderness, managing his division so as to halt his old friend Winfield Scott Hancock's corps on May 5. Later that night, however, he was frustrated in his attempts to consolidate his position.*

*I* went to General Hill who was sick. Seated on a camp stool before his camp fire he said, shaking me by the hand, "Your division has done splendidly today; its magnificent fighting is the theme of the entire army." I replied, "Yes, the division has done splendid fighting, but we have other matters to attend to just now." I described to him the almost inextricable mixing up of Wilcox's troops and my own. "Let me take one side of the road and form line of battle, and Wilcox the other side and do the same; we are so mixed, and lying at every conceivable angle, that we cannot fire a shot without firing into each other. A skirmish line could drive both my division and Wilcox's, situated as we now are. We shall certainly be attacked early in the morning." Hill replied, "Longstreet will be up in a few hours. He will form in your front. I don't propose that your division shall do any fighting tomorrow,

the men have been marching and fighting all day and are tired. I do not wish them disturbed."

A second and third time I saw Hill and begged him to order Wilcox to get his men out of the way. Wilcox saw Hill and seconded my efforts. The last time I saw Hill he got vexed and said, "D—— it, Heth, I don't want to hear any more about it; the men shall not be disturbed." The gravity of the situation was such that I determined to lay the matter before General Lee. I hunted for his tent one hour but could not find it. The only excuse I make for Hill is that he was sick.

I walked the road all night; when I imagined I saw the first streak of daylight, I ordered my horse and with half speed rode down the Plank Road to see if Longstreet was coming. I rode two or three miles in the direction of Mine Run. No Longstreet. I hurried back.

*Ambrose Powell Hill's combativeness on the battlefield quickly gained him a reputation as one of Lee's most aggressive commanders. Promoted to lieutenant general in 1863, Hill found the change from division to corps command difficult and was, furthermore, hampered by a recurring kidney disease. Illness forced him temporarily to relinquish his command on May 8.*

# The Wilderness—May 6

For his second day in the Wilderness, Grant planned to concentrate his force against Hill's Third Corps on the Orange Plank road. Hancock's II Corps, reinforced with four V Corps brigades under Wadsworth and three VI Corps brigades under Getty, was to smash into Hill's front and northern flank, while Burnside's IX Corps slipped into the gap between Ewell and Hill and swung south, attacking Hill's rear.

Lee realized the danger to Hill and instructed Longstreet to shift his First Corps onto the Orange Plank road. Longstreet started from his bivouac at Richard's Shop but lost his way while taking a shortcut and, as the sun rose, had not yet arrived when the massive Federal juggernaut slammed into Hill's line.

The Confederate Third Corps collapsed and stampeded to the rear. Lee, from his headquarters in Widow Tapp's field, watched as the remnants of Hill's corps streamed past and Federal soldiers began spilling onto the Tapp farm close behind. As Lee was contemplating defeat, a brigade of Texans and Arkansans, the vanguard of Longstreet's anxiously awaited corps, marched into view to his rear on the Plank road.

Lee, elated at the seemingly miraculous appearance of the reinforcements, was swept up by the moment and attempted personally to lead the Texas and Arkansas troops in a countercharge. The men refused to advance until the general went to the rear. Meanwhile Longstreet's two divisions, under Major General Charles W. Field and Brigadier General Joseph B. Kershaw, arrived and pitched into the Federals, driving them back several hundred yards east of the Tapp farm. Longstreet had saved the Army of Northern Virginia from disaster.

Longstreet was then informed of an unfinished railway grade that led past Hancock's left flank. Eager to maintain the initiative, he sent his aide, Lieutenant Colonel G. Moxley Sorrel, with four brigades drawn from the First and Third Corps, along the grade to a point opposite Hancock's flank. While Sorrel's force struck the end of the Union line, the rest of the First Corps attacked from straight ahead. The Confederates rolled up the Union formation, Hancock later admitted, like a "wet blanket."

Wadsworth tried to lead a counterattack north of the Orange Plank road only to be mortally wounded. In the confusion, however, some Virginia troops mistook Longstreet and his staff for Yankees and fired at them. Several men were killed, including General Micah Jenkins. Longstreet himself was severely wounded and knocked out of action for several months.

While combat raged along the Plank road, Burnside was failing miserably in his assigned task of coming in behind the Rebel left. A single Confederate brigade under Brigadier General Stephen D. Ramseur frustrated his first attempt to pass between Ewell and Hill. Then he became hopelessly entangled in the underbrush and Rebel reinforcements arrived to block him, ensuring that the IX Corps was lost to the Union effort for the rest of the day.

But Lee, too, was experiencing frustrations. The Confederate attack had become disorganized in the wake of the Longstreet mishap, and several hours passed before Lee could reorder his scattered forces on the Plank road. Hancock used the lull to rally his retreating troops and prepare a strongly fortified line along the Brock road. At 5:00 p.m. Lee attacked this new position.

The Federals slaughtered the Confederates as they charged, but then Hancock's log-and-earth barricades caught fire. Taking advantage of the acrid smoke billowing into the Yankees' faces, the Rebels leaped over the fortifications; but Hancock's artillery drove them back, and in short order the breach was sealed. That closed the day's actions on the Orange Plank road.

While this bloody stalemate was being played out, equally fierce but inconclusive combat erupted again along the Orange Turnpike. At daybreak Sedgwick and Warren attacked Ewell, who repulsed them once again. Gordon, whose Georgians made up Ewell's northernmost element, scouted behind Sedgwick's formation and discovered that its right flank dangled unprotected. He urged Ewell and his division chief, Major General Jubal A. Early, to exploit this opportunity, but Early objected. He feared—incorrectly, it developed—that Burnside's men were massed nearby. Toward the end of the day, Gordon persuaded Ewell to attack anyway. Shortly before sundown, three of Ewell's brigades crumpled the upper end of Sedgwick's line. Darkness, however, prevented Gordon from exploiting the breakthrough.

The Battle of the Wilderness had ended. Lee stood entrenched firmly in place and confidently awaited Grant's next move.

*On May 6 Hancock punched through Hill's line and was set to swamp Lee's army when Longstreet arrived, repulsed the Yankees, and launched a flank attack that rolled up Hancock's line. Subsequently, Gordon hammered Sedgwick's right flank north of the turnpike, and the day closed with the Rebels in a strong position.*

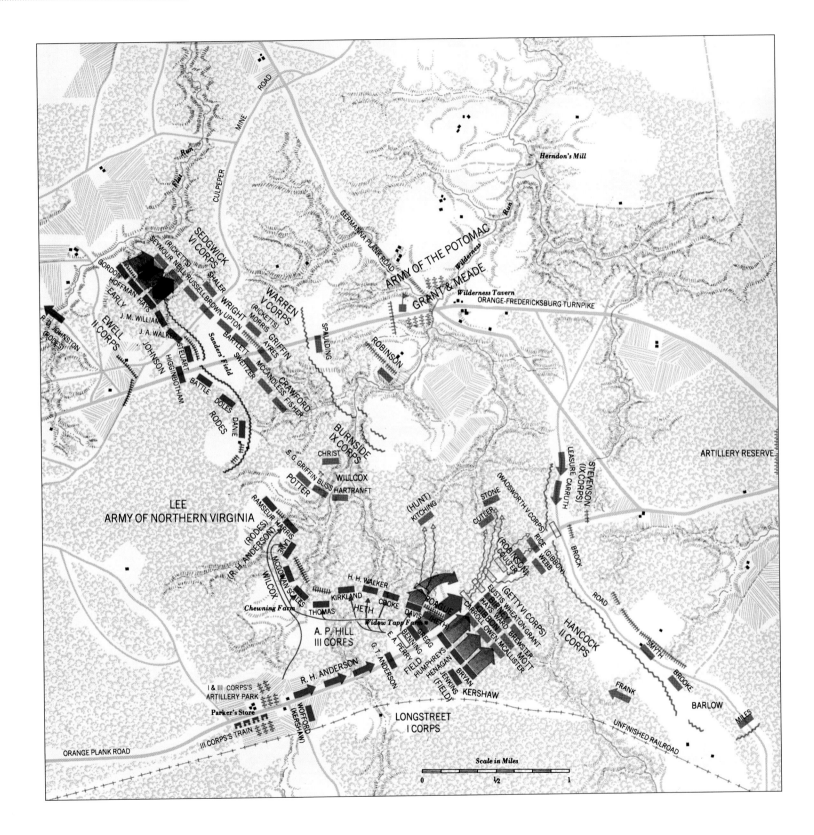

## LIEUTENANT COLONEL WILLIAM T. POAGUE

### ARTILLERY BATTALION COMMANDER, THIRD CORPS

*Poague, one of Lee's ablest artillerists, deployed his guns on May 5 along a rise on the Widow Tapp's farm to support A. P. Hill's defense of the Orange Plank road. Reconnoitering early the following morning, Poague became alarmed by the lethargy and unpreparedness of Hill's troops.*

As I went along the Plank Road . . . I was surprised to see the unusual condition of things. Nearly all the men were still asleep. One long row of muskets was stacked in the road. Another row made an acute angle with the road and still another was almost at right angles, and here and there could be seen bunches of stacked guns.

I asked an officer the meaning of the apparent confusion and unreadiness of our lines and was told that Hill's men had been informed that they were to be relieved by fresh troops before daylight, and were expecting the relieving forces every minute. I asked where the Yankees were. He didn't know certainly, but supposed they were in the woods in front. He struck me as being very indifferent and not at all concerned about the situation. I could not help feeling troubled, although I supposed somebody knew about how things were.

Just after I had gotten back to the battalion and placed the recaptured gun in position, pop! pop! began the skirmishers and soon a terrific outbreak of musketry showed that the enemy were attacking in force. For I knew that our troops could hardly be making the attack with our lines situated as I had found them to be. For a long time the firing seemed to be stationary and then gradually it began to draw nearer. Soon our men were seen to be falling back slowly on the right of the road, through a thick growth of blackjack. None of our wounded retired by the road but kept in the dense woods. I could yet do nothing to help our sorely pressed men because the firing indicated that the combatants were very close together and all across the road from our position.

Closer and closer the uproar came and at last the enemy's skirmishers appeared at the edge of the thicket in our front and opened fire on us. I had directed our men to pile up rails, logs, etc., at each gun for protection from bullets that now came constantly our way. Knowing that the skirmishers in our front meant a line of battle behind them, I ordered a slow fire to the front with short range shells. To our surprise no force showed itself, for I surely expected our guns to be charged. I had one gun in the road . . . which was used with effect in causing the approaching hostiles to leave the road for the brush.

Still our troops were being pressed back until they were nearly on our flank. Several pieces on the right of the battery were turned to fire obliquely across the road on their advancing lines as indicated by the firing, for not a man could be seen in the tangle of the Wilderness.

*Alfred N. Proffitt, a 22-year-old private in the 18th North Carolina of Lane's brigade, was shot in the head as the Federals overran Hill's right flank. He survived, although the Minié ball remained lodged in one of his sinuses. Years later, after Proffitt experienced a violent sneeze, the Yankee bullet (above) popped out of his nose.*

## LIEUTENANT COLONEL WILLIAM H. PALMER
### STAFF, LIEUTENANT GENERAL A. P. HILL

*Expecting Longstreet's First Corps to arrive before daylight, Lee and A. P. Hill chose to let Hill's tired soldiers sleep rather than redeploy the scattered units against a possible enemy assault. But Longstreet was still on the march when Hancock's Yankee juggernaut stormed into the Rebel front and flank. Palmer, a twice-wounded veteran, recalled the near disaster that resulted from his superiors' misjudgment.*

As soon as it was light General Hill rode to the left to examine the ground in the interval between General Ewell's troops and his, leaving me at the fire by the right gun of Poague's battalion. Shortly after he left I looked across the field and saw General Longstreet loping his horse across the open. I had served in his brigade with the First Virginia Infantry, and knew him well, but had not seen him

*General James Longstreet, Lee's trusted "War Horse," rested his hard-marching soldiers for eight hours on the evening of May 5, a delay that contributed to the near-destruction of Hill's corps. But once he reached the field, Longstreet brilliantly executed a counterattack that turned the tide of battle in the Rebels' favor.*

since his Chickamauga and Knoxville campaign. As I grasped his hand I said, "Ah, General, we have been looking for you since 12 o'clock last night. We expect to be attacked at any moment, and are not in any shape to resist." His answer, "My troops are not up, I have ridden ahead," was drowned in a roar of musketry. He rode off to form his troops in the road, and in a moment General Hill returned, and together we rode to the main road. As far as we could see the road was crowded with the enemy moving forward; our troops slowly and in order retiring, except just at the road, where they were holding fast. General Hill directed me to ride to the guns, and to order them to fire obliquely across the road. McGowan's brigade were for the most part through the guns and forming behind him. There were a few of our troops in front. General Hill said it could not be delayed, the guns must open. The sixteen guns firing, the last one reaching the enemy far in rear, did great execution, as the road was packed with Federal troops. It was unexpected, as no artillery had been used the day before, except one gun in the road, which was soon silenced by the enemy's skirmishers. It enabled us to hold at the road, and soon the Texas brigade of Longstreet's corps filed behind the guns, and as they moved into position General Longstreet rode down the line, his horse at a walk, and addressing each company said, "Keep cool, men, we will straighten this out in a short time—keep cool."

## COLONEL WILLIAM F. PERRY
### BRIGADE COMMANDER, FIRST CORPS

*Galvanized, Longstreet's soldiers hurried forward as they neared the battlefield. The brigades of Generals John Gregg and Henry L. Benning pushed past Hill's demoralized men and charged across Widow Tapp's field, while Perry's five Alabama regiments deployed astride the Orange Plank road. Formerly president of East Alabama Female College, Perry enlisted as a private and ended up a brigadier general.*

The progress made before light was slow. The night was dark, and we seemed to be on a narrow country road. As it grew light the speed of the men was quickened. At sunrise firing was heard in the distance, and about the same time the direction of our march changed almost at a right angle to the left. The distance to the scene of the engagement was now probably about five miles, and it was traversed with the greatest possible speed.

The first visible sign of battle that we encountered was the field hospital, through the depressing scenes of which our line of march lay. We were now on the Orange plank-road, and began to meet the wounded retiring from the field. At first there were few; but soon they came in streams, some borne on litters, some supported by comrades, and others making their way alone. Close behind them were the broken masses of Heth's division, swarming through the woods, heedless of their officers, who were riding in every direction shouting to gain their attention.

The brigades, pressing on with increasing speed, lapped each other, and now in some places filled the road with a double column of march. The only encouraging feature of the situation was the manner in which the men bore up under the depressing influences around them. They were just now rejoining their old comrades and idolized commander, after a separation of eight months. They saw that this reunion had occurred at a crisis when lofty qualities were in demand and great things were to be done; and they rose with the emergency. The stronger the pressure upon them, the greater the rebound and the firmer their resolution seemed to become. They urged the retreating soldiers to reform —come back—and aid them in beating the enemy. In a tone that indicated the belief that such an announcement was of itself sufficient to inspire renewed hope and courage, they informed them that they were "Longstreet's boys," returned to fight with them under "Old Bob."

## PRIVATE EDWARD H. FRARY
### 97TH NEW YORK INFANTRY, BAXTER'S BRIGADE

*Advancing in the center of Wadsworth's division, Frary's regiment helped drive Hill's left flank to the Orange Plank road before Poague's artillery and Longstreet's reinforcements halted the Yankee advance. Frary, a farmer drafted into the Union army in July 1863, was grievously wounded by an exploding shell and left for dead. He spent the next nine months in a military hospital.*

On the morning of the 6th, firing began as the first light of day showed through the trees. Soon after sunrise a charge was ordered along the whole line covered by the 5th corps. As we drove the enemy from the line they had occupied the evening before, we could see the evidence that our fire had been effective as there were dead men laying all about. Just in the rear of a large tree were six bodies fairly piled on one another.

Just before we reached the plank road, I was struck by a spent ball on the left knee, cutting through pants and flesh, striking my knee cap, cracking it, and causing me to measure my length on the ground. On getting up, and finding that I was all together, I continued on with the line. We struck the plank road at an angle and wheeled slightly to the right, still driving the enemy. Men on both sides were falling, either dead or wounded, like leaves from the trees, until it seemed to be only a question of a little time when we would entirely destroy each other. Finally we came to a halt as we reached a line of their works and they opened up a battery from front and right oblique on us, at close range, with terrible effect. One shell which exploded just to my right caused three deaths and three others wounded. Two of the dead were twin brothers by the name of Fisher.

Just after that, as I was with right knee on the ground, resting left elbow on left knee, and aiming my Enfield at a Johnny standing at the

*The 13th North Carolina Infantry was issued this unique variation of the Confederacy's "second national" flag a month before the Battle of the Wilderness. During the rout of Hill's corps the banner was captured by Sergeant Stephen Rought of the 141st Pennsylvania, who killed the colorbearer with a blow from his musket butt.*

*Yankee troops of Wadsworth's division, formed in line of battle, fight their way through the woods north of the Orange Plank road. "The smoke and rattle of musketry all conduced to a fearful confusion," one Federal recalled. "In this chaos it was almost impossible to distinguish friend from foe."*

right end of our ambulance, a shell exploded above and so close to my head that I heard the rending of the iron of the shell. A piece of it struck my gun on the stock, knocking it out of my hands, and hit the side of my shoe as it reached the ground. At this same instant, I felt that my whole left side was torn out. It was one awful terrible agonizing sensation as though all creation had fallen in upon me, crushing and tearing my body apart, piece by piece. My first thought was that the piece of shell had gone through my body. The concussion from the shell had partly thrown me back so that when I straighted up partially, the blood gushed out of my mouth and nose as though pumped.

My captain ordered two men, W. H. Gray and Columbus W. Ford, to carry me back to the rear and stay with me. We started back, they carrying me as best as they could, by holding me up under my arms.

That was agonizing to me so I begged them to lay me down so I could die in peace. Even then I was wondering that I could be conscious when I was torn open as I supposed I was. They sat me down by the side of the road. We could see and hear shells come tearing down the road and through the woods. I was still bleeding from nose and mouth. With others' help the boys carried me back a ways. When I was becoming faint, I begged them to lay me down, which they did. I bid them goodby

# "We all saw that Gen. Lee was following us into battle—care and anxiety upon his countenance—refusing to come back at the request and advice of his staff."

as my vision dimmed, supposing that for me it was the last of earth. Thoughts of my wife and children back at home came to mind. With a mental prayer that God would care for them, I became unconscious. The boys returned to the company and reported me dead. In the field report of those terrible days, I was so reported. (While being carried back, Gray had unbuttoned my clothes and found a bullet sticking about half out of my back and found a hole in my neck.)

Toward sundown I recovered consciousness so far as to understand that I was yet in the land of suffering and living.

*This battle flag of the 5th Texas was presented to the regiment by Mrs. M. J. Young in the spring of 1862 and carried at the Wilderness, where 60 percent of the unit fell. The flag was retired the following October and returned to Mrs. Young.*

## PRIVATE ROBERT CAMPBELL
### 5TH TEXAS INFANTRY, GREGG'S BRIGADE

*The 20-year-old Campbell, detailed as a courier on General Gregg's staff, was awed by the sight of Robert E. Lee personally leading the Texans into battle. Posted on the right flank of the Texas Brigade, Campbell's regiment charged across the Tapp field, then swung south to engage Federal troops on the other side of the Orange Plank road. Only 77 of the 188 men in the 5th Texas emerged from the fight unscathed, and every one of its officers was killed or wounded.*

As we stood upon this hill, Lee excited and in close consultation with Longstreet. . . . The cannon thundered, musketry rolled, stragglers were fleeing, couriers riding here and there in post-haste, minnies began to sing, the dying and wounded were jolted by the flying ambulances, and filling the road-side, adding to the excitement the terror of death. The "Texas brigade," was in front of Fields' division—while "Humphrey's brigade" of Mississippians led the van of Kershaw's division.

The consultation ended. Gen. Gregg and Gen. Humphrey were ordered to form their brigades in line of battle, which was quickly done, and we found ourselves near the brow of the hill, Gregg on the left—Humphrey on the right. "Gen. Gregg prepare to move," was the order from Gen. L.

About this time, Gen. Lee, with his staff, rode up to Gen. Gregg—"General what brigade is this?" said Lee.

"The Texas brigade," was General G.'s reply.

"I am glad to see it," said Lee. "When you go in there, I wish you to give those men the cold steel—they will stand and fire all day, and never move unless you charge them."

"That is my experience," replied the brave Gregg.

By this time an aid from General Longstreet rode up and repeated the order, "advance your command, Gen. Gregg." And now comes the

*A Texas district judge and a staunch secessionist, John Gregg was elected to the first Confederate Congress but resigned his seat to become colonel of the 7th Texas Infantry. Gregg saw extensive action in the war's western theater, and in January 1864 he was given command of the famed Texas Brigade.*

point upon which the interest of this "o'er true tale" hangs. *"Attention Texas Brigade"* was rung upon the morning air, by Gen. Gregg, *"the eyes of General Lee are upon you, forward, march."* Scarce had we moved a step, when Gen. Lee, in front of the whole command, raised himself in his stirrups, uncovered his grey hairs, and with an earnest, yet anxious voice, exclaimed above the din and confusion of the hour, *"Texans always move them."*

. . . never before in my lifetime or since, did I ever witness such a scene as was enacted when Lee pronounced these words, with the appealing look that he gave. A yell rent the air that must have been heard for miles around, and but few eyes in that old brigade of veterans and heroes of many a bloody field was undimmed by honest, heart-felt tears. Leonard Gee, a courier to Gen. Gregg, and riding by my side, with tears coursing down his cheeks and yells issuing from his throat exclaimed, "I would charge hell itself for that old man." It was not what

Gen. Lee said that so infused and excited the men, as his tone and look, which each one of us knew were born of the dangers of the hour.

With yell after yell we moved forward, passed the brow of the hill, and moved down the declivity towards the undergrowth—a distance in all not exceeding 200 yards. After moving over half the ground we all saw that Gen. Lee was following us into battle—care and anxiety upon his countenance—refusing to come back at the request and advice of his staff . . . the brigade halted when they discovered Gen. Lee's intention, and all eyes were turned upon him. Five and six of his staff would gather around him, seize him, his arms, his horse's reins, but he shook them off and moved forward. Thus did he continue until just before we reached the undergrowth, not, however, until the balls began to fill and whistle through the air. Seeing that we would do all that men could do to retrieve the misfortunes of the hour, accepting the advice of his staff, and hearkening to the protest of his advancing soldiers, he at last turned round and rode back to a position on the hill.

## CAPTAIN D. AUGUSTUS DICKERT
### 3D SOUTH CAROLINA INFANTRY, HENAGAN'S BRIGADE

*While Gregg's brigade blunted the Federal assault in Widow Tapp's field, Colonel John W. Henagan's South Carolinians—the lead brigade of Kershaw's division —wheeled into the woods south of the Orange Plank road. Henagan's men held their fire as the stampeding remnants of Hill's corps passed through their formation, then dressed the line and charged the oncoming Federal ranks. Dickert, who wrote a history of the brigade, chronicled the desperate struggle that followed.*

As soon as the musketry firing was heard, we hastened our steps, and as we reached the brow of a small elevation in the ground, orders were given to deploy across the road. Colonel Gaillard, with the Second, formed on the left of the road, while the Third, under Colonel Nance, formed on the right, with the other regiments taking their places on the right of the Third in their order of march. . . .

The line had not yet formed before a perfect hail of bullets came flying overhead and through our ranks, but not a man moved, only to allow the stampeded troops of Heath's and Wilcox's to pass to the rear. . . . While forming his lines of battle, and while bullets were flying all around, General Kershaw came dashing down in front of his column, his eyes flashing fire, sitting his horse like a centaur—that superb style

*Shortly before the outbreak of war Franklin Gaillard sat for this portrait with his children, Maria and David. After graduating from South Carolina College, Gaillard prospected for gold in California, then returned to his native state and became an influential editor of newspapers in Winnsboro and Columbia. He suffered a mortal head wound while leading the 2d South Carolina at the Wilderness.*

# "Both armies stood at extreme tension, and the cord must soon snap one way or the other, or it seemed as all would be annihilated."

as Joe Kershaw only could—and said in passing us, "Now, my old brigade, I expect you to do your duty." . . . It seemed an inspiration to every man in line, especially his old brigade, who knew too well that their conduct to-day would either win or lose him his Major General's spurs, and right royally did he gain them. The columns were not yet in proper order, but the needs so pressing to check the advance of the enemy, that a forward movement was ordered, and the lines formed up as the troops marched.

The second moved forward on the left of the plank road, in support of a battery stationed there, and which was drawing a tremendous fire upon the troops on both sides of the road. Down the gentle slope the

brigade marched, over and under the tangled shrubbery and dwarf saplings, while a withering fire was being poured into them by as yet an unseen enemy. Men fell here and there, officers urging on their commands and ordering them to "hold their fire." When near the lower end of the declivity, the shock came. Just in front of us, and not forty yards away, lay the enemy. The long line of blue could be seen under the ascending smoke of thousands of rifles; the red flashes of their guns seemed to blaze in our very faces. Now the battle was on in earnest. . . . The roar of the small arms, mingled with the thunder of the cannon that Longstreet had brought forward, echoed and re-echoed up and down the little valley, but never to die away, for new troops were being put rapidly in action to the right and left of us. Men rolled and writhed in their last death struggle; wounded men groped their way to the rear, being blinded by the stifling smoke. All commands were drowned in this terrible din of battle—the earth and elements shook and trembled with the deadly shock of combat. Regiments were left without commanders; companies without officers. The gallant Colonel Gaillard, of the Second, had fallen. The intrepid young Colonel of the Third, J. D. Nance, had already died in the lead of his regiment. The commander of the Seventh, Captain Goggans, was wounded. . . .

Still the battle rolled on. It seemed for a time as if the whole Federal Army was upon us—so thick and fast came the death-dealing missiles. Our ranks were being decimated by the wounded and the dead. . . . The enemy held their position with a tenacity, born of desperation, while the confederates pressed them with that old-time Southern vigor and valor that no amount of courage could withstand. Both armies stood at extreme tension, and the cord must soon snap one way or the other, or it seemed as all would be annihilated.

### PRIVATE CHARLES A. FREY
150TH PENNSYLVANIA INFANTRY, STONE'S BRIGADE

*One of several Pennsylvania regiments sporting bucktails in their caps, the 150th advanced in the rear rank of Wadsworth's division. The 20-year-old Frey, although ailing with chronic rheumatism and diarrhea, stuck by his comrades as the Bucktails clashed with Longstreet's troops east of Tapp's field.*

At five o'clock A.M. we were ordered into ranks. All night long troops had been brought up and placed in position, and by morning our lines were all properly established, and we were ready to fight a fair, square, stand-up battle. The sun rose with unclouded brilliancy. As its first rays came streaming through the woods, we moved forward on the enemy's position. To a looker-on, I think the advance that morning was the grandest display of military strength that was ever seen on this continent. We press on in six parallel lines of battle, and as the mighty host advances along the plank road, it seemed as if nothing could check its progress. Our brigade was in the third line from the front.

The front line had not proceeded over a hundred yards before it came upon the enemy, who, judging from the quantity of corn meal scattered over the ground, must have been drawing rations. The battle opened at once. They give way before the fierce attack of our front line, fighting, however, as they retire; and for more than a mile they are borne steadily back, and it looked as if we would have an easy day of it. But their batteries have now got into position, and are throwing shells through our ranks at a terrible rate. At this juncture Longstreet's corps arrives and advances to the attack. Our foremost line, which has been doing such splendid fighting, is now checked, and then falls back. The second steps to the front and pours in its volleys. It bears up bravely for a while, but at last is also compelled to give way before the desperate onslaught of the enemy. Now is our turn. As the men composing our

first and second lines take refuge in our rear, we move to the front, and General Wadsworth riding up to our regiment says: "Give it to them, Bucktails!" We pour in one close, deadly volley, and they stagger under the terrible fire. The general shouts: "Boys, you are driving them; charge!" Our brigade, now the front, charges fiercely, driving them back some distance; but a fresh line comes to their support, fires a volley in our very faces, and sends us back over the ground we had just gained, charging us in return. A new line comes to our aid, pours its fire upon the opposing ranks, compelling them to give way; and again we charge over the same ground, only to be driven back in turn, on our reserves, as reinforcements come to the help of the enemy. The battle now becomes close and bloody. Charges and countercharges are made in quick succession. Five times we traverse the same ground, led by General Wadsworth, who sits on his horse with hat in hand, bringing it down on the pommel of his saddle with every bound, as he rides at the head of the column. Then as the bullets strike among his men like hail, and they begin to recoil, he rides slowly back in their midst, speaking kindly to them, with ever a smile on his pleasant countenance, which shows no concern for the storm of lead and iron raging around him.

*The commander of Company G of the 150th Pennsylvania, Captain Horatio Bell, had earlier served as acting regimental commander. He was among 22 men in the 150th who were killed during the two days of fighting in the Wilderness.*

## LIEUTENANT COLONEL G. MOXLEY SORREL

STAFF, LIEUTENANT GEN-
ERAL JAMES LONGSTREET

*Sorrel, the son of a Savannah businessman, left the Georgia Central Railroad in 1861 to join Longstreet's brigade as an aide. Dashing and ambitious, he soon became the general's chief of staff. At the Wilderness he led the daring flank assault on Hancock's corps.*

there is a fine chance of a great attack by our right. If you will quickly get into those woods, some brigades will be found much scattered from the fight. Collect them and take charge. Form a good line and then move, your right pushed forward and turning as much as possible to the left. Hit hard when you start, but don't start until you have everything ready. I shall be waiting for your gun fire, and be on hand with fresh troops for further advance."

A slight pause in the activities of the armies occurred. Gen. M. L. Smith, an engineer from General Headquarters, had reported to Longstreet and examined the situation on our right, where he discovered the enemy's left somewhat exposed and inviting attack; and now came our turn. General Longstreet, calling me, said: "Colonel,

*Brigadier General James Wadsworth (above) was, at the age of 56, one of the oldest field officers in the Union army. A Harvard-educated patrician and a leading figure in the Republican Party, he was appointed to division command following an unsuccessful 1862 campaign for the governorship of New York. Wadsworth was shot from his horse with a mortal wound while riding along the embattled Union line (left).*

No greater opportunity could be given to an aspiring young staff officer, and I was quickly at work. The brigades of Anderson, Mahone, and Wofford were lined up in fair order and in touch with each other. It was difficult to assemble them in that horrid Wilderness, but in an hour we were ready. The word was given, and then with heavy firing and ringing yells we were upon Hancock's exposed left, the brigades being ably commanded by their respective officers. It was rolled back line after line. I was well mounted, and despite the tangled growth could keep with our troops in conspicuous sight of them, riding most of the charge with Mahone's men and the Eighteenth Virginia. . . . A stand was attempted by a reserve line of Hancock's, but it was swept off its feet in the tumultuous rush of our troops, and finally we struck the Plank Road lower down. On the other side of it was Wadsworth's corps in disorder. (I had last seen him under flag of truce at Fredericksburg.) Though the old General was doing all possible to fight it, his men would not stay. A volley from our pursuing troops brought down the gallant New Yorker, killing both rider and horse.

There was still some life left in the General, and every care was given him by our surgeon. Before they could get to him, however, some of his valuables—watch, sword, glasses, etc.—had disappeared among the troops. One of the men came up with, "Here, Colonel, here's his map." It was a good general map of Virginia, and of use afterwards.

## SERGEANT ELNATHAN B. TYLER
### 14TH CONNECTICUT INFANTRY, CARROLL'S BRIGADE

*Tyler writes vividly of the unstoppable Rebel assault against the Federal left. After shifting along the unfinished railroad to a point just south of Hancock's force, Sorrel's brigades slammed into the naked flank of the Union line. Yankee Colonel Robert McAllister's brigade offered little resistance before fleeing through Colonel Samuel Carroll's troops, who gave way in turn. Shot through the hips, Tyler was carried off by his retreating comrades.*

The real shock of the day came shortly after noon when Longstreet, that master of impetuous charges, massed a large body of men and precipitated them upon a portion of our line he may have had reason to think a little weak. This attack struck our line a little to the left of the Fourteenth's position. We quickly changed front, moved to the left and then forward in a countermarch in the direction of the advancing foe. Before opening fire we had to let the broken and deplet-

ed remnants of a regiment that had been stationed on this part of the line fall back into or through our ranks. That done we opened fire. How defiantly and continuously that rebel yell of the oncoming foe held its own even above the volleys of musketry, and this was wholly a battle of infantry and musketry. Still onward they come. Our men had halted and keeping their line in as good shape as possible were awaiting the shock. But we were not idle; the men, many of them lying close upon the ground, some of them resting on one knee, were firing rapidly and low. Officers and file closers were cheering them and encouraging them, sending the wounded to the rear and strengthening the ranks by using their rifles as freely as the men. And now they had come so near we began to distinguish the brown and butternut colored uniforms among the trees and our rifles had distinct targets and the increasing closeness of their shots showed they too were having the same advantage. Now we could see them still more plainly. They were not coming fast, simply moving forward slowly, steadily, and Oh, so obstinately and surely! We could not check them. I am sure our Sharp's rifles never did better service for the few brief minutes than now, but their yells and their volleys and their advance seemingly was not to be stayed. There could only be one result, unless speedily reinforced, we should be overpowered and captured within five minutes. The volleys from our rifles were growing weaker and scattering. Our color-bearer had planted the flag staff firmly on the ground and kneeling or lying beside it upheld it with his upstretched arms.

## LIEUTENANT COLONEL CHARLES H. WEYGANT
### 124TH NEW YORK INFANTRY, WARD'S BRIGADE

*Caught in a crossfire from their left flank and rear, Hancock's brigades crumbled before the Confederate charge. Regiments like Weygant's that had been distinguished for valor in earlier battles were swept away. Weygant recounted his futile efforts to rally the panicked men in his 1877 history of the "Orange Blossoms" —the unit's nickname, referring to its origins in Orange County, New York.*

A terrific racket broke out in the woods to our left, and bullets began to fly thick and fast above and among us, passing lengthwise of the Union line. The grand assault which Lee had intended to make at an early hour in the morning had come at last. . . .

Hurrying the 124th into line, I caused it to change front to the left, so as to face toward whence the bullets came, and attempted to prevent

*Colonel Charles Griswold of the 56th Massachusetts Infantry was killed while making a valiant attempt to stem the Rebel offensive on the Orange Plank road. His line thrown into disorder by fleeing troops, Griswold seized the regimental flag shown here and ordered an advance. "He was extremely brave," a comrade recalled, "shot through the jugular vein while holding the colors, which were covered with his blood."*

enveloped line, like heat lightning from a cloudy horizon, and pouring into our disorganized host a continuous fire, so terrible in its effect as to leave the ground over which we passed strewn afresh with hundreds, yea, thousands of dead, wounded, and dying. Hancock's officers, in their frantic efforts to rally their men on a new line, planted their colors on nearly every rising piece of ground they came to; and, waving their swords and gnashing their teeth, shrieked the order, *"Rally men, rally for God and your country's sake, rally,"* but to no purpose. The colors were no sooner planted by those in front, than they were swept away, and in some instances trampled under foot, by those from the rear, who, while doing their best to get out of range of the enemy's bullets, continually echoed and re-echoed the *Rally men, rally.*

At one place about a mile and a half in rear of the farthest point of our advance, on the banks of a little stream that ran through this vast, weird, horrible, slaughter-pen, a skeleton line of mixed troops was partially formed; and for a moment it looked as if a sufficient number might be rallied there, to at least check the thus far almost undisputed advance of Longstreet's lines. Gathering a corporal's guard of the 124th about me, I sprang over the stream, and bidding my color-bearer (Corporal Washington Edwards) unfurl our flag, planted it on the half-formed line; but almost the next moment a heavy volley coming from the woods to our rear and left, told that a fresh and unexpected body of the foe was close upon us, and away went our men again in an instant. I now became thoroughly disheartened, and, abandoning all hopes of gathering my command south of the Rapidan, sheathed my sword, and moved back with the rabble.

the further spread of the disaster, but I might as well have tried to stop the flight of a cannon ball, by interposing the lid of a cracker box. Back pell-mell came the ever swelling crowd of fugitives, and the next moment the Sons of Orange were caught up as by a whirlwind, and broken to fragments; and the terrible tempest of disaster swept down the Union line, beating back brigade after brigade, and tearing to pieces regiment after regiment, until upwards of twenty thousand veterans were fleeing, every man for himself, through the disorganizing and already blood-stained woods, toward the Union rear.

The foe meantime pressed rapidly forward, lighting up the dim forest with powder flames which continually flashed from his smoke-

## CAPTAIN FRANCIS W. DAWSON
### STAFF, LIEUTENANT GENERAL JAMES LONGSTREET

*At noon, with the Yankees falling back toward the Brock road, Longstreet rode east on the Orange Plank road to follow up his success with a renewed assault on the enemy. Dawson describes how, in a replay of the Stonewall Jackson tragedy a year earlier, Longstreet's group was fired upon by the 12th Virginia and other units of William Mahone's brigade, who had mistaken the party for retreating Federals.*

Longstreet, with Colonel Sorrel, Captain Manning, of the Signal Corps, and myself, with some couriers, rode down the Plank-road at the head of our column. Just then, General Jenkins, who commanded a South Carolina brigade in our corps, rode up, his face flushed with joy, and, shaking hands with Longstreet, congratulated him on the result of the fight. Turning then to his brigade, which was formed in the road, Jenkins said: "Why do you not cheer, men?" The men cheered lustily, and hardly had the sound died away when a withering fire was poured in upon us from the woods on our right. Jenkins, rising in his stirrups, shouted out: "Steady, men! For God's sake, steady!" and fell mortally wounded from his saddle. Longstreet, who had stood there like a lion at bay, reeled as the blood poured down over his breast, and was evidently badly hurt. Two of General Jenkins' staff were killed by the same volley. What others thought I know not. My own conviction was that we had ridden into the midst of the enemy, and that nothing remained but to sell our lives dearly. The firing ended as suddenly as it began, and we learned that Longstreet had been wounded and Jenkins had been killed, as Jackson was, by the fire of our own men. It was but the work of a few minutes. We lifted Longstreet from the saddle, and laid him on the side of the road. It seemed that he had not many minutes to live. My next thought was to obtain a surgeon, and, hurriedly mentioning my purpose, I mounted my horse and rode in desperate haste to the nearest field hospital. Giving the sad news to the first surgeon I could find, I made him jump on my horse, and bade him, for Heaven's sake, ride as rapidly as he could to the front where Longstreet was. I followed afoot. The flow of blood was speedily staunched, and Longstreet was placed in an ambulance.

*Shot through the neck and shoulder, Longstreet (center) maintains his composure as General Micah Jenkins (left) reels with a mortal head wound. "I settled back to my seat and started to ride on," Longstreet recalled, "when in a minute the flow of blood admonished me that my work for the day was done."*

*Weakened by illness and suffering from painful carbuncles on his back, Brigadier General Micah Jenkins climbed out of an ambulance to lead his troops against the Yankee line at Brock road, exclaiming, "We shall smash them now!" Jenkins' sword and scabbard (below) were damaged by the fatal volley from Mahone's Virginians.*

# COLONEL ASBURY COWARD
## 5TH SOUTH CAROLINA INFANTRY, JENKINS' BRIGADE

*Coward, like his boyhood friend Micah Jenkins, was the scion of a wealthy South Carolina planter and a graduate of the Citadel. In 1854 he and Jenkins founded the King's Mountain Military Academy at Yorkville. The two young men continued their close association in the army, and when Coward learned of Jenkins' wounding, he hastened to his stricken comrade. Later that afternoon Coward himself was severely wounded leading a charge on the Federal breastworks along the Brock road.*

After we had marched in line about 100 yards through brush and woods, we came upon a line of men, about two small regiments, lying down or kneeling directly in the path of our march.

I had to halt my men and on inquiry found it was General Mahone's Brigade, who had just halted there. Seeing at the time a flag passing along the tunpike, I ran toward it through the intermediate thicket to inquire what troops they were. It was the Second South Carolina, one of the regiments of Jenkins' Brigade. I could not understand why they were marching in columns of fours, while I was marching in line of battle.

As I turned, I saw that Mahone's men had commenced, on the right, to fire by file. Thinking only of the danger to the Second Regiment, I rushed back to stop the firing by voice and gesture.

But not until I reached the line was the firing stopped.

At that moment Mahone walked up and enquired why the firing had stopped. I explained why I had stopped it. He then asked me who had started it. I told him the firing had begun in his right company. I

# "The order came for the Second Brigade to advance, which it did in the face of a terrible, murderous fire, the bullets raining upon the men like hailstones."

went on to say that they might be able to explain how it started there.

He went off in the direction of his right company in a very agitated state.

The incident had just taken place when Major R. M. Sims came to me and said: "That firing has wounded both General Longstreet and General Jenkins, one in the throat and the other in the temple . . . and I fear both are fatally wounded."

I ran toward the group of trees that he indicated and found men lifting General Longstreet, litter and all, into an ambulance. Jenkins had just been placed on a litter. General Kershaw, who had remounted his horse, was urging haste; for the enemy's cannon was throwing shells at the cluster of trees. Fortunately, the shots were passing high but were nevertheless dangerous.

I knelt by the friend of my life since I entered The Citadel, my alter ego. Taking his hand in mine, I said: "Jenkins . . . Mike, do you know me?"

I felt a convulsive pressure of my hand. Then I noticed that his features, in fact his whole body, was convulsed.

The haste urged by General Kershaw prevented any further stay at his side. He was lifted into an ambulance and carried to the rear.

Dazed, I returned to my Regiment.

## CAPTAIN LEANDER W. COGSWELL
### 11TH NEW HAMPSHIRE INFANTRY, S. G. GRIFFIN'S BRIGADE

*Shortly before 2:00 p.m., eight hours late, Burnside's IX Corps arrived to support the Federal attack on the Orange Plank road. But it was the Rebels who were now attacking, and as the Yankees approached, three Confederate brigades swung north to meet them. Cogswell described the savage encounter in his 1871 regimental history.*

The Eleventh had the advance of the brigade, and when the centre was reached a line of battle was formed, and an advance was made until the Third Division was reached, the men of which were lying upon the ground, hesitating to advance. The order came for the Second Brigade to advance, which it did in the face of a terrible, murderous fire, the bullets raining upon the men like hailstones. Just

*The senior officers of the 11th New Hampshire—Colonel Walter Harriman (left) and Lieutenant Colonel Moses Collins—were among the 56 casualties their regiment sustained during Burnside's advance through the woods north of Widow Tapp's field. Collins was shot dead and Harriman taken prisoner; a minister and former New Hampshire state treasurer, he was elected governor two years after the war.*

as the order came, "Charge!" Lieutenant-Colonel Collins was shot through the head, a bullet entering his forehead, and he fell dead. On went the brave boys with such an impetuosity that the first intrenchments were carried, and many prisoners captured. The woods were on fire, the smoke was dense, the work of no other regiment could be seen . . . and still the men, flushed with success, moved on, until ascertaining themselves to be far in advance of any other regiment, Colonel Harriman called a halt. He then, wishing to find where the rest of his brigade was, as well as to report his own success, sent back Captain Edgerly of the brigade staff, who was with the Eleventh, and who was captured and shot; then Corporal Franklin was sent, and he also was captured. Captain Tilton was next dispatched, and barely escaped capture. Finally, Lieutenant Frost was dispatched, and received this message from General Griffin: "Tell Colonel Harriman to hold the line, if he can." Before this order was received a line of rebels was seen coming upon our left flank, and Colonel Harriman said, "To the rear, and form a new line to the foe!" and when the second line of the enemy which had been carried was reached, the colonel ordered a halt. "We

can hold them here," he said, but with rebels in the rear, on both flanks, and, in fact, all about them, the men, seeing that resistance was useless, fell back as best they could; and in this retreat some were killed and some were captured, among the latter being Colonel Harriman.

. . . The only wonder is that more of the men were not captured. Sergeant Edmunds, of Company D, and [myself] were the last men who saw Colonel Harriman before his capture. Every man was making good his escape, if possible. Just after the log entrenchments were reached, where Colonel Harriman had hoped to make another stand, the smoke lifted enough to disclose the fact that the rebels were close upon us and on both flanks, and all making substantially for the same point. When Colonel Harriman was captured . . . many bullets whizzed about his head as he was seen when the smoke lifted. . . .

Colonel Harriman could not help falling into the hands of the enemy, —as many another one did,—for at this point the rebels fairly swarmed, and had the Eleventh Regiment not commenced to fall back when it did, hardly a man could have escaped capture.

## COLONEL ST. CLAIR A. MULHOLLAND
### 116TH PENNSYLVANIA INFANTRY, SMYTH'S BRIGADE

*The appearance of Burnside's force on the Confederate left slowed Lee's offensive for roughly two hours, enabling Hancock's battered units to rally on the II Corps reserve at Brock road. The Yankees hastily strengthened their line of log breastworks and cleared a field of fire to their front. Mulholland, a 25-year-old Irish immigrant, describes the furious Rebel assaults that commenced shortly after 4:00 p.m.*

*I*t was a morning of intense anxiety to the men. For hours they listened to the continuous roll and the musketry and cheers of the Union Army and they knew that their people were driving everything before them as huzzas and roar of the firing continued to recede and get further away. But towards noon the Union cheers became less frequent and the firing came nearer. Then the Confederate yell rose loud and wild and the Union line began to come back. The wounded poured out of the woods in streams and everything told of disaster to the Union arms. The victorious enemy halted before reaching the point where the regiment lay and although ready and anxious and more than willing the men did not get an opportunity of firing a shot until towards evening. Towards five o'clock, Captain Megraw,

who had been out visiting the picket line, rushed in, tumbled over the breast-work and called out: "They are coming—get ready!" Instantly everyone was in line and very wide awake, although many were resting and dozing a moment before.

A few shots were heard on the picket line which was but a short distance in front, and almost without warning a Confederate line of battle stood within fifty yards of the slight works; they covered the regimental front and began firing. The fight was short and sharp. The men replied vigorously for a few moments, then the breastwork, which was built up with dry fence rails and logs, caught fire. The wind fanned the flames, and soon the whole line in front of the regiment was in a blaze. The smoke rolled back in clouds; the flames leaped ten and fifteen feet high, rolled back and scorched the men until the heat became unbearable, the musket balls the while whistling and screaming through the smoke and fire. A

*In this Alfred Waud sketch Yankee soldiers rescue a stricken comrade from the burning woods, using muskets and a blanket as a makeshift litter. Scores of dead and wounded were consumed by the flames as the fire swept east toward the Brock road.*

scene of terror and wild dismay, but no man in the ranks of the regiment moved an inch. Right in the smoke and fire they stood, and sent back the deadly volleys until the enemy gave up the effort and fell back and disappeared into the depths of that sad forest where thousands lay dead and dying. Soon the fire communicated to the trees and bush, and in less than an hour, acres of ground over which the armies had struggled and fought during the two awful days, was a mass of fire. This was the saddest part of all the battle. How many poor, wounded souls perished in the flames none but the angels who were there to receive their brave spirits will ever know.

## LIEUTENANT COLONEL CHARLES H. WEYGANT
### 124TH NEW YORK INFANTRY, WARD'S BRIGADE

*Scattered by Sorrel's flank attack, Weygant's soldiers fell back to the log breastworks along Brock road and rallied to the colors. The 124th New York and the other units of Ward's brigade, posted just south of the intersection with the Orange Plank road, repulsed several Rebel charges. But when the woods caught fire, flames and smoke began to force Ward's men from their works—an opening the enemy was quick to exploit.*

About three P.M. the Confederate advance struck and immediately drove in our pickets, who had barely time to make their way through the slashing, and crawl over the works, ere their pursuers appeared in solid battle line, and the combat re-opened with a terrific crash of riflery all along the lines; but so impetuous and persistent was the advance of the victorious foe, they were half-way through the slashing and within thirty yards of our works before we could bring them to a stand.

Occasionally one of our number would fall dead—pierced through the brain—or be carried to the rear wounded in the head, hand, or shoulder. Beyond this the rapid fire of the foe had but slight effect on our line, behind its bullet-proof cover; over the top of which we, with deliberate aim, hurled into their exposed but unwavering line an incessant and most deadly fire. Again and yet again did their shattered regiments in our front close on their colors, while fresh troops from the rear moved up and filled the gaps. . . .

During the contest the woods between the lines, at a short distance to the left of Ward's brigade, took fire. And just when the enemy—after having withstood our deadly volleys for over an hour—began to show signs of exhaustion, and a Union force was being made ready for a charge when the critical moment should arrive, a strong wind suddenly sprang up, and carried the fire to our log breastworks, along which the

*At the climax of the Confederate assault on May 6, troops of Mott's division break for the rear as two regiments of Jenkins' brigade momentarily gain the smoldering Yankee breastworks at the Brock road. The colorbearer depicted in Alfred Waud's sketch—mistakenly dated May 9—may represent Colonel Asbury Coward, who seized the 5th South Carolina's battle flag from a fallen soldier and planted it atop the parapet.*

# 'Presently huge clouds of strong black pine smoke, such as almost eats one's eyes out, rolled over and completely enveloped our regiment."

flames spread with wonderful rapidity. Several regiments to the left of the 124th, unable to withstand the heat and smoke, abandoned the works, though several individual members of these commands remained until their hair was singed, for the smoke and flames were blown directly into their faces. Presently huge clouds of strong black pine smoke, such as almost eats one's eyes out, rolled over and completely enveloped our regiment.

At this critical moment the Confederates rushed up and occupied the deserted works to our left; seeing which the Union reserve, posted as a second line about fifty yards to our rear, opened fire, and, supposing our regiment had moved down the road to the right, or fallen back behind them, with the regiments which had been stationed on our left, sent a volley right into the cloud of smoke which hid us from their view. Fortunately their aim was so high that the most of their bullets passed over our heads. . . .

A determined charge in front of an opening in the works about twenty rods to our right, had cleared the way for a battery which had been run out and placed in such a position as to rake the outer face of our breastworks, which, for the distance of full seventy rods, ran perfectly straight; and were now heavily manned with Confederate troops. As soon as these batterymen, with guns double shotted with canister, began mowing down the foe, our infantry rushed back to the now blackened and smoking works—for the flames, having consumed the most combustible portion of the dry bark from the logs, had subsided—and opened a most deadly fire into the very faces of the bleeding foe on the opposite side. Presently the batterymen were ordered to cease firing, when, with a tremendous shout, over the works rushed the Union line with clubbed muskets, swords, and bayonets, right at the now totally demoralized Confederates, who broke for the rear, and fled in the wildest disorder across the slashing and down through the woods again.

*Praised by a subordinate as "tried and faithful," Vermonter Albert Buxton—captain of Company H, 2d U.S. Sharpshooters—was among 26 men in the regiment killed outright or mortally wounded in the fighting along the Orange Plank road.*

*On the afternoon of May 6 Alfred Waud sketched mounted officers of Sedgwick's VI Corps surveying their lines north of the Orange Turnpike while smoke billows from the guns of Lieutenant Jacob Federhen's Massachusetts battery, deployed atop the knoll at left. Following a brief clash with Ewell's Confederates that morning, Sedgwick's troops spent much of the day digging rifle pits and piling up logs and brush for shelter from the incessant and deadly fire of Rebel sharpshooters.*

## PRIVATE ISAAC G. BRADWELL

### 31ST GEORGIA INFANTRY, GORDON'S BRIGADE

*All day long the fiery Gordon advocated an attack on the northern flank of Sedgwick's line, exposed when Burnside shifted to the Federal left. But the proposal was repeatedly overruled by Early and Ewell, and the hours passed. Finally, with the battle raging along the Brock road to the south, Ewell acceded to Gordon's request. Bolstered by Pegram's and Johnston's brigades, at sunset Gordon launched a furious charge, described here by Bradwell, against the Yankee position.*

The order to advance was now given, and the skirmishers ran up the hill and were on the enemy, then cooking their evening meal on thousands of small fires, secure, as they thought, behind the breastworks. Poor fellows! None of them suspected the bolt that was about to strike them. Suddenly, and only a few yards away, the long line of gray-clad soldiers appeared and opened on them seated in groups about the fires with their guns stacked back of their works. Never was lightning from the clouds more unexpected, and confusion

reigned supreme. About this time the main line came on the scene, and so anxious were they to open fire that they disregarded the orders and poured a deadly volley into the confused enemy, endangering very much the lives of our sharpshooters, who fell on their faces, shouting back to us not to shoot until we had passed over them. No attention was paid to this, and we were at their works. The regiment to which I belonged was on the extreme right of the brigade, and my company formed the right of the regiment. It so happened that the most of the company was on the right of the enemy's works. The enemy, rolled up in a confused mass behind their defenses, supposed we were the only troops making the attack and, seeing us in the dim light of their fires, opened on us with a heavy fire. All the company leaped over to the left side, and I found myself the only survivor remaining on that side. Thinking perhaps the fire on the left side, where my comrades had gone, was less severe and afforded some hope of life, I jumped over the men fighting there. No sooner had I done so than two or three of my comrades fell dead by my side, and the fire from the great mob, only a few feet in our front, was too hot for us. It was like the old saying about jumping out of the frying pan into the fire. So I again crossed the works, while my comrades moved to the left, but at the same time advancing on the enemy, who continued shooting in the direction of their abandoned works. The other regiments to the left were now sweeping on through the forest almost unopposed, shooting at the fleeing enemy whenever seen, like sportsmen driving game through the woods, with little or no loss to themselves. . . .

I now made my way through the forest, illuminated only by the flashing of guns and the explosion of Confederate shells, looking for comrades with whom I could unite to assist in the fighting. Finally I saw a small gray-clad soldier standing behind a tree, from which he was shooting toward the enemy's works. I asked him what command he belonged to, and he said: "Hays's Louisiana Brigade." Ah! then, I felt that I had found a friend I could rely on. I told him not to shoot over there any more, as he might injure our own men. He replied indignantly: "They are Yankees." This was true, but I was not sure of it. I told him I was going to see, and he said he would go too. So we started and were soon standing on the breastworks. Out in the woods we could see a great number of men in such confusion. Not knowing exactly who they were, we went in among them and found from their uniforms and their foreign accent that they were Yankees. The fire from the Confederates was cutting them down around us, and the brigade looked like an army of fireflies in the forest as they advanced a long line through the woods. My comrade stuck close to my side, and I whispered: "They are Yankees. Let us run out." We elbowed our way to their front and bolted. For the first hundred yards of our retreat out of this situation I suppose we struck the ground a few times, but we gradually slackened our pace until we came to a long line of Confederates brought up to assist our brigade if needed. They were sitting and lying about on the ground and kindly allowed us to pass on when we told them that we had just made our escape from the enemy. Following the line of works, we soon saw ahead of us a number of small fires kindled out in the field where we first made the attack, around which were Confederate soldiers and Yankee prisoners. As soon as I reached the opening I met a comrade who informed me that our company (I, 31st Georgia) had captured two generals— General Seymour, of New York, and General Shaler—and their fine horses. Pointing to a small fire, he said: "There they are." And my curiosity led me to draw near and see them and hear what they had to say. General Seymour was talking to his captors as familiarly as if he had been one of them. He told them it was only a matter of time

when we all would be compelled to come back into the Union. He was a tall, handsome young officer with a very pleasing address. General Shaler was short and thick-set and seemed too mad to say a word, gazing sullenly at the little fire before him, while his fellow prisoner chatted with our men, all of whom took a great liking to him. These two generals in the confusion as our men were sweeping through the woods rode into our company, supposing they were their own men. They were made to surrender and dismount. In doing so General Seymour patted his fine dappled iron-gray on the hip and said: "Take good care of him, boys; he is a fine animal." Just at this time Lieutenant Compton, who was leading the company, was shot in the ankle. His men put him on Seymour's horse and went to the rear with their prisoners.

*Union brigadier generals Truman Seymour (left) and Alexander Shaler were captured when their formations disintegrated in the face of Gordon's assault. A West Point-educated veteran of the Mexican War, Seymour had been a member of the Federal garrison that surrendered Fort Sumter. Two years later he was severely wounded during the Federal siege of Charleston. Shaler, whose brigade was first to break, was a wealthy New York militia officer who had recently commanded a prisoner of war compound at Johnson's Island, Ohio.*

# LIEUTENANT COLONEL THOMAS W. HYDE

### STAFF, MAJOR GENERAL JOHN SEDGWICK

*Fearing the collapse of the entire VI Corps line, Sedgwick and his aides galloped among the wavering ranks urging them to stand fast. A 23-year-old Bowdoin College graduate, Hyde had earlier commanded the 7th Maine and joined his old regiment as it stood fast in the face of Gordon's onslaught.*

Our 3d division, which had recently joined the corps, had the right of our line, and about five o'clock Gordon struck them square on the flank. They crumbled up, and our first intimation of it was throngs of excited men pushing through the bushes for the rear. The general sent part of us off to the right to rally them, and went straight down the road himself, wherever he went holding his line by his personality. Arthur McClellan and Captain Hayden succeeded with

me in getting several hundred men together in a clearing, and were pushing them forward in a tolerable line with several colors, when a brigadier-general, in full uniform, burst out of the woods and frantically ordered them to halt, and at the same moment Gordon's troops struck us. Our line, having lost momentum, disintegrated at once. Had they been in motion, I think they would have kept on. Hayden was shot through both his legs, McClellan's horse was killed, and I threw myself between my horse's neck and the fire and barely escaped capture. Soon I met a colonel, mounted, whose face bore the most abject expression of terror I ever witnessed. I asked him if our line held. He said, "It was all gone." I asked where were the 7th Maine. He answered they were wiped out. This was pretty bitter news, and I took the direction from

*Colonel John Wilson of the 43d New York Infantry, a devout Baptist and a much-admired veteran of 15 battles, was fatally wounded as his regiment wheeled to face Gordon's assault. When Wilson's sack coat (far right) was returned to his widowed mother, the inside pocket was found to contain a half-smoked cigar, which the colonel had snuffed out when the alarm was sounded.*

which he had come, with the idea of verifying it or sharing their fate, but I only succeeded in running the gauntlet of Gordon's fire again. Then I got back to the main road. I found many guns in position, and Crawford and the Pennsylvania reserves marching up, having been sent us by Grant as a reinforcement. I told Crawford where he had better put his troops, and then went to the 5th corps line, and down it to ours, which had stood like a rock, and on to the 7th Maine holding its extreme right, refused. To my joy I found the regiment had changed front to rear on the 10th company, and with the 43d New York had stopped the rout, but at a great cost; about half were killed and wounded, and the colonel, lieutenant-colonel, and major of the 43d had been killed near our colors. But there was brief time for condolence.

## LIEUTENANT COLONEL HORACE PORTER

### STAFF, LIEUTENANT GENERAL ULYSSES S. GRANT

*Born to a prominent Pennsylvania family—his father served two terms as governor—Porter graduated in 1860 with honors from West Point, where he was adjutant of the Corps of Cadets. Porter joined Grant's staff in November 1863 and became a valued aide and confidant.*

It was now about sundown; the storm of battle which had raged with unabated fury from early dawn had been succeeded by a calm. . . . It was felt that the day's strife had ended, unless Lee should risk another attack. Just then the stillness was broken by heavy volleys of musketry on our extreme right, which told that Sedgwick had been assaulted, and was actually engaged with the enemy. . . . It was soon reported that General Shaler and part of his brigade had been captured; then that General Seymour and several hundred of his men had fallen into the hands of the enemy; afterward that our right had been turned, and Ferrero's division cut off and forced back upon the

# "The most immovable commander might have been shaken. But it was in just such sudden emergencies that General Grant was always at his best."

Rapidan. . . . Aides came galloping in from the right, laboring under intense excitement, talking wildly, and giving the most exaggerated reports of the engagement. . . . Such tales of disaster would have been enough to inspire serious apprehension in daylight and under ordinary circumstances. In the darkness of the night, in the gloom of a tangled forest, and after men's nerves had been racked by the strain of a two days' desperate battle, the most immovable commander might have been shaken. But it was in just such sudden emergencies that General Grant was always at his best. Without the change of a muscle of his face, or the slightest alteration in the tones of his voice, he quietly interrogated the officers who brought the reports; then, sifting out the truth from the mass of exaggerations, he gave directions for relieving the situation with the marvelous rapidity which was always characteristic of him when directing movements in the face of an enemy. . . .

A general officer came in from his command at this juncture, and said to the general-in-chief, speaking rapidly and laboring under considerable excitement: "General Grant, this is a crisis that cannot be looked upon too seriously. I know Lee's methods well by past experience; he will throw his whole army between us and the Rapidan, and cut us off completely from our communications." The general rose to his feet, took his cigar out of his mouth, turned to the officer, and replied, with a degree of animation which he seldom manifested: "Oh, I am heartily tired of hearing about what Lee is going to do. Some of you always seem to think he is suddenly going to turn a double somersault, and land in our rear and on both of our flanks at the same time. Go back to your command, and try to think what we are going to do ourselves, instead of what Lee is going to do." The officer retired rather crestfallen, and without saying a word in reply.

# Slaughter at Spotsylvania

Fog and smoke hung over the Wilderness on the morning of May 7. So did an eerie calm, seeming out of place after the recent violence. General Grant, pondering the bloodshed, concluded that further attacks against the Rebels in the chaos of the Wilderness would be fruitless.

Grant made plans to shift his army southeast to Spotsylvania Court House, an important crossroads on the route to Hanover Junction, where the Rebels' main rail supply lines met. At Spotsylvania, the Yankees would be astride the best route to Richmond. Lee would be forced to attack Grant there or race to a blocking position to protect the Confederate capital.

During the day Grant issued orders for the 10-mile march to Spotsylvania. General Warren's V Corps would take the lead on the Brock road, moving out under cover of darkness.

Lee suspected that his foe might make such a move, and as a precaution he had ordered a

*Located 10 miles south of the Wilderness battlefield, Spotsylvania Court House became the focal point of the contending armies, as Grant sought to interpose his forces between Lee's Army of Northern Virginia and Richmond.*

rough track cut through the forest to connect his right flank to a road that led to Spotsylvania. Then, reports of Federal activity on the afternoon of May 7 convinced Lee that Grant might well be heading south.

Lee ordered Major General Richard H. Anderson, who had taken over the First Corps from the wounded James Longstreet, to march his divisions on the Rebel right flank down the newly cut route toward Spotsylvania. Richard Ewell and A. P. Hill would follow with their corps.

The Federal march that night went slowly, the men dead tired and the road clogged with wagons and ambulances carrying wounded. It was after midnight when General Meade arrived at Todd's Tavern—about five miles from the court house—with the lead elements of Warren's corps. There, Meade was incensed to find the way blocked by, of all things, Major General Philip Sheridan's Union cavalry.

Through most of May 7 two divisions of Sheridan's troopers had clashed with Jeb Stuart's Rebel cavalry around Todd's Tavern. Brigadier General Wesley Merritt's Federals had managed to drive Major General Fitzhugh Lee's division several miles down the Brock road, where the Rebel line held. Then, at dark, Sheridan had inexplicably ordered Merritt to withdraw back toward the tavern, giving Fitz Lee the opportunity to strengthen his barricades across the Brock road.

Meade rode forward and angrily ordered Merritt to get back into action and clear the road of Confederates. The horsemen rode off into the early-morning darkness and soon ran into the improved Rebel defenses. Despite repeated attempts Merritt could make little headway.

By 6:00 a.m. Warren's infantry took over the job of opening the way to Spotsylvania Court House. Leading the V Corps advance was Brigadier General John C. Robinson's division, which had little trouble pushing forward, despite resistance by the Rebel cavalry. After having fought a five-hour delaying action, Fitz Lee and his men now fell back to a low ridge known as Laurel Hill.

The Rebel cavalry commander had been looking for reinforcements all morning. Finally, one of his couriers found the head of Anderson's approaching column at the Block House Bridge on the Po River. Anderson immediately sent the brigades of Brigadier General Benjamin G. Humphreys and Colonel John Henagan racing ahead to support Fitz Lee at Laurel Hill.

Robinson's Federals, meanwhile, were exhausted from hours of marching but exhilarated to be driving the enemy. As they approached Laurel Hill, Warren rode up and ordered Robinson to attack quickly—before the Rebels dug in. Thinking that they faced only a small contingent of enemy cavalry, the Yankees advanced across a clearing—and were met by furious volleys from the two brigades sent by Anderson, which had arrived in the nick of time.

Robinson's troops were bloodily repulsed, and Robinson himself was badly wounded. As the morning wore on, Warren put in the rest of his corps, which nonetheless was unable to dent the Rebel line. General Meade now realized he was facing more than cavalry.

With the Union attack stalled, Meade ordered Sedgwick's newly arrived corps to form on Warren's left and attack "with vigor and without delay." But by the time Sedgwick got into position, around 5:00 p.m., the 17,000 Confederates of Ewell's corps were coming in on Anderson's right. The Federal assault was ill coordinated and halfhearted, and it, too, failed. When darkness brought a halt to the fighting, the Yankees' route to Spotsylvania remained blocked.

The Confederates spent the morning of May 9 strengthening their earthworks and waiting for an attack. By afternoon the Rebel front resembled a north-pointing V tipped by a strong salient—called the Mule Shoe for its shape—in the center. Anderson's corps stood on the Rebel left, Ewell's corps occupied the Mule Shoe, and A. P. Hill's corps—commanded by Jubal Early, because Hill was sick—held the right.

Meade and Grant also deployed their forces for battle. Hancock's men took up position on Warren's right, while Sedgwick remained on Warren's left.

During the morning, Grant lost one of his best generals. While inspecting his corps' forward line, "Uncle John" Sedgwick was shot and killed by a Rebel sharpshooter. Horatio Wright was named to replace him as corps commander.

That afternoon Grant ordered Hancock to take his troops across the Po River on a flanking move around Anderson's left. But darkness caught Hancock before he could reach the Block House Bridge, and that night Robert E. Lee adroitly shifted two brigades from Early's corps to intercept the Union probe. On the morning of May 10 Hancock found Confederates blocking his way on the far bank of the Po.

Grant, thinking that Lee's move to stop Hancock must have weakened the Confederate line elsewhere, recalled Hancock's troops to assist in a frontal attack by Warren's corps. But when

Warren's assault came about 4:00 p.m., it failed utterly to break the Confederate line. Three hours later Warren tried again, and again he was repulsed. Then, farther east, Meade decided to send the VI Corps against the Mule Shoe salient. Wright assigned the assault to a young brigade commander, Colonel Emory Upton.

Upton meant to try a new form of attack—a concentrated force sent to hammer a narrow front, break through, and then fan out in the enemy's rear. In the cover of pine woods he formed his troops—a force of 12 proven regiments—into a compact mass. He instructed the men to charge without pausing to fire and load.

Upton's troops swept across a 200-yard gap in front of the Rebel works. Many of the leading troops fell, but others clawed their way through the tangled abatis and threw themselves over the parapet. "Numbers prevailed," Upton wrote, "and, like a resistless wave, the column poured over the works."

The Confederate defenders broke and ran. Unfortunately for the Yankees, however, the troops that were to follow up and exploit the breakthrough never made it to the Mule Shoe. Lee and Ewell launched a counterattack, feverishly shifting regiments to the endangered spot. The fresh troops in gray battered Upton's men back.

The outcome was a bitter disappointment for Upton, but the attack encouraged General Grant. It had shown that Lee's mighty works could be smashed. That night, an orderly overheard Grant say to Meade, "A brigade today, we'll try a corps tomorrow."

The next day, May 11, Grant deployed his forces for a massive assault on the Mule Shoe, shifting Hancock's corps to a position directly north of the salient. With his formations massed like Upton's for a concentrated blow—but on a much larger scale—Hancock would attack at first light on May 12.

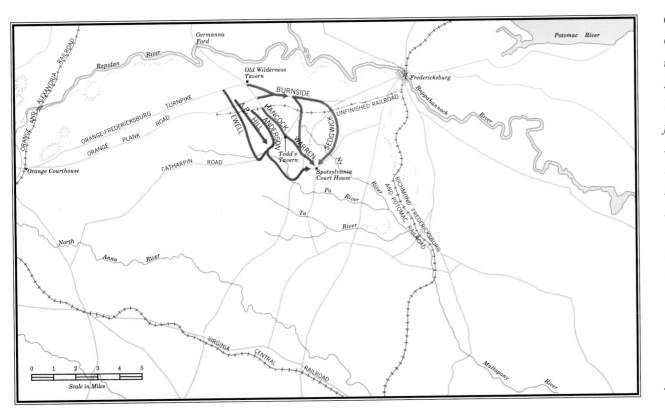

*On the morning of May 7 Grant ordered his army to resume the advance toward Richmond. Led by Warren's V Corps, the Federals set out for Spotsylvania Court House. Sedgwick's VI Corps marched east before turning south, followed by Burnside's IX Corps. Hancock's II Corps, which had remained to screen the movement, followed Warren. Divining Grant's intentions, Lee ordered Anderson to make a night march to Spotsylvania, where his men arrived just in time to block Warren.*

At dawn, in a heavy fog, 20,000 men advanced on the apex of the Mule Shoe. With Brigadier General Francis C. Barlow's division in the vanguard, the Union juggernaut obliterated the blunt end of the salient within minutes, shattering Major General Edward "Allegheny" Johnson's division at the point of impact. Thousands of Yankees swarmed into the Mule Shoe and spread out, dislodging brigade after Rebel brigade.

Facing disaster, Lee's commanders swung into action. Gordon counterattacked, followed by several brigades from Early's corps, while on their left Major General Robert E. Rodes flung his troops against the Yankee tide. The furious counterthrust staggered the Federal attack, which was by now losing momentum.

Grant responded by sending in more troops—this time against the west side of the salient where the line bent southward, a place that came to be known as the Bloody Angle. Lee countered by pumping more brigades into the Mule Shoe.

By noon, a grisly equilibrium of forces had set in at the Bloody Angle. Through the afternoon the slaughter continued in the rain. Men stood on bodies and fired blindly at the enemy just a few yards away. Wounded men suffocated in the mud, and corpses filled the trenches.

Not until after midnight did the battlefield fall silent. The struggle for the Mule Shoe was over. In two days of fighting at Spotsylvania, May 10 and 12, nearly 6,000 Confederates had been killed or wounded, and almost 4,000 captured. Grant's toll: 10,920 casualties.

There followed days of maneuver over muddy roads in a relentless downpour. On May 13 Grant began shifting Warren's and Wright's corps to a position east of Spotsylvania Court House, intending to turn his enemy's right flank. Lee moved some of his units from the Confederate left southward to counter the Yankees.

This time Grant reasoned that Lee must have weakened his left near the Mule Shoe when he shifted troops to his right. The Union commander ordered Hancock to attack again over the same bloody ground.

When Hancock's Federals charged on May 18, however, they encountered not a thin gray line but Ewell's stubborn veterans, supported by 29 pieces of artillery. The Rebel cannon fire stopped the attack cold. In yet another try at cracking the Rebel line, the Federals had lost about 2,000 more men—yet this grim total was a mere footnote to the carnage wrought at the Mule Shoe six days before.

## LIEUTENANT COLONEL G. MOXLEY SORREL
### STAFF, LIEUTENANT GENERAL JAMES LONGSTREET

*With Longstreet seriously wounded, Sorrel was well placed to advise Lee on a new commander for the First Corps, having served on Longstreet's staff since 1861. Sorrel's own fortunes rose as the war continued, and his talent for leading men in battle earned him a brigadier general's commission in October 1864. He commanded a brigade in William Mahone's division with skill and gallantry until a gunshot wound in his right lung at Hatcher's Run the following February took him out of action for the rest of the war.*

At sunrise, on the 7th, I was summoned to the Commander-in-Chief and promptly reported. General Lee received me most kindly and at once withdrew under a neighboring tree. "I must speak to you, Colonel," he opened, "about the command of the First Corps." He then in substance went on to say that the two major-generals of the corps present were too recent for the command (Pickett does not appear to have been thought of) and an officer must be assigned. He had three in mind: Major-Generals Early, Edward Johnson, and Richard H. Anderson, and did me the honor to invite my opinion. "You have," he said, "been with the corps since it started as a brigade, and should be able to help me."

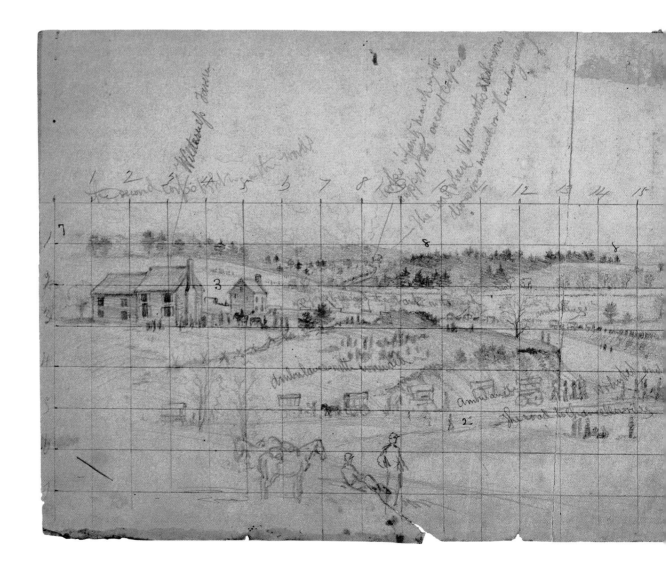

At once I saw the need of giving all the assistance possible and that I must use every care in judgment.

Thanking the General for his unprecedented confidence, I said that probably Early would be the ablest commander of the three named, but would also be the most unpopular in our corps. His flings and irritable disposition left their marks, and there had been one or two occasions when some ugly feelings had been aroused while operating in concert. I feared he would be objectionable to both officers and men. "And now, Colonel, for my friend Ed. Johnson; he is a splendid fellow." "All say so, General," was my answer—and I fully believed it—"but he is quite unknown to the corps. His reputation is so high that perhaps he would prove all that could be wished, but I think that some one personally known to the corps would be preferred."

This brought the commander to Gen. Richard H. Anderson, and I was led to say, without presuming to criticize him or point out his merits or demerits (there are probably plenty of both), "We *know him* and shall be satisfied with him." He was long a brigadier with us, tried and experienced; then a major-general until withdrawn to make up the Third Corps.

"Thank you, Colonel," said General Lee. "I have been interested, but Early would make a fine corps commander." Being dismissed, I hastened back to camp, full of thoughts as to who was to command us.

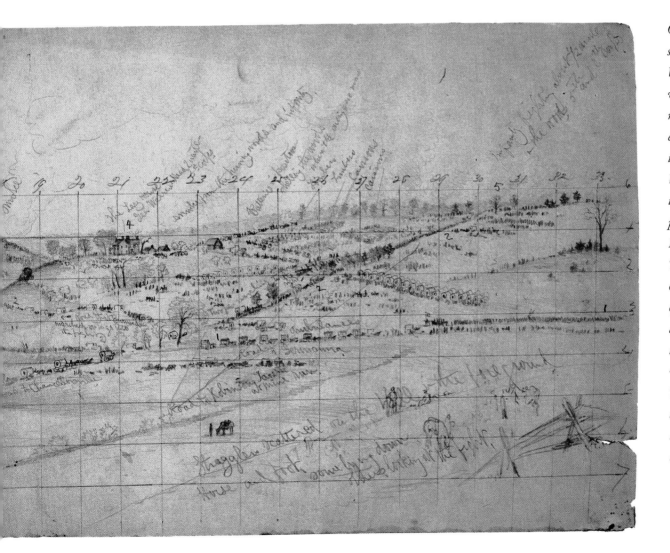

*On May 7 Edwin Forbes sketched this view of the Wilderness looking southwestward from a slight eminence near Wilderness Tavern. Forbes' key identifies the Orange Turnpike (#2), Wilderness Tavern (#3), the Lacy house (#4), and the positions of the Army of the Potomac's four corps (#5–#8). The drawing also shows wagon trains and massed batteries of the army's reserve artillery, as well as ominously long trains of ambulances headed west toward Fredericksburg. The grid pattern was added by an engraver at Leslie's Illustrated to facilitate making a woodblock plate for printing.*

It looked from the General's closing words as if it would be Early (I am sure he preferred him), but no, Anderson was the man. Later, the same day, came the order assigning chivalrous, deliberate "Dick" Anderson to the command of the First Army Corps and it was not very long before he was made lieutenant-general.

*After participating in the capture of Fort Sumter and serving on the Gulf Coast, Richard H. Anderson was ordered to Virginia, where he commanded a brigade and then a division, rising to the rank of major general by July 1862. After succeeding Longstreet in command of the First Corps on May 7, Anderson saved the day with hard marching and skillful maneuvering to block the Federal advance toward Spotsylvania Court House.*

## PRIVATE ALEXANDER HUNTER

### 4TH VIRGINIA CAVALRY, WICKHAM'S BRIGADE

*After two years as a foot soldier Hunter transferred to the cavalry in 1863. Captured in January 1864, he escaped from Point Lookout prison and returned to his regiment. He was wounded near Todd's Tavern late on May 7 when Federal cavalry maneuvered to seize the roads leading to Spotsylvania Court House.*

The men had by this time warmed up to the work before them, and when Lieutenant James sprang out and ordered a charge they answered with a will. The opposing force, evidently under the impression that we had received heavy reinforcements, gave ground and were pushed back across a swamp, fighting at every step and inflicting upon us quite a severe loss. Through the wood into a miry, boggy, swampy piece of land the line advanced in skirmish order.

Just then Dick Martin and I crossed the road, and as we spied the dead horse of the officer who went down by our first volley, we both rushed to it. I to secure a handsome leather haversack suspended from the pommel, and Dick to get the saddle, which was an unusually fine one, and which Dick was green enough to think he could bear safe and undisturbed to the rear. The rider lay near; he was a captain of cavalry, and a ghastly hole in his throat showed where he got his death wound. I unstrapped the haversack, which was full of something, and slung it around my neck. I never did a better day's work than I did then, for without that haversack I would have fared badly.

We two were about seventy-five yards in advance of the company, and noticing a Virginia snake fence near, which separated the forest from a field, both Martin and I crawled up to it and looked through the rails. One glance was enough; the field was literally full of Yankees, and a line of battle a half mile long was just in motion in our direction. Dick ceased to covet the saddle. He threw it off his shoulders and we fled back to the company just as a rattling volley came from our left, killing two men and wounding three. I rushed to Captain Payne and told him that there were thousands of Yankees in our front, and that we had better make tracks—and make them long and fast. Captain Payne was so nervous with this new species of warfare that he could not see how to get his command out. Martin also told what he had seen to Lieutenant James, and that astute officer had a soldier's instinct. He gave command to the company to right about face and retreat.

There was no panic; the men shouted and joked with one another as they sought the rear, stopping every few seconds to turn and fire in the direction of the wild hurrahs, which sounded so strangely in the woods. . . .

Just then a line of battle appeared on the rim of the woods opposite and advanced across the field. They wore the yellow-seamed jackets of the cavalry. Our rifles began to ring out, and many of them dropped, but our scattering volley only served to spur them up. With a loud hurrah they poured a volley in our direction. . . .

with thirst, struck for the spring. I filled my cap with water, and taking a few gulps kept on at a two-forty gait. . . .

Disregarding the cries of surrender, I zigzagged as I ran, and when about to sink upon the ground breathless, I heard the rattling of small-arms on the farther end of the field and saw the blue smoke curling from behind the fence. This showed where our line of battle was stationed; so making a final spurt I reached the fence and dropped on the ground like a log. I could not have run ten yards more if all the Yankee army, with Ben Butler at the head, had been marching up the hill.

## PRIVATE FRANK WILKESON
### 11TH BATTERY, NEW YORK LIGHT ARTILLERY

*Many exhausted Union soldiers felt certain that Grant would withdraw the Army of the Potomac behind the Rapidan in the wake of the severe mauling it had suffered in the Wilderness at the hands of Lee's Rebels. In his 1887 memoirs, "Recollections of a Private Soldier," Wilkeson recounted his conversation on that subject with some passing Vermont soldiers on May 7. Wilkeson was awarded a commission in the Regular Artillery the following month.*

That evening the troops began to pour out of the woods in columns. The infantry soldiers marched soberly past the artillery. There were no exultant songs in those columns. The men seemed aged. They were very tired and very hungry. They seemed to be greatly depressed. I sat by the roadside, in front of the battery, waiting for it to move, and attentively watched the infantry march past. Many of the soldiers spoke to me, asking if there was authentic news as to where they were going. Some of these men were slightly wounded. I noticed that the wounded men who stuck to their colors were either Irish or Americans, and that they had the stride and bearing of veterans. There was a gap in the column, and my battery moved on to the road, and other batteries followed us. We marched rapidly and without halting, until we reached a point where another road, which led in the direction of the right of our battle-line, joined the road we were on. Here we met a heavy column of troops marching to the rear, as we were. The enlisted men were grave, and rather low in spirits, and decidedly rough in temper. Marching by my side was a Vermont Yankee sergeant whose right cheek had been slightly burnt by a rifle-ball, not enough to send him to the rear, but sufficient to make him irritable and ill-tempered.

*The buildings of Todd's Tavern cluster around the intersection of the Brock and Catharpin roads in this photograph taken after the war. Confederate horsemen fought here to wrest control of the intersection from Federal cavalry probing toward Spotsylvania. Grant and Meade made their headquarters here on the evening of May 7.*

Thrice happy were the long-legged ones. Every Black Horseman discounted his record that day as a runner. Through the woods, across swamps, into briers we tore, with the Yankees close behind, yelling like mad and sending pattering bullets after us. At last we reached a large field fully half a mile across, with a large farm-house in the center, and now it was neck or nothing, with the blue-coats not a hundred yards behind. A squad of us aimed for the house, and nearly crazed

He talked bitterly of the fight. His men talked worse. They one and all asserted that the army was not whipped, that they had not been properly handled in the two first days' fighting, and that the two days' fighting had resulted in a Confederate loss almost, if not quite, equal to ours, as the fighting was generally outside of the earthworks.

"Here we go," said a Yankee private; "here we go, marching for the Rapidan, and the protection afforded by that river. Now, when we get to the Chancellorsville House, if we turn to the left, we are whipped— at least so say Grant and Meade. And if we turn toward the river, the bounty-jumpers will break and run, and there will be a panic."

"Suppose we turn to the right, what then?" I asked.

"That will mean fighting, and fighting on the line the Confederates have selected and intrenched. But it will indicate the purpose of Grant to fight," he replied.

Then he told me that the news in his Sixth Corps brigade was that Meade had strongly advised Grant to turn back and recross the Rapidan, and that this advice was inspired by the loss of Shaler's and Seymour's brigades on the evening of the previous day. This was the first time I heard this rumor, but I heard it fifty times before I slept that night. The enlisted men, one and all, believed it, and I then believed the rumor to be authentic, and I believe it to-day. None of the enlisted men had any confidence in Meade as a tenacious, aggressive fighter. They had seen him allow the Confederates to escape destruction after Gettysburg, and many of them openly ridiculed him and his alleged military ability.

Grant's military standing with the enlisted men this day hung on the direction we turned at the Chancellorsville House. If to the left, he was to be rated with Meade and Hooker and Burnside and Pope—the generals who preceded him. At the Chancellorsville House we turned to the right. Instantly all of us heard a sigh of relief. Our spirits rose. We marched free. The men began to sing. The enlisted men understood the flanking movement. That night we were happy.

*Passing Federal columns in this sketch by Forbes cheer General Grant on the evening of May 7 as they realize that he has turned his forces southward onto the Brock road. Staff officer Horace Porter recalled that the excited soldiers "swung their hats, tossed up their arms, and pressed forward to within touch of their chief, clapping their hands, and speaking to him with the familiarity of comrades."*

### PRIVATE JOHN COXE

#### 2D SOUTH CAROLINA INFANTRY, HENAGAN'S BRIGADE

*After service in Hampton's Legion, Coxe reenlisted, joining the 2d South Carolina just before the Battle of Chancellorsville. Henagan's brigade, part of Kershaw's division, was one of the lead elements of Anderson's corps that occupied Laurel Hill just in time to block the Federal V Corps on May 8.*

We made a fair supper on the contents of the haversacks of the dead enemy, and as darkness came on we began to "go to bed" between earth and sky. But the "dull god" sleep was not to preside over us that night. At about half past seven a mounted officer dashed along the line and in sharp but suppressed speech said: "Attention, men! Fall into line!" Of course we privates jumped into line of battle and were sure the enemy was creeping up to us through the bushes. But the next moment the command, "By the right flank, march!" was given, and away we went in quick time through the thickets as best we could. Never before nor afterwards did I experience such a trying night march. On we went, with never a halt, over rough places, little streams, swamps, and through next to impenetrable thickets. The stars were bright, but there was no moon. A little before dawn we struck a road at a left oblique angle and followed the left end, thence on to a bridge over a little stream, and thence on to a crossroads, where at the first show of dawn we found Gen. J. E. B. Stuart and staff in the saddle.

Stuart was smiling, and in a moment he was all action. He turned the head of our regiment at right angles to the left and into the road leading north up a gentle slope. Open fields were on the right and thick pine woods on the left. Halfway up the slope Stuart and his staff wheeled our brigade into line of battle and double-quicked us up to the top of the low hill. There we found some of Stuart's cavalry dismounted behind fence rail breastworks in the open on both sides of the road, and advancing up the other side of the hill there was a heavy Federal

line of battle. The dismounted cavalry quickly fell back through our ranks, and we as quickly occupied their position behind the rails. Our regiment, the 2d, was on the left and the 3d on the right of the road. Large fields were in our front, except some open pines on the right, where the 3d Regiment took post. In the field directly in our front were a large two-story farmhouse and outbuildings.

At this time Stuart was the only Confederate general officer in sight and, figuratively speaking, just as cool as a piece of ice, though all the time laughing. He rode right along the lines and, with the help of his staff, personally posted all the regiments of the brigade. On rushed the solid lines of the enemy with every apparent confidence of rushing over us and capturing that hill, which was in truth the key of that route to Richmond. Stuart rode along our line, continually cheering us and telling us to hold our fire till the Federals were well in range. "And

*Cavalry commander Jeb Stuart conducted a brilliant delaying action to slow the Federal V Corps on the Brock road. A South Carolina soldier recalled Stuart's laughing admonition as he hurried Anderson's infantry into position on Laurel Hill—"Run for the rail piles, the Federal infantry will reach them first, if you don't run."*

then," he said, "give it to them good and hold this position to the last man. Plenty of help is near at hand." He also told us that we had been sent to him to hold that hill at all hazards.

The position of the 3d Regiment on the opposite side of the road was a little in advance of ours, and when the Federal line got up to a large wild cherry tree on the right side of the road the 3d fired a solid and withering volley into it, and this was quickly followed by a similar volley by our regiment. The Federals seemed completely surprised, staggered, and as we continued our rain of lead into their ranks broke and retreated in great disorder down the hill and took shelter in a woods in their rear. But before they got back to the woods we saw one of their men turn back and run up the road toward us, and when he got near the cherry tree he stooped down and picked up the body of one of his comrades, put it on his shoulder, and rapidly walked back into his own lines. No Confederate gun was trained on that man. We all admired his pluck and imagined the picked-up body was that of his kinsman or friend. . . .

The field in our front was blue with the dead and wounded Federals. They were Grant's van, under Warren, with orders to seize these heights of Spottsylvania Courthouse, and as prisoners they told us they imagined that the hill was held by a small force of our cavalry.

## LIEUTENANT COLONEL CHARLES L. PEIRSON
### 39TH MASSACHUSETTS INFANTRY, LYLE'S BRIGADE

*Exhausted from its march, Colonel Peter Lyle's brigade crossed the Spindle farm west of the Brock road into volleys of musketry from Brigadier General Benjamin G. Humphreys' waiting Mississippians. Peirson survived the engagement but was put out of action by a wound at Hatcher's Run in August.*

*Captain William Watts Parker raised his Richmond battery in March 1862 from youths of that city aged 14 to 18. At Laurel Hill Parker's "Boy Battery" occupied the fork of the Brock and Old Court House roads, south of the Spindle farm. Its guns played a key role in repelling the attacks of the Federal V Corps on May 8. Parker was promoted to major just weeks before the war's end.*

The enemy's line was formed on a ridge across the Brock Road, near its junction with a road leading to the Block House, and was protected by an incomplete breastwork, with small pine-trees felled for abatis and a rail fence parallel with the line to the front. The enemy were hard at work finishing their breastworks. They were two brigades of Kershaw's division of Longstreet's corps.

Lyle's brigade, in which my regiment was, charged over 500 yards of open, badly gullied, ground under a rapid fire from the enemy's muskets and from the artillery we had so nearly captured. The troops went over the rail fence, into the abatis, and up to within 30 feet of the works, getting shelter then from the slope of the hill and the felled pine-trees. Here they lay to recover their wind, easily keeping down the fire of the enemy of their front, who fired hurriedly and aimlessly, and while waiting saw the 3d brigade (Marylanders) advancing gallantly across the field to their support. The latter, however, after getting halfway to the rebel works, broke under the enemy's fire from the right and retreated in confusion, General Robinson being shot in the knee while trying to rally them. The remaining brigade was too far to the right and rear to assist in this assault. Lyle's brigade, having rested these few minutes, started to go over the works, and would have gone over, but at this moment, discovering a fresh brigade of the enemy advancing in line of battle upon our left, I (a lieutenant-colonel, upon whom the command had devolved, so few were the men who had reached this spot) reluctantly gave the order to retire, and the command fell back in some confusion, but re-formed when clear of the flanking fire, and taking advantage of the accidents of ground checked the advance of the enemy. The sun was so hot, and the men so exhausted from the long run as well as from the five days and nights of fighting and marching, that this retreat, though disorderly, was exceedingly slow, and we lost heavily in consequence from the enemy's fire. My own experience was that, while wishing very much to run, I could only limp along, using my sword as a cane. My color-bearer was shot by my side, and unheeding his appeal to save him, I could only pass his colors to the nearest man, and leave the brave fellow to die in a rebel prison. The flanking brigade of the enemy, which so nearly succeeded in surrounding us, was part of Longstreet's corps (now under command of General R. H. Anderson), and it was his line we had so nearly broken.

## PRIVATE GEORGE C. BUCKNAM
### BATTERY C, MASSACHUSETTS LIGHT ARTILLERY

*When the shattered units of the V Corps reeled back across the Spindle farm, Captain Augustus P. Martin's battery narrowly escaped losing their guns to Humphreys' Mississippians. Later that day, Bucknam was ramming home a cartridge in his 12-pounder cannon when a spark ignited the flannel bag containing the gunpowder. The premature discharge blew away his right hand and part of his left.*

The Battery took its position on the crest of the hill—and as soon as our Infantry had advanced far enough we opened fire with our six cannon firing 2 & 3 shots a minute right over the heads of our infantry. The smoke from our guns [with] the air being so heavy . . . didnt lift but laid close to the ground, so we could see

*In this drawing by Edwin Forbes, V Corps commander Gouverneur K. Warren (above and inset), grasping a tattered regimental color, tries to rally the men of Colonel Andrew W. Denison's Maryland brigade. The Marylanders suffered more than 200 casualties at Laurel Hill when they charged the Confederate works west of the Old Court House road.*

*Captain Augustus P. Martin ably led Battery C of the Massachusetts Light Artillery at Second Manassas and Gettysburg and commanded an artillery brigade of the V Corps late in 1863. He returned to his battery of six 12-pounder Napoleons on May 3, 1864, and was severely wounded at Laurel Hill by a bullet in the neck.*

the shot and shell were dropping all around so much that we got behind the trees for safety. I got behind a pine tree large as a flour barrell —when a 10 lb shot struck it about 10 feet over my head and made the slivers fly and I got out of that out into the road . . . the Battery went down the road about half a mile and turned in off the road into a field of little low pine woods none over 30 ft. high down to 6 ft. high—we drove right in straight from the road—and then began to see how many [of] the boys were gone, 15 gone 8 killed & 7 wounded besides the Capt.

## SERGEANT FRANK M. MIXSON
### 1ST SOUTH CAROLINA INFANTRY, BRATTON'S BRIGADE

*As nightfall brought the fighting of May 8 to an uneasy halt, the weary soldiers of both armies toiled to improve their defenses. Mixson, a resident of Coles Island, South Carolina, recalled the formidable earthworks he and his companions constructed despite having inadequate tools. Mixson fought through the Wilderness campaign and was wounded in the left hand at Fort Harrison on the James River in September 1864. He surrendered at Appomattox.*

nothing in front of us—but our Capt. being on his horse back could see over better than we could—he being between my gun and [the] next one he sprang from his horse and hollered to us, "Boys give them Hell" they were coming—while we were doing all that mortal man could do our tongues hanging so low out of our mouths were liable to step on them . . . the smoke in front of our guns lifting we see the Rebs right on us, and we limbered up to move off the field and in doing so the two lead horses on my piece got a bullet through them and killed them both in their tracks . . . we cut their traces and left the horses where they fell—and went down to go through the [gate] when the piece of mine and another undertook to go through the gate together, and of coarse only wide enough for one gun, they got locked together and couldnt move and the Rebs were right at our heels then as they had about annihalated our infantry . . . Capt. Martin had been shot in the neck, a flesh wound, it devolved on first Lieut Aaron F. Wolcott, when the guns were locked together, to double shot each gun and rip them apart which we did with good effect and went down the road flying— but the Rebs were very close to us then and could trouble us in the open—so the guns went down the road it seem to be every man for himself, and the end for us all—we struck into the woods that lined the road, and it seemed as if the Rebs were shelling them altogether, for

The men, of their own accord, commenced to cut down pine trees to build breastworks. The only tools we had for this purpose were the little hand axes, about three inches wide, which some of the men had. These they had carried in their belts and used them to chop wood for fires. But now they put them to bigger use and would not hesitate to jump onto a pine tree that would square twenty inches; and it was surprising how soon they would have it down, cut off, trimmed up and cut off again. Then the whole company would take it up, place it in position. We worked this way for some hours into the night. All the while the whole skirmish line was pretty warmly engaged. That was a great incentive to us, and we worked until we had to quit because we were just broken down. But we had put up some log work which would be a great protection before we did quit. We got a very good night's sleep, and next morning, after eating what little we had, we felt real good and ready to go to work again on our breastworks. This we did, and while our skirmish line was fighting in our front and the hard fight going on "at the angle" on our right, we worked. And by afternoon we had a set of breastworks of which we were proud. The Yankees did not attack our part of the line during the day—only kept our pickets heavily engaged.

Now, this night was Company E's time for picket, and before dark we were carried out to the line, relieving the company already there. Our company had at this time sixteen men, all told, and we had to cover the entire front of the whole regiment. Consequently, we were not at regulation distance apart when we deployed as skirmishers. We, however, relieved the other company and fell in behind a rail fence. We expected an

advance at any moment. Our orders were to hold the ground as long as we could. After dark three of us rallied together and remained so. This made some distance from one squad to another, but it was the best we could do. Where each three men were we "let the fence down," making a jam, and then, getting in this, we had right good protection. There were in one jam Eddie Bellinger, Job Rountree and myself. Well, at midnight they advanced, and it was hot for some time. Eddie Bellinger and myself could load our guns lying down on our backs, but Job could not do it. He was used to hunting squirrels around Mixson's Mill Pond and Joyce's Branch and had never had to lie down to load. He thereupon proposed to Eddie and me that if we would do the loading he would do the shooting. This we readily agreed to, and Job would stand up, exposing himself from waist up. As soon as we would get a gun loaded we would pass it to him, and he would throw the empty gun back for another loaded one. We had three guns and worked them so fast that they got so hot we stopped loading for fear they would not stand it. We finally drove this advance back, after an hour's hard work. We were not disturbed any more till morning.

*An abatis—a barricade of tree branches with sharpened points—protects a line of Confederate trenches on Laurel Hill in this postwar photograph. By the time the armies met near Spotsylvania Court House, the experience of fighting in the Wilderness had taught both sides a brutal lesson in the value of well-constructed defenses.*

## LIEUTENANT COLONEL MARTIN T. MCMAHON
### STAFF, MAJOR GENERAL JOHN SEDGWICK

*McMahon, a 25-year-old native of Canada, served as chief of staff of the VI Corps. On May 9 he was standing near his chief when the much-loved Sedgwick was mortally wounded by a Rebel sharpshooter's bullet. In 1891 McMahon was awarded the Medal of Honor for gallantry at White Oak Swamp.*

Shortly after daylight he moved out upon his line of battle. We had no tents or breakfast during that night or morning. The general made some necessary changes in the line and gave a few unimportant orders, and sat down with me upon a hard-tack box, with his back resting against a tree. The men, one hundred feet in front,

*Shocked gunners and staff officers cluster around General Sedgwick (above and inset) in this painting by soldier Julian Scott. Surgeon Emil Ohlenschlager checks the prostrate figure for signs of life, while Colonel Charles H. Tompkins gestures for aid. Staff officers Martin T. McMahon, Thomas W. Hyde, and Charles A. Whittier (left to right) kneel behind the general. The bullet that struck Sedgwick in the left cheek was fired by a Rebel marksman nearly half a mile distant.*

were just finishing a line of rifle-pits, which ran to the right of a section of artillery that occupied an angle in our line. The 1st New Jersey brigade was in advance of this line.

After this brigade, by Sedgwick's direction, had been withdrawn through a little opening to the left of the pieces of artillery, the general, who had watched the operation, resumed his seat on the hard-tack box and commenced talking about members of his staff in very complimentary terms. He was an inveterate tease, and I at once suspected that he had some joke on the staff which he was leading up to. He was inter-

rupted in his comments by observing that the troops, who during this time had been filing from the left into the rifle-pits, had come to a halt and were lying down, while the left of the line partly overlapped the position of the section of artillery. He stopped abruptly and said, "That is wrong. Those troops must be moved farther to the right; I don't wish them to overlap that battery." I started out to execute the order, and he rose at the same moment, and we sauntered out slowly to the gun on the right. About an hour before, I had remarked to the general, pointing to the two pieces in a half-jesting manner, which he well understood, "General, do you see that section of artillery? Well, you are not to go near it today." He answered good-naturedly, "McMahon, I would like to know who commands this corps, you or I?" I said, playfully, "Well, General, sometimes I am in doubt myself"; but added, "Seriously, General, I beg of you not to go to that angle; every officer who has shown himself there has been hit, both yesterday and to-day." He answered quietly, "Well, I don't know that there is any reason for my going there." When afterward we walked out to the position indicated, this conversation had entirely escaped the memory of both.

I gave the necessary order to move the troops to the right, and as they rose to execute the movement the enemy opened a sprinkling fire, partly from sharp-shooters. As the bullet whistled by, some of the men dodged. The general said laughingly, "What! what! men, dodging this way for single bullets! What will you do when they open fire along the whole line? I am ashamed of you. They couldn't hit an elephant at this distance." A few seconds after, a man who had been separated from his regiment passed directly in front of the general, and at the same moment a sharp-shooter's bullet passed with a long shrill whistle very close, and the soldier, who was then just in front of the general, dodged to the ground. The general touched him gently with his foot, and said, "Why, my man, I am ashamed of you, dodging that way," and repeated the remark, "They couldn't hit an elephant at this distance." The man rose and saluted, and said good-naturedly, "General, I dodged a shell once, and if I hadn't, it would have taken my head off. I believe in dodging." The general laughed and replied, "All right, my man; go to your place."

For a third time the same shrill whistle, closing with a dull, heavy stroke, interrupted our talk, when, as I was about to resume, the general's face turned slowly to me, the blood spurting from his left cheek under the eye in a steady stream. He fell in my direction; I was so close to him that my effort to support him failed, and I fell with him.

Colonel Charles H. Tompkins, chief of the artillery, standing a few feet away, heard my exclamation as the general fell, and, turning, shouted to his brigade-surgeon, Dr. Ohlenschlager. Major Charles A. Whittier, Major T. W. Hyde, and Lieutenant-Colonel Kent, who had been grouped near by, surrounded the general as he lay. A smile remained upon his lips but he did not speak. The doctor poured water from a canteen over the general's face. The blood still poured upward in a little fountain. The men in the long line of rifle-pits, retaining their places from force of discipline, were all kneeling with heads raised and faces turned toward the scene; for the news had already passed along the line.

## LIEUTENANT CHARLES A. STEVENS
### 1ST U.S. SHARPSHOOTERS, CROCKER'S BRIGADE

*Stevens survived two wounds during the war, one at Mechanicsville in the Seven Days' fighting and a second at Cold Harbor in 1864. He was mustered out of the sharpshooters in September 1864 and in 1892 wrote the unit's history. Late on the afternoon of May 9 riflemen of the sharpshooters' Vermont company sparred with Rebel units along the Po River. Here Stevens describes a novel method the Vermonters thought up to extend the range of their breech-loading Sharps rifles.*

Some of the Vermonters tell how they were detached from the regiment for special sharpshooting, as they approached the high ground overlooking the valley of the Po, for the purpose of driving away a rebel signal party—some 1,500 yards off—as Gen. Hancock did not wish to have the enemy observe his movements. One of our batteries did open on them, but the distance was too great for canister, while "the saucy rebels only laughed at shell." Our Sharps rifles being sighted

*This Forbes sketch provides a view from behind the center of the Union line on May 8. Reserve batteries (#10) stand near the Alsop house (#3), while Grant and his staff (#11) watch Federal infantry marching south on the Brock road (#4). In the middle distance smoke rises from a Coehorn mortar battery (#13) firing at the Rebel trenches from just west of the spot (#6) where Sedgwick was shot. On the horizon behind the trees are Anderson's Confederates (#1) and Spotsylvania Court House (#7).*

for 1,000 yards only, the green-coats resorted to an experiment by cutting and fitting sticks to increase the elevation, when a few expert shots tried what they could do, a staff-officer with his field-glass watching the result. It became soon apparent, however, from the way the men in the distant tree top—the improvised signal station—looked down, according to our officer's report, when the bullets began to whistle near them, that our riflemen were shooting under; so, longer sticks were fitted for

sights, and now the rebels began to look above, showing that the balls went over. Cutting the sticks down a little, they were finally sighted about right, when the rebs began to dodge about, according to the officer with the glass, for our men could not distinguish them with the naked eye, but could see the tree and the flags. The result was, that as soon as the entire detail got to shooting, the surprised rebs abandoned their station in a hurry—their signaling proved a signal failure.

## COLONEL ST. CLAIR A. MULHOLLAND

### 116TH PENNSYLVANIA INFANTRY, SMYTH'S BRIGADE

*With the Federal advance stalled at Laurel Hill, Grant dispatched the II Corps toward the Po River to probe the Confederate left flank. Late on the evening of May 9 lead Yankee elements, including Mulholland's 116th Pennsylvania, pushed across the Po but were halted by darkness and increasing Rebel resistance. The next day Mulholland received a slight scalp wound but returned to his command. On May 31, near Cold Harbor, a serious bullet wound ended his military career.*

No sooner had the line halted for the night in the pitch dark forest, than the regiment was detailed for picket along with several hundred members of a German regiment. The picket force moved very cautiously and were as noiseless as could be until the head of the column reached the bank of the stream at the Block House Bridge. The regiment in perfect silence filed to the right and was deployed along the bank, the officers issuing their orders in whispers and the men groping their way and finding their posts as best they could in the intense darkness. All went well until the picket (composed of the One Hundred and Sixteenth) was in position to the right of the bridge. Every man seemed to instinctively feel the necessity of getting into position without the enemy, who was supposed to be on the other side of the river, being aware of his presence, and the success up to a certain point was remarkable.

But when the German detail filed to the left of the bridge and began deploying in the darkness, matters were very different. Tin cups rattled now and then, and the officers gave their orders in tones loud enough to be heard on the further bank of the stream. Then a man fired his musket. Some one else promptly followed, and the whole detail began blazing away into the darkness. The roar for a few moments was deafening. It seemed impossible to quiet the excited Teutons, and notwithstanding the exertions of their officers, who ran from post to post calling out

*A New Orleans lawyer and politician who had served in the Mexican War, Brigadier General Harry Thompson Hays was wounded while in the trenches with his Louisiana "Tiger" Brigade at Spotsylvania on May 9. Earlier in the war Hays had been a highly regarded regimental and brigade commander under Stonewall Jackson.*

to stop firing, the noise was continued for ten or fifteen minutes. Not a shot was fired in return, and no sound was heard to indicate that the Confederate pickets were on the other side of the stream, and it is not at all likely that any were there, but the man who fired the first shot on the Union side, and so brought on the trouble, was the direct cause of the failure of all the plans for turning the flank of the enemy's line, for the volleys of musketry echoing through the still woods notified Hill of the presence of the Union Army, and when morning broke, his men were discovered hard at work entrenching and getting artillery in position to cover the passage of the bridge. Hancock and Barlow were on hand early examining the crossing, and at once saw how impracticable it would be to force a passage at that point. Brooks with his brigade crossed the stream lower down, however, and pushing forward half a mile, discovered the left of the enemy's line, and found it strongly fortified, and the movement against Lee's left flank was abandoned.

# Spotsylvania—May 10

Late on May 9, Grant dispatched Hancock's II Corps in a maneuver against the left flank of Lee's line, believing this to be the weak spot in the Confederate defenses. The plan was for Hancock to cross the Po River on the Block House Bridge the next morning and plow into the end of Lee's position. Then, as the Confederate line collapsed, Warren's V Corps and Wright's VI Corps were to attack from the north, and Burnside's IX Corps was to push into Spotsylvania Court House from the northeast.

Lee reacted decisively to turn Hancock's deployment to his advantage. During the night, he shifted Brigadier General William Mahone's division of the Third Corps to the Block House Bridge to oppose Hancock. He also dispatched Henry Heth's Third Corps division on a mission to move around to the west and then turn north to slam into Hancock's open right flank.

Early on May 10 Heth's men appeared in strength south of Hancock, who had already been stopped by Mahone's blocking force. Trumped by Lee's maneuvers and threatened with destruction, Hancock managed to pull all of his formations to safety except Francis Barlow's division, which was hit hard by Heth's four brigades. Using dogged delaying tactics, Barlow was able to extricate most of his division; but it had been a close call for the Union II Corps. By late afternoon both sides had consolidated and dug in.

The moves against Hancock alerted Grant that Lee had drawn troops from some portion of his line. Grant decided to assault across Lee's entire front to develop the vulnerable spot. To afford his commanders ample time to prepare, he scheduled the attack for 5:00 p.m.

Warren, anxious to redeem his reputation after the fiascos at Saunders' Field on May 5 and Laurel Hill on May 8, petitioned Meade for permission to attack Laurel Hill before the time set by Grant. Meade agreed, and at 4:00 p.m. the V Corps, in conjunction with Brigadier General John Gibbon's division of the II Corps, attacked Richard Anderson's well-prepared First Corps line on Laurel Hill. The attackers never stood a chance. Anderson's Confederates mowed them down as they charged across the open expanse that lay before the Rebel works. Warren's attack not only failed in its own right but also was to have dire consequences later that day.

A major component of Grant's 5:00 p.m. attack was to be a charge by select units from the VI Corps led by Colonel Emory Upton. This hard-fighting brigade commander planned to send a deep, powerful formation of 12 veteran regiments forward without pausing to fire. After they breached the Rebel earthworks, they were to spread left and right to widen the gap. A supporting force commanded by Brigadier General Gershom Mott would then swoop into the breach and consolidate Upton's gains. Simultaneous attacks by the Union V and IX Corps were expected to complete the destruction of Lee's force.

The plan quickly unraveled. Because of Warren's abortive attack at 4:00 p.m., Grant postponed his general assault. Mott, however, was not informed of the delay and attacked promptly at 5:00, only to be driven back. Upton, who was ignorant of Mott's misadventure, attacked at 6:30 and met with spectacular success. His sledgehammer formation overran the sector of Ewell's line commanded by Brigadier General

George Doles and opened a gap for Mott to move into. Mott's force, of course, never showed up, and Upton's warriors soon found themselves marooned from the rest of the Federal army as Lee skillfully brought up reinforcements and counterattacked. After a protracted struggle costing him more than 1,000 soldiers, Upton managed to withdraw. A superb opportunity for the Union had come to naught.

The other components of Grant's grand assault also fizzled. Following Warren's debacle, Hancock assumed command of the II and V Corps, and at 7:00 p.m. he launched another attack against Laurel Hill. Anderson's Confederates repelled most of the assault force, although Brigadier General J. H. Hobart Ward's brigade managed to break through the Confederate line. But, as had happened with Upton, reinforcements were not forthcoming, leaving Ward's soldiers no choice but to submit to capture or to withdraw through a gantlet of Rebel fire.

Burnside's advance also went nowhere. Lee had drawn Heth and Mahone from Burnside's sector to oppose Hancock on the Po. This was the vulnerable portion of Lee's defenses that Grant had been seeking. Burnside, however, moved with his usual temerity, and his advance ground to a halt well short of its objective at Spotsylvania Court House.

May 10 had been an extraordinarily bloody day for the Federals, and they had nothing to show for it. By masterfully shuffling his units, Lee had deflected Grant's blows and maintained his position in front of Spotsylvania Court House. In many respects, May 10 had been the gray-haired Confederate's finest day as a defensive commander.

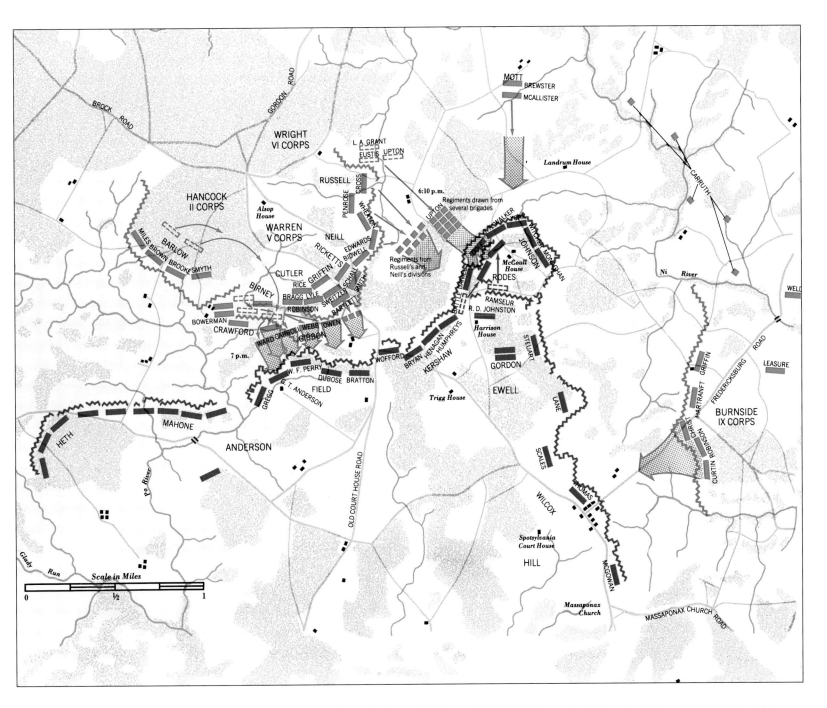

*May 10 witnessed a flurry of Union attacks. Early in the morning, Hancock tried to assail Lee's left flank but was repulsed. Then Warren assaulted Anderson's corps on Laurel Hill and was driven back. Toward evening, Upton led 12 regiments in a massed blow against the Mule Shoe's western face and broke through. Mott, however, failed to support Upton, who had to pull back. The day closed with an abortive drive by Burnside against Lee's right flank.*

## PRIVATE JOHN W. HALEY

### 17TH MAINE INFANTRY, CROCKER'S BRIGADE

*With his corps across the Po by dawn on May 10, Hancock resumed his maneuver against Lee's left. Haley's unit was part of a two-regiment reconnaissance led by Major James C. Briscoe that pushed south across Gladys Run. Briscoe's force collided with Heth's division as the Rebels swept northward in an attempt to trap Hancock's overextended command.*

Of the actual position of Lee's force we had no knowledge. It might be a long way off or it might be close by. Soon after deploying we passed down into a hollow. This was Glady Run, and on the high ground of the other side we saw something that we mistook for Rebel skirmishers. We thought them uncommon civil to allow us to approach so near without making some kind of show of hostility. When we all had crossed the stream, we prepared to charge, but a nearer view showed them to be nothing but stumps, which by some singular circumstance were situated equal distances apart on the end of the hill and all of a line.

This bugbear now disposed of, we moved on and reached a point perhaps a mile and a half from the Po. A clearing showed another run, and we were just starting up an eminence in the woods when suddenly the familiar *Whish! Whish!* and *Zip! Zip!* informed us we had at last stirred up our nest of hornets. We immediately put ourselves in position to engage them. It didn't take long for us to find out that we were working at a decided disadvantage, both as to position and numbers.

They were well-supported and had entrenchments, while we were out on open ground and far in advance of any of our army, our right flank in the air and our left the Devil knew where. Briscoe now urged us on, but we refused to move another step in that direction. He grew livid with rage and swore several shocking oaths in quick succession, but this didn't move us a hair. The bullets became more and more plentiful as we stood behind the trees, trying to make up our minds

what to do. To go farther was to invite annihilation of our entire force. To advance was folly; to retreat promised death or wounds at best. Briscoe swore, threatened, entreated. It was no go. He then tried to bully us by drawing his sword and threatening to "cut our d——d heads off," but we didn't budge. We firmly refused to sign our death warrants or be driven or bullied any further by him or any other drunken pimp. Just at this moment, as he was trying to get us to advance again, a bullet struck his horse, nearly unseating him. He kept to the road all this time and would have been brought down but for the fact that the enemy could hear him giving orders to us to go forward, and no doubt they thought we should soon all be their game. Seeing now that they were not likely to accomplish this purpose, they turned on him and peppered his poor old nag. Briscoe wheeled about and put the spurs to what was left of the animal. With surprising agility and brilliancy of execution he made tracks for the rear, yelling as he departed, "You must all now look out for yourselves and, if anyone gets out, he might have a chance to make coffee."

What an incentive to action—the privilege of making coffee. Major Briscoe is one of the last whom I would have thought capable of such a cowardly and unfeeling act. Had I not been an eyewitness and participant, it would be incredible. No thanks to him that we were not shot or gobbled and sent to Richmond to enjoy a spell at Libby Prison or Belle Island.

Thought of the terrors of these dens proved sufficiently stimulating to make us attempt an escape and to succeed. We moved over the ground in a manner calculated to astonish our Southern friends. The Rebs pursued us with all the speed attainable, but we, having so much more at stake, almost *flew.* Also, we had the promise of Briscoe's coffee to spur us on. And we did outrun Johnny Reb and did come first to the river. A goodly portion of our flight was through a section of underbrush so dense a rabbit couldn't have skinnied through without leaving behind most of his hair. By dint of great deal of puffing, sweating, and blowing we worked out of the thicket.

The Rebs in the meantime had projected themselves through the gap between us and the 4th Maine and seized the road and the crossing. Seeing this, we made no attempt to reach the crossing, but jumped into the stream and made our way across. It may be said that all this scrabble caused us to indulge in sundry unscriptural remarks concerning the Rebels in general and Briscoe in particular. We jumped into the Ta with a strong suspicion that we should sink to rise no more, the water being of that peculiar color that prevents one from seeing the bottom. If we could swim with our duds on, it was well; otherwise we would drown.

"We firmly refused to sign our death warrants or be driven or bullied any further by him or any other drunken pimp."

*Shortly after the fighting at Spotsylvania, General Hancock (center), surrounded by staff officers at II Corps headquarters, poses for one of Mathew Brady's photographers with his three division commanders—Major General David B. Birney (right of Hancock) and Brigadier General John Gibbon (next to Birney), both of whom had spent their boyhood in the South, and Brigadier General Francis C. Barlow (left of Hancock, against tree). All but Birney had been wounded the previous summer at Gettysburg, and Hancock's injuries would plague him throughout the campaign.*

*Thomas G. Stevenson gained his brigadier's star serving on the North Carolina coast in December 1862 and commanded a brigade on Morris Island during the siege of Charleston. One of Burnside's commanders, Stevenson was killed by a sharpshooter on May 10 as he rested under a tree awaiting orders to advance his IX Corps division.*

The shots of the Rebels grew nearer and nearer and we couldn't stop to deliberate. So in we went, but instead of disappearing beneath the river, we found ourselves standing on the bottom with water only up to our waists. Such a sudden halt was too much; it nearly upset my equilibrium. (I was affected very much like the cow who was struck by a locomotive and thrown into a field nearby. She wasn't hurt, but she was much surprised.) I had on long-legged boots, which soon filled with water. I had to stop and turn it out, thereby exposing my corporeal substance to considerable risk. But no catastrophe came to pass and I was soon out of the way.

We floundered out on the other side, and when Johnny Reb saw we had eluded him, he grew red in the face and commenced to pepper us, even firing at a lot of our wounded who were being brought across. The chivalrous conduct on the part of our Southern "gentlemen" is unbelievable. They call us "vulgar Yankees," yet I never knew a Yankee so vulgar as to fire on wounded men who were being carried from the field.

## PRIVATE CHARLES A. FREY

### 150TH PENNSYLVANIA INFANTRY, BRAGG'S BRIGADE

*Throughout the day on May 10, Warren's V Corps probed the Rebel lines on Laurel Hill. By late afternoon Warren had received orders to storm the enemy earthworks, supported by Hancock's II Corps. Frey and his comrades prepared for the attack with a sense of impending doom. "The men regarded the effort as hopeless from the start," recalled a chaplain, "and the officers failed to secure any enthusiasm in their troops."*

After dinner we were moved forward to the works, and the troops occupying them were ordered out into the woods in front. Picket firing had been kept up pretty regularly, but now it became general along the line, and a battery off on our left, with an enfilading range, began throwing shells which did great execution. It seemed to me as if our left pivoted on that battery, and the right, in swinging forward, gave it a chance for a raking fire all the time. The works behind which we lay were no protection, as the shells passed lengthwise of them, flying over us in a continual stream. At last a long cone-shaped shell came bounding along the top of the intrenchments, and striking a short distance to the left of our regiment, came down among us, hitting Captain George W. Sigler (Company I) on the left arm, and then, dropping to the ground, lay within ten feet of me. Every man kept his place in the ranks, but hugged the earth closely, expecting the missile to explode at any moment. It seemed almost certain death to stay there, yet no one felt like getting up in such close proximity to a shell which might burst before he could get away. I took one glance at the grim messenger of death which rested so near; then, flattening myself to mother earth, awaited the issue. My next sensation was that of sudden changes from hot to cold, accompanied by the wish that the ground would open and let me down. After enduring this unpleasant feeling for several minutes, which seemed like so many hours, and no explosion having taken place, I began to feel more comfortable, and finally ventured to raise my head high enough to take a peep at the shell. There it lay, as dangerous-looking as ever, but with no sign of a burning fuse about it. If it was that kind of a shell, the fuse had gone out; but I am inclined to think it was of the percussion variety, in which case it was perfectly harmless as long as left alone. . . .

Our second brigade was out in front, but the firing became too severe for it, and part of the line fell back to the breastworks, soon to be ordered forward again. . . . All this while that battery on our left was keeping up a constant fire, some of its shells bursting uncomfortably close. . . . I was intensely interested in the battery, and kept wishing it was a hundred miles away. . . .

Corporal Theodore Clay Howard was only 17 years old when he enlisted in Parker's Richmond Battery in March 1862. His short stature—he stood only 5 feet 4 inches tall—earned him the nickname Little Corporal. On this photograph Howard carefully recorded that he had had his right ear "shot in two" at Chancellorsville. At Laurel Hill on May 10 the four rifled guns of Parker's battery maintained a deadly enfilading fire on the brigades of Brigadier General Lysander Cutler's V Corps division as it attempted to cross the open fields of the Spindle farm.

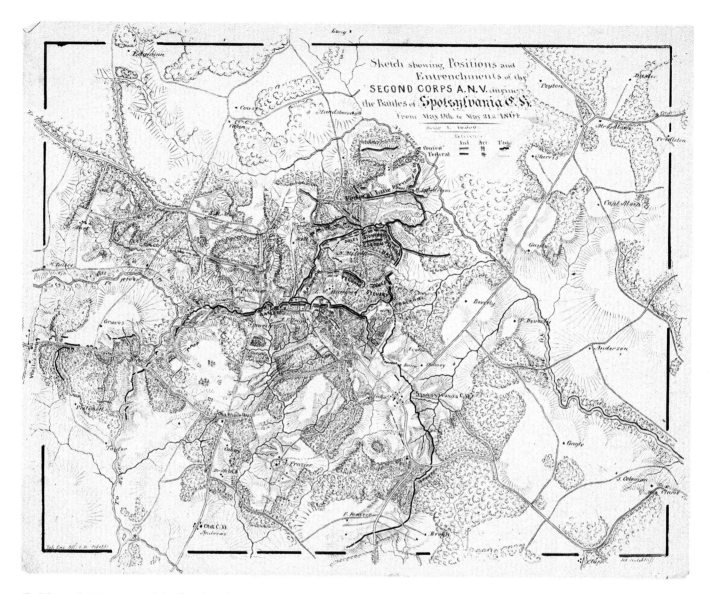

*By May 10 Lee's army occupied a line of works that resembled a ragged V, with a salient, dubbed the Mule Shoe, extending from its center. Major Jedediah Hotchkiss, chief topographical engineer of the Second Corps, made this map showing the Mule Shoe and the other earthworks held by the Army of Northern Virginia (red) around Spotsylvania Court House. Hotchkiss prepared his maps from rough field notes he made during campaigns.*

The afternoon was drawing towards a close, and we all wished that we might be ordered back to our line of works, seeing no advantage in being kept out in that exposed position and having so many men sacrificed, while we in turn could inflict but little loss on the enemy, who was well protected by his intrenchments. We were now moved a little further to the right, and a line of battle was formed in front of us, we constituting a second line, with a third and fourth at short intervals in our rear. The meaning of this was not clear to us; but to tell the truth I did not like the looks of things, and the massing of so many men at this point naturally suggested that some desperate work was before us.

After the troops were all formed, a staff-officer passed down the line and gave an order to the brigade commanders, who in turn gave it to the commanders of regiments. The order was something like this: "You are to charge the works in front of you. Second, third and fourth lines uncap your guns and fix bayonets. First and second lines, will lead the charge, closely followed by the third and fourth, and all will rush right on and over the works. Twelve pieces of artillery fired in the rear will be the signal to advance to the charge. The time will be six o'clock."

That order rang in our ears like the reading of a death sentence.

We were now commanded to lie down. No one spoke; none felt like speaking; every man was busy with his own thoughts. Musketry firing had ceased, but it seemed that that infernal battery off on the left knew exactly where we lay. How it knew, I cannot say, as we were in a wood, hid from sight. It opened fire, one of its shells striking in the first line—I think in the 149th regiment—wounding several men, one of whom had his leg torn off. The next one that came along passed perhaps a foot above my head, and striking in our company rolled three men around, but—strange to say—only one of them, Sergeant S. H. Himmelreich, was wounded. Oh! how I inwardly cursed that battery, and, at the same time, our own guns for not silencing it. I imagined that our artillery was lying in the rear, out of danger, not caring whether we were all killed or not; but was told afterwards that it could find no position from which it could reach this particular battery.

I now lay with my face close to the ground and closed my eyes. While resting in this attitude, I fancied I heard the twelve cannon-shots in the rear which were to be the signal for us to start. The troops rose to their feet and moved forward, first with a regular step, until one half of the distance had been passed over and the enemy had opened on us with musketry and artillery; then on a run, with men dropping out in great numbers, killed or wounded. We press on until two-thirds of the space separating the opposing forces has been traversed, when a black line appears before me. I could not picture myself going beyond that line. I could not imagine the possibility of ever getting back. Then the thought suddenly occurred to me: this is death! May the gathering years of all future time ever blot from my memory the anguish of mind and soul that I suffered during the next twenty minutes, expecting every moment to hear the signal to advance to the charge, and to meet what seemed to me certain death.

At last, when all hope seemed dead, a staff-officer passed down the line and delivered this message: "The charge will not be made this evening. General Warren says the loss of life would be too great to risk it."

## CORPORAL CLINTON BECKWITH

### 121ST NEW YORK INFANTRY, UPTON'S BRIGADE

*At 6:00 p.m. on May 10, two hours after an unsuccessful attack against Lee's entrenched army by Warren's V Corps, Colonel Emory Upton led a chosen force of 12 regiments in a bold attack that broke into the Mule Shoe salient. Beckwith describes the assault from its powerful start to its dismal finish.*

We were ordered to fix bayonets, to load and cap our guns and to charge at a right shoulder shift arms. No man was to stop and succor or assist a wounded comrade. We must go as far as possible, and when we broke their line, face to our right, advance and fire lengthwise of their line. Colonel Upton was with our regiment and rode on our right. He instructed us not to fire a shot, cheer or yell, until we struck their works. It was nearly sundown when we were ready to go forward. The day had been bright and it was warm, but the air felt damp, indicating rain. The racket and smoke made by the skirmishers and batteries, made it look hazy about us, and we had to raise our voices to be heard. We waited in suspense for some time. Dorr I. Davenport with whom I tented, said to me, "I feel as though I was going to get hit. If I do, you get my things and send them home." I said, "I will, and you do the same for me in case I am shot, but keep a stiff upper lip. We may get through all right." He said, "I dread the first volley, they have so good a shot at us." Shortly after this the batteries stopped firing, and in a few minutes an officer rode along toward the right as fast as he could, and a moment afterward word was passed along to get ready, then "Fall in," and then "Forward." I felt my gorge rise, and my stomach and intestines shrink together in a knot, and a thousand things rushed through my mind. I fully realized the terrible peril I was to encounter (gained from previous experience). I looked about in the faces of the boys around me, and they told the tale of expected death. Pulling my cap down over my eyes, I stepped out, the extreme man on the left of the regiment, except Ser-

*Brilliant and ambitious, Emory Upton graduated eighth in the West Point class of 1861. Two days after his innovative May 10 assault against the Mule Shoe, he was promoted to brigadier general. He later rose to command a division in the Shenandoah Valley campaign. Suffering from an incurable disease, Upton committed suicide in 1881 at 42.*

geant Edwards and Adjutant Morse who was on foot. In a few seconds we passed the skirmish line and moved more rapidly, the officers shouting "Forward" and breaking into a run immediately after we got into the field a short distance. As soon as we began to run the men, unmindful of, or forgetting orders, commenced to yell, and in a few steps farther the rifle pits were dotted with puffs of smoke, and men began to fall rapidly and some began to fire at the works, thus losing the chance they had to do something, when they reached the works to protect themselves. I got along all right and there were a number of us in the grass-grown unused road, and several were shot, but I could not tell who, because I was intent upon reaching the works. We were broken up some getting through the slashing and the abatis. By this time the Rebels were beginning to fire the second time, and a rapid but scattering fire ran along the works which we reached in another instant. One of our officers in front of us jumped on the top log and shouted, "Come on, men," and pitched forward and disappeared, shot. I followed an instant after and the men swarmed upon, and over the works on each side of me. As I got on top some Rebs jumped up from their side and began to run back. Some were lunging at our men with their bayonets and a few had their guns clubbed. Jim Johnston, Oaks and Hassett, were wounded by bayonets. One squad, an officer with them, were backing away from us, the officer firing his revolver at our men. I fired into them, jumped down into the pits and moved out toward them. Just at this time, our second line came up and we received another volley from the line in front of us and the battery fired one charge of cannister. Colonel Upton shouted "Forward"

and we all ran towards the battery, passing another line of works, and the men in them passed to our rear as prisoners, or ran away after firing into us. Continuing we ran over the battery taking it and its men prisoners, and on beyond, until there was nothing in our front, except some tents by the roadside and there was no firing upon us for a few moments, of any magnitude. I looked into the ammunition chest of the battery to see if I could find something to put in the vents of the guns to prevent their being fired again in case we had to leave them. . . . I broke off a twig in the vents of two guns, but we were ordered to go to the works and moved to the right. While moving as ordered, some Rebel troops came up and fired a volley into us. We got on the other side of the rifle pits and began firing at them and checked their advance. It was now duskish and it seemed as though the firing on our front and to our right became heavier, and the whistle of balls seemed to come from all directions and was incessant. I said to the man next to me "I guess our men are firing from the first line. We had better go back there. I don't believe our men carried the works on the left." . . . He answered "The fire is all from the Rebs." In a moment a battery opened upon us and we fell back to the first line over which I got and came across some of the regiment. . . . We could now see the flashes of the guns and knew they were coming in on us. . . . I knew that we could not stay there.

## SERGEANT WILLIAM S. WHITE
### 3D COMPANY, RICHMOND HOWITZERS

*A clerk from Lunenburg County, Virginia, White joined the Howitzers and served throughout the war. When Upton's infantry drove them from their fieldpieces, White and his fellow artillerists had the presence of mind to take their rammers and other implements with them, rendering the battery's guns useless to the enemy.*

About nine A.M., we were ordered to open upon the enemy in our front, and our battery succeeded, after a few well directed shots, in driving them back, or, at least in keeping them quiet. This was only a heavy skirmish line of the Federals.

But they remained quiet only a short time, and then they poured the Minie balls into us, with a hearty good will. Then they opened on us with their artillery, and though it was impossible for them to see us from their batteries, yet they struck inside of our battery every shot. After firing some fifty or sixty rounds, we "ceased firing" but now and

*Confederate prisoners taken during Upton's charge rush to the rear past the Shelton house in this sketch by Alfred Waud. The Yankees wanted to quickly clear the large number of Rebel prisoners from the salient, and prisoners and guards alike were anxious to escape from the fire-swept fields between the lines. Most of the captives were Georgians from Doles' brigade, but among their number were also a few from Brigadier General Junius Daniel's brigade, including Private James T. Corum (below) of the 45th North Carolina. Corum was held first in prison at Point Lookout, Maryland, then transferred to Elmira, New York. He died there of disease on April 8, 1865.*

then would put in a feeler, by way of a generous reminder. Their sharp-shooters being so close to us, annoyed us no little. Later in the after-noon, they concentrated their artillery upon us, and dealt the death missiles with an unsparing hand—literally the earth quaked and trem-bled 'neath the shock, but we were ordered not to reply to their artil-lery, and we waited for their infantry. Having no especial cause to stand up in the open field, most of us took our seats behind the breastworks, and many of us went to sleep. On our left, some heavy fighting was going on, and the news passed down the line, that we had driven the enemy several miles. Loudly roared the brazen-mouthed cannon, chanting their deep bass notes of death, in solemn harmony with the treble notes of the fatal Minie musket. The enemy's cannon cease—for a moment, a death-like stillness hangs over the line.

'Tis the *pause* of death—the Angel Azrael for a moment droops his blood-reeking wings and rests on the field of battle.

"Make ready, boys—*they are charging!*" Every man sprang to his post and the enemy come swooping through the woods on our right and *in front of Dole's brigade.* We pour a few rounds of canister into their ranks, when we are ordered to "Cease firing—our men are charging!"

A long line of Confederate infantry is seen rapidly advancing towards the enemy's line, and we jump upon the breastworks, loudly cheering them in their supposed charge; but, good Heavens, something is wrong—those Confederates have no muskets! And though 'tis hard to believe, yet a second's glance sufficed to show us that they had surrendered without firing a shot and were going to the Yankee rear as fast as their cowardly legs would carry them. Between that line of Confederates and our battery is one dense mass of Federal infantry, advancing rapidly, and at a trail arms; they were but a short distance from us, but so far to our right that we could not fire into them without killing our own men. Again we sprang to our guns and put in a shot anyway and anywhere we could; but no artillerists could stem the torrent now nor wipe away the foul stain upon the fair banner of Confederate valor.

The fourth detachment fights its gun until the first gun is captured, the second gun is captured, the third gun is captured, and its own limber-chest with its No. 6 (Dr. Roberts) captured! Nearly every man in the detachment a *recruit*—gentlemen recruits, I doff my hat to you!

Our support was breaking on all sides—on our right and rear the enemy were pouring in upon us in a perfect avalanche. And now comes over us a feeling of sickening horror—not the fear of *death*, for, so help us God, we thought not of dying, but we thought of the *shame* in leaving our battery to be captured by the enemy, and that, too, almost without a struggle.

Lieutenant Paine, who was standing near the fourth gun, now asked Major Watson "What must be done?"

I heard Major Watson make no reply, but his countenance was more expressive of dejection, not of *fear*, for he was the very bravest of men.

Then Major Watson, Lieutenant Reade (our adjutant), Lieutenant Paine, and myself, together with most of the fourth detachment, sprang over the breastworks *towards* the enemy's main line, and moving obliquely to the left reëntered our lines somewhere near the Second Howitzers. Everything was in the direst confusion—all company organization was entirely broken up. Our men, being ordered to take care of themselves, got out of the enemy's way as best they could, scarcely any two of them going together, consequently I am unable to keep any account of their movements; the reader will therefore excuse the seeming egotism if I record my own adventures for the balance of the day. Time, about 5 P.M. When Major Watson left I concluded it was time for me to be *moving*, so I sprang over the breastworks also, and as I did so I hung my foot in a root or twig and came down upon the ground with a heavy thwack; then I heard one of my bosom friends say, *"There goes*

*Among the more than 1,000 soldiers of the Federal V Corps killed or wounded on May 10 was Captain John S. Stoddard of the 12th Massachusetts Infantry. A resident of Bridgeport, Massachusetts, Stoddard had risen from sergeant to captain and survived a wound at Antietam. He was 33 years old when he died at Spotsylvania.*

*poor Buck,"* but he didn't stop to see whether I had gone or not, and I reckon I would have done as much for him. However, I gallantly picked myself up and made very good time; *I* thought I was wounded, too; then going some fifty yards to the left I reëntered our lines. In rear of the Third Company was a line of hastily constructed earthworks, occupied by *five* companies of North Carolina infantry, belonging to Daniel's brigade, who had been moved from the main line in the morning, we taking their place, and I thought this small body of men would be a nucleus on which we would rally our broken line. So taking an Enfield rifle, cartridge box, etc., from a demoralized infantryman, I made for that line as soon as possible, and there found General Ewell, with several staff officers, endeavoring to rally our men. Several of our boys fall in with these five companies and Ewell orders a charge—five companies to charge as many thousand Yankees; but we do it—we advance with a "yell" and even reach our caissons, but the enemy are

# "Grant has gone to the Wilderness, crawled in, drawn up the ladder, and pulled in the hole after him, and I guess we'll have to wait till he comes out before we know just what he's up to."

too strong for us and we are literally wiped out. It looked to me as if not so many as a dozen got back. The enemy had not formed a regular line of battle, but seemed to me to be in as much confusion as we were. . . . Gallant Dick Ewell remains at his post and is manfully endeavoring to bring up the stragglers—it is getting about twilight. By Ewell's side, astraddle of a little pony, is a boy soldier of not over eleven or twelve years of age, and I may live to be a hundred years of age, but I will never forget that little boy—his pony rearing up and pawing in the direction of the enemy, and the gallant little soldier firing his tiny pocket pistol as earnestly as Murat heading a charge.

We reform again, and by this time a brigade, marching by the right flank, comes sweeping down the lines.

"By the left flank!" comes from some old veteran; that swings them into "line of battle," and we knew something had to give way.

## LIEUTENANT COLONEL HORACE PORTER
STAFF, LIEUTENANT GENERAL ULYSSES S. GRANT

*Despite the bloody repulse of his assaults in the Wilderness and at Spotsylvania, Grant remained determined to keep the Army of Northern Virginia on the defensive. In his memoirs, "Campaigning with Grant," Porter recalled the dispatch of a letter on the morning of May 11 revealing the general in chief's stubborn determination to forge ahead with his costly campaign of attrition.*

He sat down at the mess-table that morning, and made his entire breakfast off a cup of coffee and a small piece of beef cooked almost to a crisp; for the cook had by this time learned that the nearer he came to burning up the beef the better the general liked it. During the short time he was at the table he conversed with Mr. Elihu B. Washburne, who had accompanied headquarters up to this time, and who was now about to return to Washington. . . . At half-past eight o'clock the cavalry escort which was to accompany the congressman was drawn up in the road near by, and all present rose to bid him good-by. Turning to the chief, he said: "General, I shall go to see the President and the Secretary of War as soon as I reach Washington. I can imagine their anxiety to know what you think of the prospects of the campaign, and I know they would be greatly gratified if I could carry a message from you giving what encouragement you can as to the situation."

The general hesitated a moment, and then replied: "We are certainly making fair progress, and all the fighting has been in our favor; but the campaign promises to be a long one, and I am particularly anxious not to say anything just now that might hold out false hopes to the people"; and then, after a pause, added, "However, I will write a letter to Halleck, as I generally communicate through him, giving the general situation, and you can take it with you." He stepped into his tent, sat down at his field-table, and, keeping his cigar in his mouth, wrote a despatch of about two hundred words. In the middle of the communication occurred the famous words, *"I propose to fight it out on this line if it takes all summer."* . . . The staff-officers read the retained copy of the despatch, but neither the general himself nor any one at headquarters realized the epigrammatic character of the striking sentence it contained until the New York papers reached camp a few days afterward with the words displayed in large headlines, and with conspicuous comments upon the force of the expression. It was learned afterward that the President was delighted to read this despatch giving such full information as to the situation, and that he had said a few days before, when asked by a member of Congress what Grant was doing: "Well, I can't tell much about it. You see, Grant has gone to the Wilderness, crawled in, drawn up the ladder, and pulled in the hole after him, and I guess we'll have to wait till he comes out before we know just what he's up to."

*Members of a Federal II Corps battery lounge against the log revetments of their earthwork along the Brock road in this May 11 sketch by Edwin Forbes. In the background a work party hacks at the thicket of saplings that borders the road in an attempt to improve the Yankee gunners' field of fire. The weary troops of the Army of the Potomac spent most of May 11 shifting position and improving their lines in preparation for attacks scheduled for the following day.*

## PRIVATE JOHN O. CASLER
### 33D VIRGINIA INFANTRY, J. A. WALKER'S BRIGADE

*Although May 11 saw a comparative lull in the fighting, both armies kept up a constant round of skirmishing and artillery duels. When Casler and his companions labored to improve the earthworks at the point of the Mule Shoe salient, Federal artillery fire provoked a comic incident that Casler, a native of the Shenandoah Valley, recorded in his 1906 recollections, "Four Years in the Stonewall Brigade." The pathetic subject of this episode, Private D. Frank Aleshire, was captured the next day and a week later joined the Union army.*

On the 11th there was some skirmishing and heavy artillery firing from both sides, and everyone who had to be near the front had a hole dug to get into. Our line in front of our corps was crescent shaped—our division in the center, Hill's and Longstreet's to the right and left. We were exposed to shells from two directions and shells from one direction would drop in behind the works from the opposite angle. Therefore, on part of the line we had to throw dirt on each side of the ditch.

While making a ditch of this kind on the 11th they opened on us with artillery. Most of the pioneers ran to another ditch, which was already completed, for protection. Several of them, myself included, remained where we were working, and among the number was one great, big cowardly fellow named Ayleshire, of the 10th Virginia, who always carried a big knapsack and wore a No. 13 shoe. He was six feet high and could take half a plug of tobacco at one chew. At the first fire he fell flat to the ground. As the shells passed over he would attempt to rise to run to the works, but by the time he would get on his hands and knees another shell would pass over, when he would fall flat and stretch out as before. He would then attempt to rise again, but never did get on his feet to run. He kept up that motion while the shelling lasted, which was about half an hour. He had nearly pumped himself to death, and had the ground all pawed up with his feet—the balance of us laughing at him and hallooing to him to "Run Ayleshire! run Ayleshire!" If I had known I would be killed for it the next minute I could not have helped laughing at him, it was so ridiculous. I was wishing a shell would take his knapsack off without hurting him. If one had I believe he would have died right there from fright.

## LIEUTENANT COLONEL CHARLES S. VENABLE
### STAFF, GENERAL ROBERT E. LEE

*A Virginia gentleman of considerable education who had taught mathematics at the Universities of Virginia and Georgia, Venable served as a volunteer during the operations against Fort Sumter and fought as a private at First Manassas. After engineer service at New Orleans and Vicksburg, he joined Lee's staff as an aide-de-camp in March 1862.*

In Camp
May 11th 1864
I am well & God still spares me. I cannot conceal that I have been in great danger. We have had heavy fighting on yesterday & day before especially on yesterday & have repulsed every attack of our numerous enemy & Thank God on yesterday with very slight loss comparatively. . . . I think that Grant will soon give it up & go back to Washington. His losses have been enormous. His men are deserting & straggle over the whole country in his rear. We are in about 8 miles of Chancellorsville where we were one year ago. You never saw men fight like ours do. Almost to a man they behave as though death were nothing. The little 17 year olds who were recruited in the winter it is sad to see their little faces in many instances girl like, all powder begrimed & then to see them forlorn & broken down unable to follow after veterans & looking in this wilderness country for their regiments. God bless the brave boys. Their first battle frightened them but they make soldiers in a week. Yesterday a very bold attack was had on our lines by a Yankee Col. which gained our rifle pits for ten or 15 minutes but was repulsed. The Col. was killed in the pits & somebody gave us a letter of his wife found in his pocket full of baby talk about their little children. This war is terrible in its bereavements on friend & foe. Good bye my sweet one. If God calls me I hope I am willing to go leaving all to Him. But I hope the heaviest fighting is over.

# Spotsylvania—May 12

Still hoping to achieve the success that had eluded him on May 10, Grant once again made plans to attack Lee's entire entrenched line. The focus of his assault was to be a weak point in Lee's defenses, a pronounced northward projecting bulge in the Confederate line that the soldiers had dubbed the Mule Shoe.

Under Grant's latest scheme, before sunrise on May 12 Hancock's II Corps was to attack the Mule Shoe's tip, using the same massed spearhead tactic Emory Upton had demonstrated so successfully two days before—but this time with the entire II Corps. Simultaneously Burnside's IX Corps would assault the salient's eastern face. Warren's V Corps was to keep Anderson's Confederates on Laurel Hill occupied, and Wright's VI Corps was to assist Hancock. Grant's intention was to concentrate irresistible numbers against the Mule Shoe, overrun Ewell's Second Corps, and split the Army of Northern Virginia in two.

Lee unwittingly played into Grant's hand. Late on May 11 Lee misinterpreted reports of Union movements and concluded that Grant was preparing to retreat. Avid to pursue, Lee withdrew his artillery from the salient's nose and deployed it on main roads near Spotsylvania Court House, inadvertently weakening the very portion of his line that Grant had targeted.

At 4:30 a.m. on May 12, Hancock's and Burnside's men advanced through a misty drizzle. Hancock's compact force of nearly 20,000 soldiers pressed across a piece of open ground, clawed their way through obstacles strewn by the Confederates, and burst over the top of Ewell's earthworks. The exultant Federals captured 3,000 Rebels, including Major General

Edward "Allegheny" Johnson, whose division occupied the tip of the Mule Shoe, and Brigadier General George "Maryland" Steuart.

Lee reacted decisively. While Cadmus Wilcox's Third Corps division held two of Burnside's divisions at bay, Lee sent Gordon with a quickly assembled force to expel the Federals from the eastern face of the Mule Shoe. Hancock's men had become disorganized during the attack, and Gordon was able to drive them back to the earthworks. Lee then began shifting brigades from all three corps to seal the breach on the Mule Shoe's tip and western face. Ramseur's North Carolinians, followed by Brigadier General Abner Perrin's Alabamians, Brigadier General Nathaniel H. Harris' Mississippians, and Brigadier General Samuel McGowan's South Carolinians, clawed their way to the captured line of earthworks and drove the Federals out.

Grant responded by throwing in Wright's corps. Soon the Union divisions of Brigadier Generals Thomas H. Neill and David A. Russell were heaving their combined weight against a bend in the Confederate line that henceforth would be known as the Bloody Angle.

Recognizing that he could not hold the Mule Shoe against Grant's juggernaut, Lee set the remnants of Johnson's division to constructing a new line of fortifications across the salient's base. Until that project could be finished, the Rebels would have to hold the Bloody Angle.

All day and into the night, the combatants fought savagely for a few hundred yards of earthworks. Rain poured, thunder rumbled, and trenches ran red with blood. Dead and wounded soldiers lay stacked several men deep. The

survivors fought on by instinct, firing into each other's massed ranks, stabbing with bayonets, and swinging muskets like clubs. A section of Union artillery rolled to within a few yards of the Rebel earthworks and blasted away with canister. Federal Coehorn mortars threw shells that arched high overhead and fell exploding into the trenches. Civilized men fought like wild beasts in what was to be the war's most intense and prolonged bout of face-to-face combat.

To keep Anderson's corps from reinforcing the Mule Shoe, Grant ordered a reluctant Warren to assault Laurel Hill again. Once more the V Corps marched toward Anderson's frowning battlements, and once more it fell back with heavy losses.

On the other end of his line, Grant ordered Burnside to renew his stalled efforts. About 2:00 p.m. Burnside sent Brigadier General Orlando Willcox's division advancing toward a salient on the eastern segment of Lee's line, but it was repulsed by Heth's division. Near nightfall Grant tried once again by concentrating two V Corps divisions and another division from the VI Corps near the Bloody Angle. Like Grant's other attacks on May 12, this one failed.

The forces that had compressed around the Bloody Angle continued fighting until 3:00 a.m. on May 13, by which time Lee had completed his new line across the base of the salient. His weary soldiers fell back, and the Federals were too exhausted to pursue. The next morning, the sun rose over a scene of carnage that appalled even hardened veterans. And to Grant's chagrin, the Rebels faced him from a new position even stronger than the one they had vacated. His hammering tactics had failed.

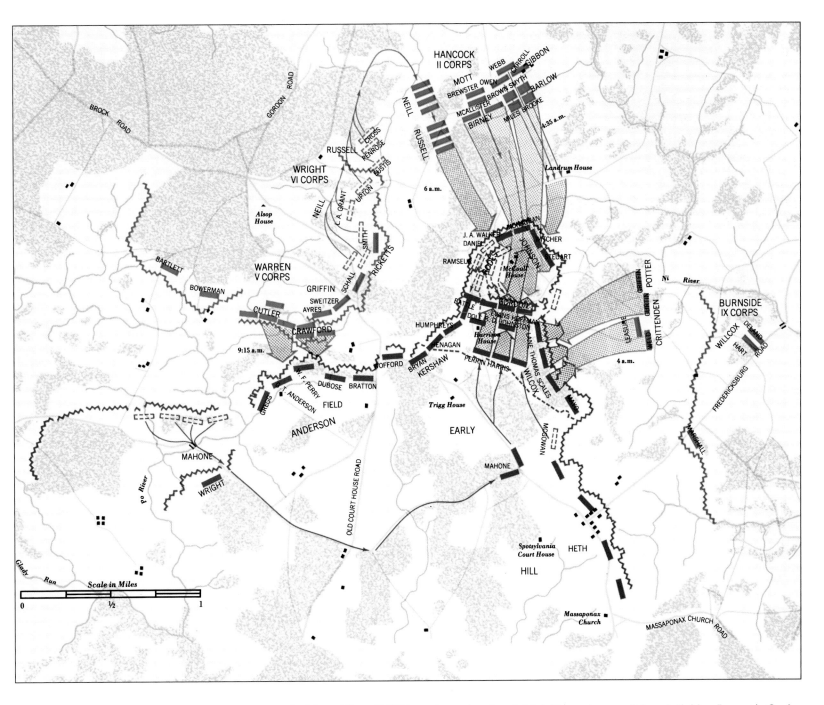

*On May 12 Hancock's II Corps advanced against the Mule Shoe and overran Johnson's division. Lee sent in Gordon to push back Hancock's men, followed by several brigades drawn from all three of his corps to support Gordon and to repulse an attack by Burnside's IX Corps from the east. Grant eventually added Wright and Warren, and fighting raged into the night. By the next morning Lee had withdrawn his forces to a new line across the Mule Shoe's base.*

# CAPTAIN ALEXANDER W. ACHESON

140TH PENNSYLVANIA INFANTRY, MILES' BRIGADE

*A junior at Pennsylvania's Washington College when the war began, Acheson enlisted with his brothers John and David—the latter of whom was killed at Gettysburg. In an 1886 newspaper article Acheson recalled his regiment's midnight march to the jumping-off point of Hancock's assault on the Mule Shoe.*

The troops fell into line and moved off through the woods to the left, down a mud road. The rain was still falling continuously. Every man in the corps was drenched with water—not a dry garment in the host; and now we went floundering through the mud, cold, sleepy, thirsty and tired. Mile after mile, and hour after hour we dragged our weary way along, saying little, as nothing was appropriate to the occasion. Sometimes a man stumbles, falls, then rises covered with mud; or another gets into a brush pile; or one trips over a stump. Once or twice we "double quick" to close up a gap. One leg strikes against the other; mud sticks to the feet; feet slip; sweat starts on the brow; legs get tired; traps get heavy, yet there is no intermission, no rest, no stop, no halt—tramp, tramp, tramp—monotony intensified.

Fatigue can not express the condition of a soldier on a march in the mud at night. It was more than that. We were fatigued by the previous day's work at the start. An hour's march and its attendant thirst had drained every canteen. It was almost impossible to replenish them, except with mud and water at our feet, because, during the darkness, should we pass within a rod of water in abundance, no one would know it. To our fatigue thirst was added, and destined to stay with us many lone hours unrelieved, unless we went down on our knees and felt for some mule track wherein the rain was accumulating. This many of the men did, while others filled their canteens with the liquid in the road, intending only to drink it could nothing else be secured after a while.

There was nothing to hear except the slosh, slosh, slosh, of the tramping thousands. Now and then a whip-poor-will uttered its mournful cry, which song was never inspiriting to a soldier who had been in battle. Or a canteen would rattle against a musket as some tired body snagged a toe and went prostrate in the mud. With the exception of these interruptions the journey was made in silence and mud—chiefly mud.

At midnight Grant's headquarters were reached, where a sentry paced before the tent. A camp fire was burning here, or trying to burn, as much as the rain would permit. The exquisite privilege was accorded the troops at this point of sitting down in the mud, resting for almost an hour and munching a hard-tack at midnight.

When our rest terminated we fell into line again and moved forward over roads infinitely worse than before. And darkness! Whew! Taking the Egyptian article as a standard of comparison ours may have been a little under size, but Pharaoh did not have any military movements to execute down a Virginia mud road. I have frequently heard soldiers wish, when pushed on a hard march, that the enemy would open on them with a battery, as it would bring an opportunity to rest. This was the leading expression now, and was canvassed back and forth among the men as we dragged our weary limbs along.

An entertainment, however, we little dreamed of was awaiting us, which we began to get intimations of about 3 o'clock A.M., May 12, when we came up with troops massed for battle. At this time we were moving immediately in the rear of our picket line and not twenty yards away from it. The firing between the pickets was not very brisk; only an occasional interchange of shots or even a volley in reply to some single shot. The atmosphere was so heavy though and the shots so close that it sounded more like cannonading. Yet the devilish hiss of the minie ball was as familiar as ever. As it whizzed past the face or cut a twig over the head the thoughts were momentarily diverted from the misery of the march.

At half-past 3 o'clock we ceased marching and formed into line of battle. . . . For one whole hour we stood silently awaiting the coming of the day, communing with our own thoughts and weighing the possibilities of the morning. And what an hour! Have you ever looked down into a gun-barrel when there was a business manager at the trigger? If so, you can appreciate that hour. Go talk with an old soldier; get him to detail his experience of skirmish, march, fight, prison, or guard-duty; ask him, "Which is the most trying?" and he will answer, "Doing nothing"—just waiting, as we stood, oppressed with anxiety, buoyed up by expectation, flattered by hope, shaken by doubt, peering out into the gloom and seeing nothing but ever and anon the flash of the skirmishers' rifle; listening intently, but hearing naught but the crack of the gun and the hiss of the ball. With the daylight unfolding upon us we moved forward.

*The formidable log-and-earth breastworks of the Mule Shoe salient impressed Confederate lieutenant McHenry Howard, who described them as "a chain or series of deep square or rectangular pits, end to end." But Howard also considered the entrenchments something of a liability. "Give a man protection for his body and the temptation is very strong to put his head under cover too," he noted. "Behind works not a few men will crouch down doing nothing."*

# LIEUTENANT JOHN D. BLACK

## STAFF, BRIGADIER GENERAL FRANCIS C. BARLOW

*The task of spearheading the attack on the Rebel salient was entrusted to Barlow's division of the II Corps. The 29-year-old commander accepted the perilous honor with grim resolve, as his aide Black recalled. Formerly adjutant of the 145th Pennsylvania, Black made a remarkable recovery after being shot through the lungs at Gettysburg. He was detailed to Barlow's staff at the outset of the Wilderness campaign and was again wounded during the siege of Petersburg.*

*At the age of 24 Lieutenant Colonel David L. Stricker was a battle-scarred veteran who had led the 2d Delaware Infantry at Antietam and Gettysburg. On May 9 Stricker was transferred by his brigade commander, Colonel John Brooke, to command of the 53d Pennsylvania; he fell in the dawn assault three days later.*

General Barlow, whose division was to lead the assault, on being informed of this fact asked, "What is the nature of the ground over which I have to pass?" The reply was, "We do not know." "How far is it to the enemy's line?" "Something less than a mile." "What obstructions am I to meet with, if any?" "We do not know." "Well, have I a gulch a thousand feet deep to cross?" And still the answer, "We don't know." "Then I assume the authority to form my division as I please, and that will be in two lines of masses." When the formation was objected to on account of the artillery that might be met within their works, Barlow replied: "If I am to lead this assault I propose to have men enough, when I reach the objective point, to charge through Hell itself and capture all the artillery they can mass in my front." After an extended controversy he carried his point and the formation decided upon was Barlow's Division to form the assaulting column, supported by Birney's Division on the right in two deployed lines, Mott's Division in rear of Birney's, and Gibbon's division in reserve in rear of Barlow and Birney.

I never remember seeing General Barlow so depressed as he was on leaving Hancock's headquarters that night; he acted as if it was indeed a forlorn hope he was to lead. His voice was subdued and tender as he issued his orders to the staff, for the formation of the command; very different from the brusque and decided manner usual for him, accompanied by the remark we had heard so many times on similar occasions, "Make your peace with God and mount, gentlemen; I have a hot place picked out for some of you to-day"; or the consoling remark that would sometimes follow, after hearing of some general officer who had particularly distinguished himself and had certain of his staff killed or wounded, "Well, gentleman, it beats Hell that none of my staff get killed or wounded."

The head of the column arrived a little after midnight at the point designated for the formation, which was a cleared strip of ground, extending from the Brown house in the direction of the Landron house. The formation of the division was: Regiments doubled on the center, closed en masse, five paces between regiments, ten paces between brigades, Colonels Miles' and Brooke's Brigades leading, and Colonels Smyth's and Brown's Brigades following, thus forming the command, composed of twenty-three regiments, into a solid square; arms at a right shoulder, officers leading their men and no commands given above a whisper. The skirmish line was deployed at one pace interval, with instructions to move forward with arms at a right shoulder and under no circumstances to fire, but as soon as they drew the fire of the enemy's pickets, to rush forward and capture every man of them, allowing none to escape to the rear and give the alarm to the main line.

It was almost four o'clock, the hour appointed for the advance, before the men were all in line and the necessary preparations completed, but the order for the forward movement was not given until half past four, owing to the intense darkness that prevailed.

The Confederate pickets were only a pistol's shot away, and, as they challenged, the low order was passed along our line, "Double-quick," replied to by a scattering volley from them, and then with a mad rush our boys were upon them and a dull thud here and there, as the butt of a musket compelled a more speedy surrender, told how well the order had been obeyed, and the way was open for the attack. And then, in the dim gray light of that early spring morning, with a mist rising from field and thicket, and while the birds were faintly chirping in the bushes and trees as they noted the coming dawn, the grand old First Division moved forward in almost perfect silence. Advancing perhaps half a mile, we passed the Landron house on our left, when a shot from the enemy's picket reserve mortally wounded Lieutenant-Colonel Stryker, a fearless and gallant soldier of the Second Delaware in command of the skirmishers protecting the left flank. A short distance beyond the Landron house our advance was obstructed by dense second-growth timber or thickets, passing through which we came to a cleared space showing a rise of ground or ridge running parallel with our line of battle. The men, taking it for granted that this was the enemy's works, contrary to order opened the yell that always accompanies a charge and sprang forward, but on mounting this crest, the red earth of a well defined line of works loomed up through the mists on the crest of another ridge, distant about two hundred yards with a shallow ravine between. Order was at once restored in the ranks and we moved quickly forward and, just as the command reached the bottom of the depression, or ravine, there belched forth from the works a volley of shot and shell that would have proved disastrous had we been in range. But, fortunately for us, the guns, in anticipation of a night attack, had been trained on the ridge we had just crossed, and so the shells passed over our heads, doing no damage. At once came the order from General Barlow repeated by every officer in the command, "Forward! Double-quick! Charge!" and with cheers and yells which were heard miles away, they rushed up against the works. Tearing away the abatis with their hands, Miles' and Brooke's Brigades dashed over the entrenchment and with bayonet and clubbed musket beat down everything before them, and before the charges could be rammed home in the smoking guns twenty-two pieces of artillery were in our possession, together with thirty-two stand of colors and over four thousand prisoners, among whom were Major General Edward Johnson, commanding a division, and Brigadier-General George H. Stewart, commanding a brigade.

*This flag of the 4th Virginia Infantry, one of two dozen Confederate colors scooped up by Hancock's corps in the collapse of the Mule Shoe salient, was captured on May 12 by Private Benjamin Morse of the 3d Michigan, part of Birney's division. Posted on the right of Brigadier General James A. Walker's Stonewall Brigade, the 4th Virginia was among the first regiments to be overrun in the Yankee breakthrough.*

## CAPTAIN WILLIAM J. SEYMOUR
### STAFF, COLONEL WILLIAM MONAGHAN

*For the first two years of the war Seymour was associate editor of the New Orleans Commercial Bulletin, a paper owned by his father, Isaac, who died leading a brigade at the Battle of Gaines' Mill. Incarcerated for three months following the Federal occupation of New Orleans, Seymour eventually made his way to Lee's army and became a volunteer aide on the staff of Hays' Louisiana Brigade. On May 12 the full weight of the Yankee onslaught struck the brigades on the Louisianans' right.*

May 12th. My birth-day, and a stirring one it was. It was nearly 3 o'clock in the morning before we could arrive at a conclusion as to the meaning of the Yankee movements, they seeming to be marching in every direction; at that hour it became apparent that they were massing very heavily in our immediate front. I immediately went to the Head Quarters of Major General Edward Johnson and communicated to him this intelligence. He quickly informed Gen. Ewell and requested that the Artillery Battalion be sent back to it's old place on Jones's right; he also dispatched orders to his Brigade commanders to be in readiness, and that Gordon's & Pegram's

*Advancing 40 ranks deep, Barlow's division surges over the earthworks along the northeastern angle of the Mule Shoe. "The Union column swept en masse over the fortifications," recalled Colonel Nelson Miles, whose brigade spearheaded the attack. "It was the first time during the war that I had actually seen bayonets crossed in mortal combat; it was a crash and a terrible scene for a few moments."*

Brigades should form behind our Brigade to assist it in repelling the expected assault. A few minutes before daylight, these Brigades were in the position assigned to them, and the men stood expectant and ready to do their whole duty on that day. It was the first time that our Brigade had been supported by two lines of battle, and we all felt confident of resisting any force that could be brought against us. But we were doomed to be disappointed, for the enemy, though massed in our front, did not attempt to assault our portion of the line. Just at dawn of day, there suddenly burst upon our startled ears a sound like the roaring of a tem-

# "Just at dawn of day, there suddenly burst upon our startled ears a sound like the roaring of a tempestuous sea."

## COLONEL ROBERT MCALLISTER
### BRIGADE COMMANDER, II CORPS

*Advancing with Mott's division in the second wave of the assault, McAllister brought his nine regiments forward to plug a gap between Barlow's and Birney's troops and struck the Rebel line at the apex of the salient. The colonel, at 51 one of the oldest Union field officers, was nicknamed "Mother McAllister" by his troops because of his devout and solicitous nature.*

pestuous sea; the woods before us fairly rang with the hoarse shouts of thousands of men. . . .

Click, click, sounded along our ranks, as each man cocked his musket and every eye was strained to discover, in the dim light of early morn, the first appearance of the Yankee line as it emerged from the woods. Some moments elapsed before we could see a single Yankee, when suddenly the enemy poured out of the woods in front of our right, and marching obliquely to the left (our right), reached the broad open field in front of Jones's Brigade. Never have I seen such an exciting spectacle as then met my gaze. As far as the eye could reach, the field was covered with the serried ranks of the enemy, marching in close columns to the attack. Thus was the time for our artillery to open, but not a shot was heard, our guns, unfortunately, not having gotten into position. The Yankees advanced with *twelve lines of battle*, and unmolested by artillery, soon reached the works behind which the remnant of Jones' Brigade, so cut up and demoralized at the Wilderness, was posted. These troops, formed in a single line and unsupported, and seeing the overwhelming force advancing against them, became panick stricken and ingloriously fled the field without firing scarcely a shot. The Yankees rushed over the works, taking Major Genl. Johnson prisoner, and capturing the Battalion of Artillery (19 guns) just arrived on the ground but not in time to unlimber and go into action. They quickly charged to the right and left, along the line of our works, taking our forces in flank and capturing the larger portion of Jones's, Steuart's, Stafford's & Walker's Brigades besides thirty-eight men from the extreme right of our Brigade who had not heard the order to withdraw.

At early dawn the order forward was given. At first we moved slowly up through the woods. When the first line reached the open field at the top of the hill, in sight of the Rebel works, we rolled out a tremendous cheer. It was taken up by the second line, and our boys started forward at a run. The first line parted in the front, leaving a long open space. Up to and partly into this space my Brigade went and struck the enemy works at the Salient. At this place the enemy had a field battery of 8 to 10 guns. I ordered some of my men to drag back the guns to our side of the works. The balance of the Brigade I ordered to push on towards the enemy.

But we soon discovered another line of Rebel works with large reinforcements coming to their aid. I ordered an about-face, retreated to the first line, and completed the hauling off of 8 guns. I found enough men in my command to man two of them. By the time the men had the guns on our side of the works and my line formed, the enemy came in force determined to dislodge us. They succeeded in carrying the works to my right up to the Salient. Encouraged by their success so far, and with traverses in their recaptured works behind which their sharpshooters could take deadly aim and be protected, our position was critical.

Many officers without men, and many men without officers—all of whom had been driven from our line to the right—came to our assistance here and fought nobly. Here we had representatives from many regiments. Brigades and Divisions were all inspired with one serious

*Private Sylvester Duboyce of the 26th Pennsylvania—a unit in McAllister's brigade—wore this privately purchased identity disk at Spotsylvania, where he received his second wound of the war. Hit in the shoulder at Gettysburg, he lost a testicle to a Rebel bullet on May 12. After the war Duboyce suspended the disk from a badge bearing the likeness of General Joseph Hooker, his former division commander.*

## PRIVATE WILLIAM P. HAINES

### 12TH NEW JERSEY INFANTRY, CARROLL'S BRIGADE

*As the assault column neared the Rebel defenses, Hancock ordered General Gibbon to shift Owen's and Carroll's brigades from the second wave to the front line, where they moved into position on the left of Barlow's division. Carroll's regiments swept down the Mule Shoe's eastern flank, taking three flags and 300 prisoners, but their casualties mounted as they neared a second line of Rebel earthworks. Haines recounted the chaotic charge in his 1897 regimental history.*

We crossed a little meadow and small stream, and silently moved up through an old field partly grown over with pines, the lower branches laden with water, which the man ahead very kindly held until you got just in the right place to receive the bath. All at once we struck their pickets and captured the whole of them, a few shots being fired; but in that damp and heavy atmosphere, the report was no louder than the snapping of caps, but sufficient to tell us that there was work ahead. We began to prick up our ears and wake up, just as our brigade commander, Carroll, shouted, "Double quick!" and we broke into a run, and all line or formation was soon lost, as each man seemed trying to outrun his fellows, and we went up that slope for about two hundred yards just like a tornado. In less time than it takes to tell it, we were in front of their breastworks, tugging and pulling at the abatis, or crawling over and through it (for it was certainly well built) just as the rebel heads began to show above the earthworks, and their leaden compliments to reach us; but we sprang on their earthworks, yelling and firing like a pack of demons, with our guns right in their faces.

As the Second Division (ours) sprang upon the works, I glanced down to our right, and saw the "Red Clubs" (First Division) breaking over their entrenchments, just like a big sea wave; and I have never yet seen any claim or dispute as to who got there first, for we all had plenty of business in front, as the Johnnies rolled out of their blankets and jumped for their guns; but we were on the earthworks above them, and they were quick to see that we had the drop on them. One big fellow, in particular, came crawling out of a shelter tent, gun in hand, and just bringing it up to this shoulder, as one of our boys covered him, and looking calmly down the barrel, gently asked, "Hadn't you better drop it?" And if his gun had been red hot he wouldn't have dropped it any quicker, showing how "a soft answer turneth away wrath." It took us but a very few minutes to clear out this line, as it

thought: we must hold this point or lose all we had gained in the morning. The contest was life or death.

These massed columns pressed forward to the Salient. The Stars and Stripes and the Stars and Bars nearly touched each other across these works. Here, on both sides of these breastworks, were displayed more individual acts of bravery and heroism than I had yet seen in the war. The graycoats and bluecoats would spring with rifles in hand on top of the breastworks, take deadly aim, fire, and then fall across into the trenches below. This I saw repeated again and again. More troops came to our aid and took a hand in the fight. A new line of troops was formed at an obtuse angle from this fighting line to stay the progress of the enemy on the right. But they no sooner formed than they were swept away by the enemy's deadly fire. . . .

The fighting lasted all day, and the rain poured down. Many of our men sunk down exhausted in the mud. Ammunition would give out, and more would be brought up. The rifles would become foul. We sent men back by companies to wash them out, after which they would return and renew the fight.

was a complete surprise; where most of them threw down their arms and surrendered right away, and our bullets and bayonets made short work of the rest. . . . As we passed on, another battery on our right was giving us their deadly compliments of canister and grape, double shotted, mowing a swath right through our ranks at every discharge, and cutting down small trees and bushes; shell bursting right in our faces with a report quicker and sharper than a lightning stroke, sending those rough, jagged, death-dealing fragments in all directions. The smell of powder and brimstone was almost suffocating, but on, on we rushed, at every step a life was lost—a man went down. . . . Our own gallant Lieutenant-Colonel, Thomas H. Davis, his tall form towering in our midst, bare-headed, his long beard flying over his shoulders in the wind, sword in hand, cheering and urging us on, went down in this terrible whirlwind of death, and gave up his sword and life. The very air was thick and hot with flashing, smoking, whirling missiles of death; the piteous, heart-rending cries and groans of the wounded, cheers and yells of defiance from the living. But still we press forward, and a few brave spirits almost reached their line; but we were so few in numbers, and nearly out of ammunition, that we saw it was hopeless, and the order was given to fall back to the first line.

*The West Point-educated scion of an old Maryland family, Colonel Samuel Sprigg Carroll was shot in the right arm in the Battle of the Wilderness but shrugged off the injury and a week later led his II Corps brigade in the charge at Spotsylvania. On May 13 Carroll, soon to be a brigadier general, was again injured by a bullet that shattered and permanently crippled his left arm.*

## LIEUTENANT McHENRY HOWARD
### STAFF, BRIGADIER GENERAL GEORGE H. STEUART

*The collapse of Colonel William Witcher's Virginia regiments at the center of the salient exposed the left and rear of Steuart's brigade, which was soon overwhelmed by a tide of attackers. Steuart and Howard were among many hundreds of Rebel troops captured. Howard spent the next six months a prisoner of war at Fort Delaware, and not long after his return, he was captured at Sayler's Creek.*

Presently a body of men in blue appeared in our front, to the right of the salient, and our men of Steuart's Brigade delivered a volley, perhaps more, which caused it to disappear. I do not think this was a considerable force and it seems probable that it was one which missed the point of the angle and was passing down in front of the works of our brigade, inside our picket line, about at the abatis.

About this time our artillery came up, rather slowly I thought, and unlimbered but had not time to fire a shot before being overwhelmed, except the two pieces in our center, which were discharged once—maybe twice. Musketry firing was now very heavy where Jones's Brigade adjoined us on our left and soon a crowd of fugitives came pouring down our line of works from the angle, showing that something must have gone wrong in that quarter. I was at this time, and had been from the beginning, at our center. The two pieces of artillery there now or shortly before fired their round—of canister as I imagined from the sound—but the six or eight guns in the angle had been overwhelmed as soon as unlimbered. I saw Captain Williamson pass by from that direction and knew from the expression of his face that something momentous had happened there but had no time to stop or question him. Soon a cloud of blue uniforms came pressing down from our left, along our works, in front of them, and, by far the greater number, completely filling the space within the angle and so directly in our rear. The pits in our center and right being, as I have described, deep and with traverses (side walls), available for defence in front, flank and rear, I thought they might be held or the enemy might be checked until reinforcements came up, as on the evening of the 10th; and, therefore, standing on the brink of one of them, I pushed passing fugitives into it until it was full and then jumped in. I remember a Federal soldier striding down the top of the embankment, foremost of his comrades, shouting and brandishing his gun above his head, and I called out to fire and a man—I think it was Bragonier, of the 10th Virginia—did so, and my impression is, with effect. And I also remember very vividly how the smoke of the discharge seemed as if it would never dissipate or float away from the spot in the heavy air and my apprehension that we would be made to pay a penalty for our temerity in firing when we were practically captured; for in a moment the edge of our pit (nearly shoulder deep), was surrounded on all sides. And I thought my apprehension was about to be realized when the Union soldiers brought their bayonets down with a threatening appearance, but it was only for the purpose of sweeping aside the bayonets of our men which were resting on the top, and we were ordered to scramble out. I retained my sword in hand, after some hesitation whether or not to throw it away or stick it in the ground. One man took it out of my hand and another came up while he was doing so and drawing a large clasp knife from his pocket and opening it (I wondered if he was going to stab me), he cut the scabbard from my leather belt, and they went their several ways with their trophies. We were ordered to their rear and in going I passed up the breastwork and out at the angle. In front of this and on my left as I

went back the ground was open and was crowded with a dense mass streaming up and I thought that if our artillery had been in position at the angle it would have inflicted a terrible loss and perhaps have checked the assault. I never saw an occasion when artillery would have done such execution. We were squeezed between this column of attack and the woods on our right and two or three times I tried to sidle into the thicket with a view to escaping, but each time was gruffly admonished to keep to the left in the open.

## BRIGADIER GENERAL JOHN B. GORDON
### DIVISION COMMANDER, SECOND CORPS

*Posted in reserve the previous day, and with instructions to support the line as needed, Gordon moved forward with his lead units, General Robert D. Johnston's four North Carolina regiments, toward the imperiled angle of the salient. At 5:00 a.m., as Johnston's brigade passed east of the McCoull house, it was met by volleys that felled Johnston and two regimental commanders. Gordon steadied the Tar Heels while his other brigades moved into position for another counterattack.*

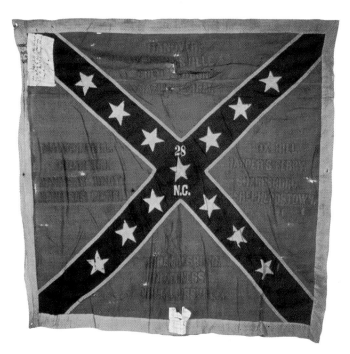

*After Hancock crushed Steuart's line, Colonel Simon Griffin's IX Corps brigade slammed into the exposed left of General James H. Lane's North Carolina brigade, overwhelming two of his five regiments. One of them, the 28th North Carolina Infantry, lost this battle flag to Corporal John M. Kindig of the 63d Pennsylvania.*

My command was rapidly moving by the flank through the woods and underbrush toward the captured salient. The mist and fog were so heavy that it was impossible to see farther than a few rods. Throwing out in front a small force to apprise us of our near approach to the enemy, I rode at the head of the main column, and by my side rode General Robert Johnston, who commanded a brigade of North Carolinians. So rapidly and silently had the enemy moved inside of our works—indeed, so much longer time had he been on the inside than the reports indicated—that before we had moved one half the distance to the salient the head of my column butted squarely against Hancock's line of battle. The men who had been placed in our front to give warning were against that battle line before they knew it. They were shot down or made prisoners. The sudden and unexpected blaze from Hancock's rifles made the dark woodland strangely lurid. General Johnston, who rode immediately at my side, was shot from his horse, severely but not, as I supposed, fatally wounded in the head. His brigade was thrown inevitably into great confusion, but did not break to the rear. As quickly as possible, I had the next ranking officer in that brigade notified of General Johnston's fall and directed him at once to assume command. He proved equal to the emergency. With great coolness and courage he promptly executed my orders. The Federals were still advancing, and

When the daring charge of the North Carolina brigade had temporarily checked that portion of the Federal forces struck by it, and while my brigades in the rear were being placed in position, I rode with Thomas G. Jones, the youngest member of my staff, into the intervening woods, in order, if possible, to locate Hancock more definitely. Sitting on my horse near the line of the North Carolina brigade, I was endeavoring to get a view of the Union lines, through the woods and through the gradually lifting mists. It was impossible, however, to see those lines; but, as stated, the direction from which they sent their bullets soon informed us that they were still moving and had already gone beyond our right. One of those bullets passed through my coat from side to side, just grazing my back. Jones, who was close to me, and sitting on his horse in a not very erect posture, anxiously inquired: "General, did n't that ball hit you?"

"No," I said; "but suppose my back had been in a bow like yours? Don't you see that the bullet would have gone straight through my spine? Sit up or you'll be killed."

The sudden jerk with which he straightened himself, and the duration of the impression made, showed that this ocular demonstration of the necessity for a soldier to sit upright on his horse had been more effective than all the ordinary lessons that could have been given. It is but simple justice to say of this immature boy that even then his courage, his coolness in the presence of danger, and his strong moral and mental characteristics gave promise of his brilliant future.

*Twenty-year-old Captain John Stanley Brooks of the Brunswick Guards entered the service as a company commander in the 20th North Carolina. Twice wounded and promoted to lieutenant colonel, he died leading his regiment in Gordon's counterattack.*

every movement of the North Carolina brigade had to be made under heavy fire. The officer in charge was directed to hastily withdraw his brigade a short distance, to change front so as to face Hancock's lines, and to deploy his whole force in close order as skirmishers, so as to stretch, if possible, across the entire front of Hancock. This done, he was ordered to charge with his line of skirmishers the solid battle lines before him. His looks indicated some amazement at the purpose to make an attack which appeared so utterly hopeless, and which would have been the very essence of rashness but for the extremity of the situation. He was, however, full of the fire of battle and too good a soldier not to yield prompt and cheerful obedience. That order was given in the hope and belief that in the fog and mists which concealed our numbers the sheer audacity of the movement would confuse and check the Union advance long enough for me to change front and form line of battle with the other brigades. The result was not disappointing except in the fact that Johnston's brigade, even when so deployed, was still too short to reach across Hancock's entire front. This fact was soon developed: not by sight, but by the direction from which the Union bullets began to come.

*With the outbreak of war 16-year-old Virginia Military Institute cadet Thomas G. Jones left his studies for duty as a drillmaster in Richmond. Later recommended for promotion by his former professor, Stonewall Jackson, Jones in 1863 was appointed to Gordon's staff. As a major he carried the flag of truce at Appomattox; he later served as governor of Alabama.*

*About 6:00 a.m. on May 12 Alfred Waud sketched General Hancock—standing at right center with hand on sword—conferring with VI Corps commander Horatio Wright at their headquarters near the Landrum house, a quarter mile northeast of the Mule Shoe. "Our troops could not be restrained after the capture of the entrenchments," Hancock said of the early phase of his attack, "but pursued the flying enemy through the forest in the direction of Spotsylvania Court House."*

## PRIVATE WILLIAM W. SMITH

### 49TH VIRGINIA INFANTRY, HOFFMAN'S BRIGADE

*With Yankee troops continuing to pour into the captured salient, Gordon gathered two brigades commanded by Colonels Clement A. Evans and John S. Hoffman—some 3,500 men—and rushed them toward the eastern flank of the Mule Shoe. When these reinforcements swung into line of battle and prepared to attack, General Lee rode forward to lead them—as he had the Texans a week earlier at the Wilderness. The 18-year-old Smith witnessed the dramatic scene.*

It was an hour of destiny. The thin line stood confronting the massing enemy in our trenches only some two hundred yards away; obscured they were, it is true, by the underbrush and in some cases by the contour of the land, but ready to push forward to the capture of the parked reserve artillery ammunition just behind us.

General Lee's headquarters were but a short distance away. . . . A moment later I noticed a quiet officer ride in front of our line. He was a large man on an iron gray horse, and had come up without retinue, even, I think, without a single staff officer or orderly. It was when he

turned face towards us and with a silent gesture of extended arm pointed towards the enemy we recognized our idolized Lee. Already the bullets were zipping past, aimed chiefly at the struggling remnant of Johnson's division, that had been overwhelmed in the trenches. What if one should kill Lee? "Get in front of him, keep the bullets off," was the instinctive feeling of each man.

Just then from the right General J. B. Gordon came dashing down the line. At the sight of Lee he reined up his handsome bay so sharply as to throw him on his haunches. It was a picture never to be forgotten. "General Lee, this is no place for you. Go back, General; we will drive them back. These men are Virginians and they have never failed me; they will not fail me; will you boys?" Then rose the oft-quoted shout: "General Lee to the rear! Lee to the rear!" "Go back, General, we can't charge until you go back." "We will drive them back, General." Some one got hold of his bridle and back through the line of the 49th Regiment Lee was led. The whole scene was not fifty paces from where I stood. . . .

"Forward!" cried Gordon, and the line stepped off with the steady tread of a dress-parade. There was no shout, no rebel yell, but, as I looked down the line, I saw the stern faces and set teeth of men who

# "Go back, General; we will drive them back. These men are Virginians and they have never failed me; they will not fail me."

have undertaken to do a desperate deed, and do not intend to fail.

With the freedom of the volunteer, I said to those next me: "Pass it down the line, boys; General Lee is looking at us." "Aye, and depending upon us, too," and the silent line moved on with long, swift strides. In a few moments we marched down into the bottom, then rising, parted the undergrowth, and were upon them, packed thick as blackbirds in our trenches. A fearful volley wrought havoc and started those in advance to get back to their line. Those behind, seeing these returning, became alarmed. Without pausing to reload, we rushed upon them, so quickly, indeed, that we did not give them time to run. Many surren-

dered upon demand; some gave us the bayonet. With these we had short, stern argument, using chiefly our clubbed guns. My gun being too short for such use and quite handy to load, I gave my stubborn opponent, who refused to surrender, the leaden contents at short range, and passed on after finding that he was beyond the need of assistance from me. As we rushed on, hundreds threw up their hands and said: "I surrender," but we could not afford to send men back from the charging line with prisoners, and would say: "Throw down your guns and go to the rear." Many did so; many obliqued to the left and finally escaped and joined their comrades, but we passed on, driving the ruck before us.

## LIEUTENANT JOHN D. BLACK
### STAFF, BRIGADIER GENERAL FRANCIS C. BARLOW

*Generals "Allegheny" Johnson and "Maryland" Steuart were taken prisoner along with some 3,000 other Rebels in Hancock's assault. Johnson was captured while flailing at the Yankees with the stout club he habitually carried into action. Steuart surrendered to Colonel James A. Beaver of the 148th Pennsylvania. Black recounts what happened after soldiers hustled the crestfallen Johnson and the arrogant Steuart to the rear.*

I reached corps headquarters as the prisoners were being formed in line preparatory to being marched to the rear, and at the time when Generals Johnson and Stewart were brought up to General Hancock, who at once stepped forward, and in that graceful and courtly manner of his extended his hand as if meeting an old comrade (which in fact he was) and exclaimed: "General Johnson, I am glad to see you." General Johnson took his hand and with tears coursing down his face, replied: "General Hancock, this is worse than death to me." With a kindly smile General Hancock answered: "This is the fate of war, General, and you must not forget that you are a soldier." He then turned and cordially offered his hand to General Stewart who drew back and remarked, "Under existing circumstances, Sir, I cannot take your

*Captain Asher W. Garber of the Staunton (Virginia) Artillery lost two guns after his infantry support collapsed during the opening assaults on the salient's eastern face. When the Rebels counterattacked, Garber rushed forward with some of his men and retook the pieces, turning them on the Yankees.*

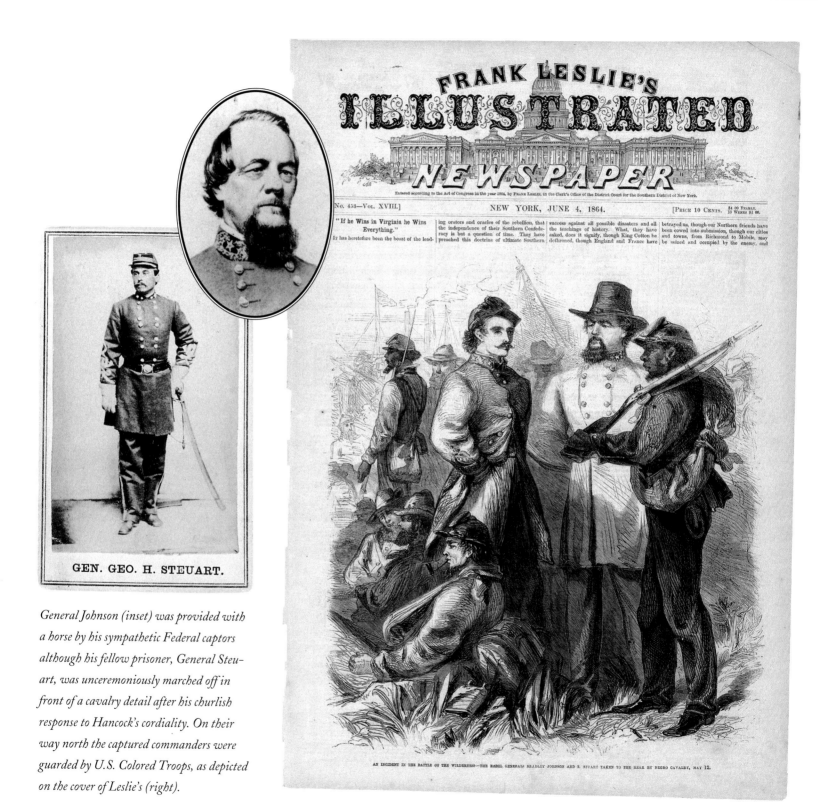

GEN. GEO. H. STEUART.

*General Johnson (inset) was provided with a horse by his sympathetic Federal captors although his fellow prisoner, General Steuart, was unceremoniously marched off in front of a cavalry detail after his churlish response to Hancock's cordiality. On their way north the captured commanders were guarded by U.S. Colored Troops, as depicted on the cover of Leslie's (right).*

hand." Quickly came that soldierly bearing and manner that had won for Hancock the title of "The Superb," and as quickly the retort, "Under any other circumstances, Sir, it would not have been offered." He turned his back on Stewart and entered into conversation with General Johnson, shortly after ordering Captain Mitchell, one of his Aides, to supply General Johnson with a horse and accompany him to General Meade's headquarters.

## CAPTAIN ALEXANDER W. ACHESON

### 140TH PENNSYLVANIA INFANTRY, MILES' BRIGADE

*By 6:00 a.m. ferocious Rebel counterattacks had pushed the Yankees back to the northern edge of the salient. Wright's VI Corps was sent forward to support Hancock's command, but it stalled along the line of captured entrenchments. Acheson was shot in the face during the action, returning to duty two months later with his wound unhealed. Stricken with chronic diarrhea in August, he resigned in November.*

After the Sixth Corps reached the ground we occupied, and seeing they were going no further, I left the works and moved forward towards the Confederate line. The object was to see if any of my men had been left between the lines, unable to get away by reason of wounds. After skirmishing over the ground our brigade had charged across, helping the wounded all that was possible, I was about returning, when a young lad was encountered belonging to Company C, 81st Pennsylvania, who was well known.

"Hello, Davis! are you hurt?"

"Yes, Captain, and I fear badly."

I got a coat and rolled it into a pillow for him, cut all his harness off, opened his blouse to relieve his labored breathing, searched over the field until a canteen was found, gave him a drink, wiped the cold death sweat from his forehead, and then shook his hand "goodby."

"Anything else, Davis?"

In a whisper he said: "Yes, take my watch and money, and send them home."

Catching the chain, I pulled at it, but found much resistance. Finally it began to yield, but the whole lining of the vest pocket over the heart was coming out with it. Slowly and with considerable pain it was finally brought to the top, when it became evident what was the matter. A bullet had struck the front case fair in the centre, gone through it, bursting open the back case and carrying the wheels into his body. As

*Captains William T. Bilbro of the 3d Alabama (left) and Orrin P. Rugg of the 77th New York were killed on May 12 in the savage fighting that raged across the Bloody Angle, on the northwestern rampart of the Mule Shoe. Bilbro had begun his wartime service as a corporal, and Rugg as a sergeant. Both had risen through the ranks to company command.*

he was suffering with the attempts to remove it, I desisted, telling him it was utterly ruined, and left it in his pocket.

Returning now to the captured line, the men were found standing in a body ten feet deep behind (or rather in front of) the earthworks. The charges and falling back had mixed them up to such an extent that it was difficult to find two of a company together. A more thoroughly mixed mass of soldiers never existed. While walking along the top of the works, General Miles was encountered, on whose staff I had served through the Mine Run campaign, during the preceding Autumn. Knowing by sight every member of his brigade . . . he asked me to continue along the works, and send all his men to the left, adjoining Colonel Carrol's brigade, where he had already collected a portion of them. This required about a half hour's work, when all the members of the brigade were sent to their places. It was but a half hour after this, and after I had returned to my regiment, that a gunshot wound was received through the face, being the fourth one in the family shot in the cheek. This terminated my work on the Spottsylvania field.

# PRIVATE ALFRED L. SCOTT

## 9TH ALABAMA INFANTRY, PERRIN'S BRIGADE

*Marching toward the sound of gunfire from its position in reserve at Spotsylvania Court House, Brigadier General Abner Perrin's brigade of five Alabama regiments was the first from Mahone's division to reach the battlefield. The Alabamians, deploying a quarter mile south of the McCoull house, were ordered to drive the Yankees from the captured salient. Scott describes the charge north to the Bloody Angle.*

Near McCoull's house the line was halted to wait for something, I never knew what, and were ordered to lie down for better protection, while waiting. A group of generals collected at the point in the line occupied by my company and engaged in an earnest and animated discussion. They were Ewell, Gordon, Rhodes, a general from Lee's staff, and General Perrin, our Brigadier. Things looked desperate and there was a considerable show of excitement. Our division commander was not present. Perrin was looking from one to the other as if at a loss for his orders. Gordon was talking rapidly and literally foaming at the mouth. Ewell's horse was standing almost over my feet. Looking around and seeing our line lying down, he exclaimed, "O For God's sakes, boys, don't lie down. It don't look well for a soldier to lie down in the presence of the enemy." Being right under his eyes, I felt there was almost a flavor of personality in his words, and though realizing their absurdity, under the circumstances, and that they meant nothing but flurry, I sprang to my feet, at once, saying, as I stood erect, "We were ordered to lie down, General." He replied, "O well, if you were to lie down, lie down, that's all right." I replied, "No, General, I don't want to do anything that looks badly in a soldier," and remained standing. He repeated, "That's all right. Lie down, lie down, if that was the order." I suppose the gallant old fellow realized that, in his excitement, he had "talked through his hat." The rest of the fellows, knowing they were in proper duty, remained as they were, and were smiling at the situation. Just then I heard Gordon say to Perrin, "I will take the responsibility and order you to charge." The sharp order, "Attention!" rang out and the whole line sprang to its feet. Then Perrin spurred his horse to the front and around the left flank of our regiment, and with the accustomed yell of our brigade, drove at the enemy with rushing step. Perrin was killed almost at the very first. We passed over him and swept back the enemy at our immediate front, but our line did not extend far enough to the right to cover the whole front of the enemy. After sweeping the open field in which stood the McCoull house we found ourselves raked in front by the heavy fire from the skirt of woods on our right. Our regiment changed

*The McCoull house, photographed here several months after the battle, stood in the middle of the Mule Shoe, 250 yards south of the Bloody Angle. As Perrin's charge passed the building, which had been "Allegheny" Johnson's headquarters, three men of the 9th Alabama were shot down in quick succession while carrying the regimental battle flag.*

front to the right and attacked the forces there. After driving them back . . . we again found ourselves under heavy fire from our right. Having already charged from the right and having gotten into the woods where the undergrowth prevented our seeing . . . we naturally supposed from the direction that we were being fired upon by our friends. . . . We never thought of returning their fire, but called to them to cease their fire, that we were friends, and called to our color bearer to "Show the flag." He held the colors up as high as he could, waving them emphatically so as to make them show over the tops of the chinquepin bushes about us. . . . But the more our colors were waved the more the fire seemed to pour into us. They were quite near us, we could see the smoke of their muskets through the leaves and catch glimpses of the guns and men themselves. I distinctly remember catching sight of the feet and legs of the line through the lower part of the bushes, where the leaves were not so thick. They seemed to have kept their flag out of sight. But I for one never dreamed of their being Yankees till there came a crash which nearly lifted off the top of my head and I saw the bushes in front of me swept by the blast of the cannon and its charge of grape fired straight into the line that was firing on us. Looking around I found that a section of our own artillery had rushed up to jam into our line without our having noticed them, in the uproar, and were now belching grape from both guns, for dear life, at our supposed friends. Calling to Peagler, I said, "Henry, those artillery men surely know what they are doing, so here goes!" We recognized them at once and our boys did not treat them as friends any more. Our first charge was straight into the angle. I passed right along the enclosure of the front of McCoull's yard. As I passed under a heavy cherry tree near the front gate I distinctly remember the shower of the bits of leaves floating to the ground in the still sultry air. They were falling in a constant steady shower from the whole tree, and as I passed through them, I remember that the sight at the moment suggested to my mind of a constant fall of snow floating to the ground with that easy quiet motion peculiar to it when there is not a breath of wind. The enemy must have been over-shooting us wonderfully; for if the bullets had been sweeping closer to the ground as thick as they were through the trees, I don't see how many of us could have gotten through.

*Abner Perrin served as a teenaged lieutenant during the Mexican War and rose from captain to brigadier general in Confederate service. Unabashedly ambitious for higher rank, Perrin remarked as his troops neared the battlefield at Spotsylvania, "I shall come out of this fight a live major general or a dead brigadier." With drawn sword he led his brigade to the charge and fell dead from the saddle with seven wounds.*

## PRIVATE BURTON R. CONERLY

### 16TH MISSISSIPPI INFANTRY, HARRIS' BRIGADE

*Nathaniel Harris' Mississippians, the second of Mahone's brigades to reach the salient, charged through the scattered survivors of Perrin's assault and fought their way to the northwestern face of the Mule Shoe, coming into line on the right of Stephen Ramseur's North Carolinians. Drenched by a torrential downpour, Conerly and his comrades began battling the Yankees at point-blank range and an hour later were joined by Samuel McGowan's South Carolina Brigade.*

Our men rushed forward with cheers, following their flags which were planted in quick succession on the trenched works. The brave Abe Mixon carrying the brigade flag, fell as he mounted the works. Our Colonel, Samuel Baker, fell a few feet from the writer, his body being in an exposed position, was riddled with rifle balls. Lieut. Col. Feltus fell soon afterwards.

The writer saw a man fall dead in the arms of Gen. Harris. This brave and good man, in this hail of death, laid him gently on the ground, with the exclamation, "Oh, my poor fellow!" Hundreds of the Federals threw down their guns and surrendered, while a triumphant yell rang out over the Confederate lines. The prisoners were ordered to the rear, numbers of whom fell dead from the shots of their own men who were rushing on us with loud "huzzahs." Many of the Federal prisoners begged us to let them stay with us, as it seemed certain death to go to the rear.

The line of works constructed by Gen. Edward Johnson was in a semicircle, and the men, to protect themselves from the enfilading fire of the enemy were in "traverses" (little short works built of poles and earth at right angles to the main line). These "traverses" were from thirty to forty feet apart. In carrying this position our brigade joined Gen. Ramseur's right. His brigade held that part of the line where we came in and our left overlapped his right. Our line was not long enough to capture the whole line, and the Federal troops still occupied the trenches on our right.

The guns which Gen. Johnson's men used were left in the trenches, and the Federals threw down theirs on the same ground. When we recaptured this position we gathered together quickly the guns found with the dead both in our front and rear, and with these guns loaded, we had practically the advantage of repeating rifles.

On the right, where the enemy was still in our trenches, the fighting was close and deadly, while the charges made on us in front came to hand to hand conflicts, in spite of our rapid firing with so many guns. The enfilading fire from our right, where the men were fighting across the "traverses" would have made our position untenable had not the "traverses" protected us. There was an incessant stream of rifle balls passing over us as well as hundreds of exploding shells. The rain poured down upon us in torrents, and the ditches were filled with water, reddened by the blood which flowed from the dead and wounded. We were forced to sit or stand on the bodies of the dead, covered with water.

At this stage of the fighting Gen. Gowan's brigade of South Carolinians, breasting the terrible storm of shot, with their men falling thick and fast at every step, their cheers mingled with the roar of musketry (the heaviest heard during the war), cannon and bursting shells, over the dead bodies of hundreds who had already fallen, rushed to our aid with the left of their brigade over lapping the right of ours, doubling our lines at this place and drove the enemy out of the trenches, capturing a number of prisoners. These had to run the gauntlet in going to our rear as on a former occasion.

The Federal troops now seemed to have renewed their efforts and made desperate charges. Hand to hand encounters occurred all during the day, The cold drenching rain continued. The flashing lightning; the bursting of shells, the tremendous and incessant roar of small arms and the yell of the soldiers, presented a scene indescribable in its terrible horror.

The trees in our rear were shot to splinters. One, eighteen or twenty inches in diameter, fell from the constant pelting of the minie balls and shells, while the bodies of the dead which lay in exposed positions were riddled beyond recognition.

During the day our ammunition ran short, and Gen. Harris called for volunteers to go to the rear and inform Gen. Ewell. Several men started to go, but none went far before they fell dead. Holden Pearson of our Company E, seeing these men fall, told Gen. Harris he would go. The General gave his reluctant consent, but looked as if he should never see him again alive. Keeping himself covered behind the trenches and moving rapidly from "traverse" to "traverse" to the left he got to a point where he could leave the line in a depression in the rear. He arrived safely at Gen. Ewell's headquarters on the field and informed him of the situation. He told Gen. Ewell how to get the ammunition to us, through the depression, and soon passing down the line, from man to man, came a steam of cartridges tied up in pieces of tent cloth. Thus we kept supplied during the remainder of the engagement, which continued nearly all night.

*Brothers William (left) and George Mackay, first cousins of General Micah Jenkins, served in Gregg's (later McGowan's) brigade. Their father died while they were away, and William resigned to operate the family plantation; he returned to service in 1863. George was killed with the 1st South Carolina during McGowan's counterattack.*

## LIEUTENANT J. F. J. CALDWELL
### 1ST SOUTH CAROLINA INFANTRY, McGOWAN'S BRIGADE

*Heeding the call for more troops, division commander Cadmus Wilcox ordered McGowan to march his five South Carolina regiments from the left of the line to reinforce Ewell's corps in the salient. McGowan's men, advancing by the flank, double-quicked in column until they reached the second line of works, where the loss of senior officers threw the brigade into confusion, as brigade historian Caldwell recalled.*

About ten o'clock, our brigade was suddenly ordered out of the works, detached from the rest of the division, and marched back from the line, but bearing towards the left. The fields were soft and muddy, the rains quite heavy. Nevertheless, we hurried on, often at the double-quick. Before long, shells passed over our heads, and musketry became plainly audible in front. Our pace was increased to a run. Turning to the right, as we struck an interior line of works, we bore directly for the firing.

We were now along Ewell's line. The shell came thicker and nearer, frequently striking close at our feet, and throwing mud and water high into the air. The rain continued. As we panted up the way, Maj. Gen. Rodes, of Ewell's corps, walked up to the road-side, and asked what troops we were. "McGowan's South Carolina brigade," was the reply. "There are no better soldiers in the world than these!" cried he to some officers about him. We hurried on, thinking more of him and more of ourselves than ever before.

Reaching the summit of an open hill, where stood a little old house and its surrounding naked orchard, we were fronted and ordered forward on the left of the road. The Twelfth regiment was on the right of our line, then the First, then the Thirteenth, then the Rifles, then the Fourteenth. Now we entered the battle. There were two lines of works before us: the first, or inner line, from a hundred and fifty to two hundred yards from us, the second, or outer line, perhaps a hundred yards beyond it, and parallel with it. There were troops in the outer line, but in the inner one only what appeared to be masses without organization. The enemy were firing in front of the extreme right of the brigade, and their balls came obliquely down our line; but we could not discover, on account of the woods about the point of firing, under what circumstances the battle was held. There was a good deal of doubt as to how far we should go, or in what direction. At first it was understood that we should throw ourselves into the woods, where the musketry was; but, somehow, this idea changed to the impression that we were to move straight forward—which would bring only about the extreme right regiment to the chief point of attack. The truth is, the road by which we had come was not at all straight, which made the right of the line front much farther north than the rest, and the fire was too hot for us to wait for the long, loose column to close up, so as to make an entirely orderly advance. More than all this, there was a death-struggle ahead, which must be met instantly.

We advanced at the double-quick, cheering loudly, and entered the inner works. Whether by order or tacit understanding, we halted here, except the Twelfth regiment, which was the right of the brigade. That moved at once to the outer line, and threw itself with its wonted impetuosity, into the heart of the battle. . . .

. . . About the time we reached the inner line, General McGowan was wounded by a Minie ball, in the right arm, and forced to quit the field. Colonel Brockman, senior colonel present, was also wounded, and Colonel J. N. Brown, of the Fourteenth regiment, assumed command, then or a little later. The four regiments—First, Thirteenth, Fourteenth and Rifles (the Twelfth had passed on to the outer line)—

closed up and arranged their lines. Soon the order was given to advance to the outer line. We did so, with a cheer and at the double-quick, plunging through mud knee-deep, and getting in as best we could. Here, however, lay Harris' Mississippi brigade. We were ordered to close to the right. We moved by the flank up the works, under the fatally accurate fire of the enemy, and ranged ourselves along the intrenchment. The sight we encountered was not calculated to encour-

*Lieutenant Colonel Isaac Foster Hunt—whose shell jacket is shown above— took command of the 13th South Carolina when his colonel fell, and at General Gordon's order led the unit forward to the embattled breastworks. The rest of McGowan's regiments followed, and under Hunt's inspired leadership they repeatedly blunted the Yankees' desperate attempts to regain the Mule Shoe.*

age us. The trenches, dug on the inner side, were almost filled with water. Dead men lay on the surface of the ground and in the pools of water. The wounded bled and groaned, stretched or huddled in every attitude of pain. The water was crimsoned with blood. Abandoned knapsacks, guns and accoutrements, with ammunition boxes, were scattered all around. In the rear, disabled caissons stood and limbers of guns. The rain poured heavily, and an incessant fire was kept upon us from front and flank. The enemy still held the works on the right of the angle, and fired across the traverses. Nor were these foes easily seen. They barely raised their heads above the logs, at the moment of firing. It was plainly a question of bravery and endurance now.

We entered upon the task with all our might. Some fired at the line lying in front, on the edge of the ridge before described; others kept down the enemy lodged in the traverses on the right. At one or two places, Confederates and Federals were only separated by the works, and the latter not a few times reached their guns over and fired right down upon the heads of the former.

# PRIVATE G. NORTON GALLOWAY
## 95TH PENNSYLVANIA INFANTRY, UPTON'S BRIGADE

*Galloway was an 18-year-old Philadelphian who joined the 95th Pennsylvania Zouaves in 1861. Captured at Salem Church in May 1863 and exchanged two weeks later, he deserted from a Federal parole camp but was arrested and returned to the regiment. He received a pardon because of previous good conduct and proceeded to display conspicuous bravery at the Bloody Angle. In 1895 he was awarded the Medal of Honor.*

At a brisk pace we crossed a line of intrenchments a short distance in our front, and, passing through a strip of timber, at once began to realize our nearness to the foe. It was now about 6 o'clock, and the enemy, reënforced, were making desperate efforts to regain what they had lost. Our forces were hastily retiring at this point before the concentrated attack of the enemy, and these with our wounded lined the road. We pressed forward and soon cleared the

*With heavy rain turning the battlefield into a quagmire, troops of Emory Upton's brigade advance against the Rebel breastworks near the abandoned guns of Lieutenant Richard Metcalf's section of the 5th U.S. Artillery. This engraving, based on sketches made by an unknown participant, depicts the surviving artillerists sheltering beside their slain battery horses at right, while pack mules and infantrymen carry up boxes of fresh ammunition.*

woods and reached an insidious fen, covered with dense marsh grass, where we lay down for a few moments awaiting orders. I cannot imagine how any of us survived the sharp fire that swept over us at this point —a fire so keen that it split the blades of grass all about us, the minies moaning in a furious concert as they picked out victims by the score.

The rain was still falling in torrents and held the country about in obscurity. . . . It was not long before we reached an angle of works constructed with great skill. Immediately in our front an abatis had been arranged consisting of limbs and branches interwoven into one another, forming footlocks of the most dangerous character. But there the works were, and over some of us went, many never to return. At this moment Lee's strong line of battle, hastily selected for the work of retrieving ill fortune, appeared through the rain, mist, and smoke. . . . The order was at once given us to lie down and commence firing; the left of our regiment rested against the works, while the right, slightly refused, rested upon an elevation in front. And now began a desperate and pertinacious struggle.

Under cover of the smoke-laden rain the enemy was pushing large bodies of troops forward, determined at all hazards to regain the lost ground. . . . The smoke, which was dense at first, was intensified by each discharge of artillery to such an extent that the accuracy of our aim became very uncertain, but nevertheless we kept up the fire in the supposed direction of the enemy. Meanwhile they were crawling forward under cover of the smoke, until, reaching a certain point, and raising their usual yell, they charged gallantly up to the very muzzles of our pieces and reoccupied the Angle.

Upon reaching the breastwork, the Confederates for a few moments had the advantage of us, and made good use of their rifles. Our men went down by the score; all the artillery horses were down; the gallant Upton was the only mounted officer in sight. Hat in hand, he bravely cheered his men, and begged them to "hold this point." All of his staff had been either killed, wounded, or dismounted.

At this moment, and while the open ground in rear of the Confederate works was choked with troops, a section of Battery C, 5th United States Artillery, under Lieutenant Richard Metcalf, was brought into action and increased the carnage by opening at short range with double charges of canister. This staggered the apparently exultant enemy. In the maze of the moment these guns were run up by hand close to the famous Angle, and fired again and again, and they were only abandoned when all the drivers and cannoneers had fallen. The battle was now at white heat.

The rain continued to fall, and clouds of smoke hung over the scene. Like leeches we stuck to the work, determined by our fire to keep the

*Captain John D. Fish of the 121st New York was appointed assistant adjutant general of Upton's brigade a month before the start of the Wilderness campaign and died at the Bloody Angle. "He was," Upton reported, "a brave, zealous, patriotic officer."*

enemy from rising up. Captain John D. Fish, of Upton's staff, who had until this time performed valuable service in conveying ammunition to the gunners, fell, pierced by a bullet. This brave officer seemed to court death as he rode back and forth between the caissons and cannoneers with stands of canister under his "gum" coat. "Give it to them, boys! I'll bring you the canister," said he; and as he turned to cheer the gunners, he fell from his horse, mortally wounded. In a few moments the two brass pieces of the 5th Artillery, cut and hacked by the bullets of both antagonists, lay unworked with their muzzles projecting over the enemy's works, and their wheels half sunk in the mud. Between the lines and near at hand lay the horses of these guns, completely riddled. The dead and wounded were torn to pieces by the canister as it swept the ground where they had fallen. The mud was half-way to our knees, and by our constant movement the fallen were almost buried at our feet. . . .

The great difficulty was in the narrow limits of the Angle, around which we were fighting, which precluded the possibility of getting more than a limited number into action at once. At one time our ranks were crowded in some parts four deep by reënforcements. . . . Our losses were frightful. What remained of many different regiments that had come to our support had concentrated at this point, and had planted their tattered colors upon a slight rise of ground close to the Angle, where they staid during the latter part of the day.

To keep up the supply of ammunition pack mules were brought into use, each animal carrying three thousand rounds. The boxes were dropped close behind the troops engaged, where they were quickly opened by the officers or file-closers, who served the ammunition to the men. . . .

Finding that we were not to be driven back, the Confederates began to use more discretion, exposing themselves but little, using the loopholes in their works to fire through, and at times placing the muzzles of their rifles on the top logs, seizing the trigger and small of the stock, and elevating the breech with one hand sufficiently to reach us. During the day a section of Cowan's battery took position behind us, sending shell after shell close over our heads, to explode inside the Confederate works. In like manner Coehorn mortars eight hundred yards in our rear sent their shells with admirable precision gracefully curving over us. Sometimes the enemy's fire would slacken, and the moments would become so monotonous that something had to be done to stir them up. Then some resolute fellow would seize a fence-rail or piece of abatis, and, creeping close to the breastworks, thrust it over among the enemy, and then drop on the ground to avoid the volley that was sure to follow. A daring lieutenant in one of our left companies leaped upon the breastworks, took a rifle that was handed to him, and discharged it among the foe. In like manner he discharged another, and was in the act of firing a third shot when his cap flew up in the air, and his body pitched headlong among the enemy.

## LIEUTENANT ABNER R. SMALL
### 16TH MAINE INFANTRY, LYLE'S BRIGADE

*With the clash at the Mule Shoe now favoring the Rebels, Grant and Meade ordered Warren to send his V Corps against the works at Laurel Hill, a mile and a half to the west. They reasoned that even if his attack failed, it would prevent enemy reinforcements from joining the battle for the Angle. Two hours passed before Warren reluctantly ordered a charge, and as Small recalled, the halfhearted effort was soon repulsed.*

The men, thoroughly exhausted, would lie at length on the cool, fresh earth, some of the timid ones hugging the bottom of the trench, painfully expressing the dread of something to come. And yet these timid ones, at the first rebel yell, would over and "at them," or draw bead on some venturesome Johnnie, and shout with derision if he was made to dodge. If they dropped him, a grim look of satisfaction, shaded with pity, passed over their dirty faces. The quiet was almost unbearable, the heat in the trenches intolerable, and rain, which commenced falling, was most welcome. Time dragged. We had not the slightest hint of what was developing. The rebels seemed very far off, and trouble ominously near.

From the right came an aide, and, quietly passing down the line of works, he dropped a word to this and that colonel; only a ripple, and all was again suspiciously still. "What was it, colonel?" [I] asked. . . . The colonel made no reply, but simply pointed up the hill. Soon he took out his watch and looked anxiously to the right. Suddenly a commotion ran down the line, followed by the command, "Attention! Forward, double-quick!" On went the brigade with a yell which was echoed from thousands of throats in front, and thrown back by the double columns in our rear. Down from the rebel right thundered shot and shell, making great gaps in our ranks, while on swept the brigade, until suddenly loomed up in our front, three lines of works—literally a tier, one above another—bristling with rifles, ready aimed for our reception. There was lead enough to still every heart present, and yet, when sheets of flame shot out in our faces, scarcely a dozen men of the regiment were hit. Then men tore madly at the abatis, and rushed on only to fall back or die. Again and again did the brigade charge, and as often came those terrible sheets of flame in our faces, while solid shot and shell enfiladed our lines. The crash which followed the fearful blaze swept away men, even as the coming wind would sweep away the leaves from the laurel overhead. Our ammunition was reduced to three rounds, when Colonel Lyle directed me to hasten to General Cutler and ask for ammunition or release. Hastening to the rear, I found the General nervously watching the effects of the shell which came crashing through the trees over his head. He came immediately forward to meet me, and said, "What is it, lieutenant?" Taking the verbal dispatch from Lyle, he replied, "Don't know that I can get a round of ammunition to your brigade. Tell Colonel Lyle to hold his position until relieved."

I was absent scarcely ten minutes, yet long enough for death to do its harvest work. "Look here," said Colonel Farnham. Partly buried in leaves and dirt lay the form of a splendid officer of the Ninetieth Pennsylvania, his head entirely shot away. Piled against his body lay six dead and dying men, all silenced by one shell. While viewing the ghastly sight, a huge shell exploded in our midst, sending Colonels Pray and Farnham to the ground, and [me] whirling like a top, neither of whom were injured. Just as the last charge was rammed home, relief came, when the brigade retired to the works in the rear, to learn that "it was not expected of the brigade to carry the works."

## LIEUTENANT THOMAS F. GALWEY
### 8TH OHIO INFANTRY, CARROLL'S BRIGADE

*Carroll's brigade lost 653 men in the daylong fight for the salient. Galwey, already a veteran company commander when just 18 years old, had been born in London of Irish parents and was a dedicated member of the secret Irish revolutionary society the Fenian Brotherhood. The day after his wounding he returned to the front and, because of the heavy losses among officers, took command of his regiment.*

About noon I was struck by a shell splinter in the calf of the leg, and was helped to the rear, about a quarter of a mile away. Here I saw acres of wounded men lying on the grass waiting for ambulances to evacuate them to the hospitals established about four miles behind the front. Amongst others was Private John Quinn of my company. I was laid near him and rendered him all the assistance in my power. I called to a surgeon of the Irish Brigade who was passing and induced him to care for his compatriot. Quinn's bowels were hanging out, and the surgeon, having pushed them in with his hand, set a handful of lint against the big hole and tied a big bandage around his body. He told me there was no hope for Quinn, but seeing a First Division ambulance, put him in it. I was sure that Quinn would die enroute. Then Sergeant Gallagher was put into one of our own Second Division ambulances, and later in the day when I was taken to the hospital tent I lay alongside of him. He was dying, but he lasted until four in the afternoon. They then carried him out and buried him in a little clump of trees. I made a headboard for him out of the side of a cracker box.

This was not my first trip to a hospital. After having my leg dressed I was able to look about me. We were some miles from the battle but of

*Edwin Forbes made this drawing of a V Corps divisional hospital behind the Union lines at Spotsylvania. More than 3,500 Federal wounded were evacuated during fighting on May 12. "The proportion of severe wounds was unusually large," medical director Thomas McParlin reported, "not over one-fourth of the number being able to walk back to the hospitals."*

course could very plainly hear both the artillery and musketry. There was one noise which seemed to be one continuous sound: the tearing of linen for bandages. This hospital was a vast assemblage of wall-tents or marquees, laid out in sections for the various corps, divisions, and brigades. Men were more or less attended by their own surgeons, and kept in the company of their comrades, thus being more easily identifiable in case of death.

Certain tents here and there were reserved for operations. In them were performed the amputations and most of the probing for balls and shell fragments. Next to our tent was one for operations and, as the walls of the tents were raised three or four feet high for a better circulation of air, we could see and of course hear the operations. Still, the surgical business had become something of an old story.

*Eighteen-year-old Cary Robinson left his studies at Columbian College in Washington, D.C., to join the 6th Virginia Infantry, one of Mahone's regiments. His exemplary conduct during the May battles led to his promotion to sergeant major. After he was killed in action in October, a fellow soldier said of Robinson, "Christian & hero— none nobler has perished."*

# LIEUTENANT COLONEL JOHN W. MCGILL

## 18TH NORTH CAROLINA INFANTRY, LANE'S BRIGADE

*Hoping to break the impasse, Grant ordered Burnside to renew the attacks against the salient's eastern flank. Three brigades advanced but were checked when Lane's men hit the Yankee left. McGill, at 21 one of the youngest field officers in Lee's army, was disgusted by Mahone's failure to support the Tar Heels' counterattack.*

About 3 o'clock P.M. the Brigade was ordered to assault the left flank of the enemy. . . . In this engagement, the Regiment was fired into from the rear by some of Mahone's Brigade, who were to support the assaulting column but failed to do so, and thereby necessitated a retreat. During this retreat, Capt. Buie, an officer of tried gallantry was spoken to in a very abrupt, and insulting manner by Genl. Mahone. I do not remember how this occurred, and as Capt. Buie is

now absent wounded, I have no means of ascertaining. This I do know, however, that while assisting Lt. McCallum off the field, (who had been badly wounded near me in the retreat) that a man on horse back, (who I afterwards learned was Genl. Mahone) rode up to a squad of eight or ten men (having a lot of prisinors under guard) a short distance in front of me and enquired if there was any Officer present. I replied that I was an Officer. He then demanded, using the expression, "Where in Hell are you taking these men to" I informed him that I was taking them to their command which I saw forming near a house, about two hundred yards in front of our line before Spottsylvania C.H. He (Genl. Mahone) then ordered me back to the front with these men remarking that the "d——d North Carolinians were deserting his brave Virginians." I then replied to him that I thought that it was just the reverse, and as I saw that the Brigade was forming at the house above mentioned, and *did not see any good* that I could accomplish by needlessly exposing myself and my men to the fire of the enemy's artillery, I did not obey his order. Whereupon he commenced abusing the Brigade generally. I endeavored to stop him from this by stating the circumstances, but as he disregarded my statement, I remarked to him that he might "go to Hell" or any where else but as for me, I would form with my command and accordingly moved forward, with about (30) thirty men of the Brigade, who had joined me while talking with Genl. Mahone.

"I remarked to him that he might 'go to Hell' or any where else but as for me, I would form with my command."

## LIEUTENANT CHARLES A. STEVENS
### 1ST U.S. SHARPSHOOTERS, CROCKER'S BRIGADE

*Fighting in line of battle rather than in their traditional role as skirmishers, the 1st U.S. Sharpshooters charged into the Mule Shoe with Birney's division and captured scores of Virginians and Louisianans. By afternoon, however, the riflemen were pinned down with thousands of other Yankees amid the bullet-swept carnage. Neither side was able to advance or willing to retreat.*

The Union artillery soon getting in position, between the cannon's deep roar and the rattle of musketry, one deafening uproar was kept up the entire day. It was one continual roar from sunrise until sunset, and after a short intermission on until midnight. Again and again did the rebels charge the position, coming up like so many fiends, to be hurled back by showers of lead and crashing shell. I counted five different charges that day, the enemy running towards us at full speed, firing as they ran, and although they often reached the works, they couldn't get over. They fought desperately, running headlong to death and destruction. They had come to us, in this fight, and they certainly did it bravely. Our men would rise quick and fire low, throwing the muzzles downward, then drop back. At one time, on the right, they gained a temporary advantage, but were finally driven away with heavy loss. Their dead and wounded were actually "piled up"—the wounded often completely covered by the dead and dying. Although they fought with the greatest determination, they were as determinedly resisted. The artillery on both sides was constantly in play, with shell and shot flying murderously about. Mens' heads were knocked to atoms by iron, others were riddled through their bodies with lead. Goodly sized trees were cut off, and brush mowed low; altogether, a most bloody carnival occurred. One tree, directly in front of Company G., some two feet through, was shot completely away by bullets alone, leaving but a bare stump full of battered lead. This stump was afterwards taken up and sent to the patent office building at Washington. Notwithstanding the enemy strove so hard to regain their old position, they signally failed in so doing—the victory belonged to the Union troops. During the day and night heavy rain wired down again, and the soldiers at the front were hardly to be recognized by their powder-blackened faces, and clothes covered with mud from their caps to their shoes, while their guns soon became dirty and rusty, and at times almost noiseless when they exploded. Heartrending scenes were on that field—the horrors of war were depicted on all sides. Men lay in all shapes, dying in position. Here, on their knees stiff

*On March 10, 1864, this national color was presented to the 51st Pennsylvania Infantry, famed as the regiment that had carried Burnside's Bridge at Antietam. At Spotsylvania the banner, one of four Federal flags lost during the repulse of the IX Corps attack, was captured by Private Leonidas H. Deane of the 12th Virginia.*

and stark—there, another kneeling in the act of loading with his arms spread, shot while ramming the cartridge—on their backs, their faces, every way. A field officer's horse just behind the writer, struck with a piece of shell, was caught quickly by the officer, who with revolver at the head, sent the wounded animal out of suffering into eternity. A piece of the same shell struck down a Sharpshooter 50 feet in front of us—Lewis E. Crowell, Company E, (N.H.)—a particularly sorrowful death. The regiment had fallen back to replenish with ammunition, and while sitting under a tree with Capt. Andrews and others of his company, the unfortunate comrade was struck under the left shoulder. He was one of three brothers, members of this company, who were ever ready for duty when called upon. Sergt. Wyatt and Gilman K. Crowell, his brother, buried him on the field further back, in the best possible manner under the circumstances. These shells were coming on all sides thick and deadly. Such was Spottsylvania—one of the hardest day's fights of the war.

## LIEUTENANT J. F. J. CALDWELL
### 1ST SOUTH CAROLINA INFANTRY, McGOWAN'S BRIGADE

*Despite the valiant determination of the Rebel soldiers and their success in shoving the Yankees back to the northern edge of the Mule Shoe, the position, Lee realized, could not be held. All troops that could be spared set to work building new entrenchments 1,200 yards to the south. In the meantime the depleted Confederate brigades would have to maintain their perilous foothold along the blood-soaked breastworks.*

We were told that if we would hold the place till dark we should be relieved. Dark came, but not relief. The water became a deeper crimson; the corpses grew more numerous. Every tree about us, for thirty feet from the ground, was barked by balls. Just before sunset, a tree of six or eight inches diameter, just behind the works, was cut down by the bullets of the enemy. We noticed, at the

*Hunkered down within arm's reach of their foe on opposite sides of an earthwork near the Bloody Angle, soldiers attempt to draw fire with hats held up on ramrods—thus luring their opponents into exposing themselves to waiting marksmen. Alfred Waud, whose sketch was likely based on accounts from survivors of the grim standoff, labeled his drawing "The toughest fight yet."*

same time, a large oak hacked and torn in a manner never before seen. Some predicted its fall during the night, but the most of us considered that out of the question. But, about ten o'clock, it did fall forward upon the works, wounding some men and startling a great many more. An officer, who afterwards measured this tree, informed me that it was twenty-two inches in diameter! This was entirely the work of rifle-balls. Midnight came; still no relief, no cessation of the firing. Numbers of the troops sank, overpowered, into the muddy trenches and slept soundly. The rain continued.

Just before daylight, we were ordered, in a whisper, which was passed along the line, to retire slowly and noiselessly from the works. We did so, and either we conducted it so well that the enemy were not aware of the movement, or else, (as I think most likely,) they had become so dispirited by our stubborn resistance of eighteen hours, that they had left only a skirmish line to keep up appearances. At all events, they did not attempt to pursue us. Day dawned as the evacuation was completed.

## LIEUTENANT JAMES E. PHILLIPS
12TH VIRGINIA INFANTRY, WEISIGER'S BRIGADE

*Colonel David A. Weisiger's five Virginia regiments, criticized by Lane for not fully supporting his brigade in the counterattack against the IX Corps, got into the fray later that day by trying to turn Burnside's left flank. Supported by Brigadier General John R. Cooke's brigade, Weisiger's men pushed northeast along the Fredericksburg road but were stopped by salvos of artillery—some coming from Rebel batteries to their rear. Phillips described the carnage in his unpublished memoirs.*

*Although limping from an ankle wound suffered in the Wilderness fighting, Sergeant William C. Smith assumed the duty of colorbearer for the 12th Virginia during the battle at Spotsylvania. After the war Smith settled in Nashville and became a noted architect and builder. A colonel of volunteers during the Spanish-American War, he died of a stroke while fighting guerrillas in the Philippines in 1899.*

We got in it very heavy. Lost a good many men. Captured men & flags by the quantity. Our color bearer was mortally wounded, W. E. Mayo, shot through the breast. Many captured. Here I lost my brother, Sergt. R. L. Phillips, Sergt. C. W. Granger Co. G killed, James Moreland, James Scriber, Co. H killed, Dr. Disoway from Co. E killed, and many others besides those carried to the rear and died. I got the watch and ring from my brother's person and was talking to Dr. Dunlap about what had occured. I had my back to the enemy, the firing was still going on. I felt a bullet pass my ear and it struck Dunlap in the right side of his neck and cut a tremendous gash. The blood squirted out and he slaped his hand over the gash and ran to the rear as hard as he could go. I said "my goodness he will die." A very few minutes later I was talking to —— one of our shells bursted which was fired from Pegram's artillery posted by the C.H. and cut down the whole color guard, killing two of them. One was Alexander Harrison the other I did not know. Allen McGee was in charge of the colors and I ran around a dogwood bush and picked them up and afterward I gave them to Sergeant W. C. Smith, Co. B. He carried them for nearly three months and had many holes shot in it and the staff was cut in three places, one above his hand and he never got scratched. . . . Was a gallant Confederate soldier and a high tone gentleman. He had besides himself three brothers in the service with Gen'l. Mahone's brigade and strange to say that neither of them was very much hurt during the whole war, and was nearly the whole time present for duty.

After my brother was killed, I did not care about anything. I made up my mind not to dodge or flinch for anything, matters not how dangerous it appeared to me. I got on a stump and the shell was flying thick & fast & bursting almost in my face yet I did not move or care if it had torn me to pieces. After awhile the firing ceased for awhile. I still sat on the stump waiting to make another charge. All of a sudden the shelling commenced again and the first one appeared to burst almost in my face. It so much surprised me that I dodged without thinking. . . . I left my brother in the woods dead along with many others, some of them I named above. I could do nothing, I being in command of two companies. Even my own captain had been wounded and gone to the rear never more to return to the Co. . . . My brother was sick when he went in the fight and had been sick for several days. I begged him not to go & his reply was "I would rather die then to have anyone say I shirked duty."

## CAPTAIN T. JAMES LINEBARGER
### 28TH NORTH CAROLINA INFANTRY, LANE'S BRIGADE

*Writing to his family on May 15, during a lull in the nearly constant marching and fighting, Linebarger acknowledged the determined and aggressive nature of Grant's campaign. Linebarger suffered wounds at Fredericksburg, Chancellorsville, and Gettysburg. He had command of the 28th North Carolina when it surrendered at Appomattox.*

*These two Waud sketches, made on the front and back of the same sheet of paper, provide a panoramic view of Barlow's—incorrectly labeled "Birney"—and Gibbon's divisions preparing to attack the new Rebel line on May 18. Advancing from the northern face of the abandoned Mule Shoe salient past decaying corpses from the earlier fighting, the Union ranks were brought to a standstill by an impenetrable abatis and driven back by a storm of artillery fire.*

*I* have for several days sought an opportunity to relieve your anxiety, but thus far have been unable to send you a letter, and even now I don't know when I can send one off, but write that it may be ready if I get an opportunity to mail it.

We have been on this campaign from the 4th, and have been four times under heavy infantry fire, besides an almost continuous shelling and skirmishing. Some portion of the army has been engaged every

day, yea, every hour since the 4th. The fighting has been generally of a desperate character, but by the blessings of Providence we have been very successful generally. I cannot undertake to give anything like a detailed account of the battle. It would fill a volume. My object is merely to relieve your anxiety by telling you that we are still both safe and well. . . .

I remarked at the outset that we have been four times hotly engaged: we have charged the enemy twice, and been twice charged by them. In our last charge we took a battery, but, failing to get support, had to fall back and leave it. We, however, *brought off more prisoners than we had men when we went in. . . .*

We are still in line of battle and skirmishing going on. Grant is not like other Yankees. Half such a whipping would have sent McClellan, Hooker, Burnside or Meade crossing to the other side of the Rappahannock, but Grant may join us again in battle at any moment. His loss has been fearful. Spottsylvania has been the theater of great events, and it seems that the end of this campaign, like the end of the war, is entirely with the future. It seems that Grant is determined to sacrifice his army or destroy Lee's. If he will charge our works a few more times, he will have expended his strength. He still confronts us, but has not made any determined assault since the 12th.

We have had a great deal of rain for the last five days, and it is still cloudy and a fine appearance for rain again this evening. I will send this off the first opportunity.

## SERGEANT WILLIAM S. WHITE
### 3D COMPANY, RICHMOND HOWITZERS

*At 4:00 a.m. on May 18 Gibbon's and Barlow's divisions, supported by three brigades from the VI Corps, advanced against Lee's new line south of the Mule Shoe. Ewell's men, who had been improving the entrenchments for a week, were ready. When the Yankees emerged from the fog they were savaged by artillery fire. White described the carnage inflicted on Colonel Matthew Murphy's brigade—newly arrived from the defenses of Washington—although White mistook it for heavy artillery.*

On come the enemy, and plainly can we see them debouching from the woods in our front and massing their troops to attack the hill on our right. Our guns are quickly trained upon them and the command "fire" is given. One by one our guns open upon them and as the thick blue smoke is blown from them we can see the deadly Napoleon shot and the unerring ten-pound rifle ball ploughing through the serried ranks of the astounded enemy. Vainly do they endeavor to press forward—again and again, we break them, and their officers uselessly dash up and down their lines, endeavoring to hurl them upon our works. The *dash* has been remorselessly extracted from these gala dressed Auger's Heavy artillerists, taken from the works around Washington to reinforce Grant, and in their *first* fight—they are but food for our gun-powder.

For one hour and a half this kind of fighting continued and every time the enemy formed for a charge we shattered their colums with artillery alone. The fourth gun fired slowly and deliberately—averaging one shot per minute—as its position was the best on the line, and our ammunition in splendid condition, it is presumable that we did fine execution. Finally the enemy, after making another abortive attempt, broke and incontinently fled, leaving us undisturbed masters of the field. Only three men in our company were wounded, two of whom were scarcely hurt. . . .

This fight has been most beneficial to us in restoring confidence to our men, for, especially on our part of the line, they have become somewhat discouraged, having suffered so severely.

The "gunner" of the fourth detachment, Corporal Miles H. Gardner, being temporarily attached to the third gun, owing to our severe loss in non-commissioned officers during the engagement of the 10th, I took my old position and acted in his stead. If there be any pleasure in fighting, it is when one is "gunner" of a splendid Napoleon gun, the men working like clock-work, ammunition in splendid order, *and no one shooting at you*. Such was the fight of to-day. . . .

. . . After the fight our infantry hung around the powder-begrimed and heated "Napoleon," patted it affectionately on the breach and muzzle, and made all manner of queer remarks concerning its effectiveness and accuracy. One strapping looking fellow sang out to his comrade, "Look here, Jim—here's *our* gun! This is the gun we pulled out'n the mud that ar' night. . . ."

Some of us walked down to the position where the enemy, in the morning, had been massing his troops for a "charge," and their dead and severely wounded, being left on the field, presented the most horrible sights we ever witnessed. Our infantry had not fired a shot—all the work had been done by the artillery. Few men were simply wounded—nearly all were dead, and literally torn into atoms; some shot through and through by cannon balls, some with arms and legs knocked off, and some with their heads crushed in by the fatal fragments of exploded shell. Horrible, horrible! They left several hundred of their dead in our front, and as it is to be presumed that many were carried off, their loss must have been severe. Our infantry were ordered not to fire until their line of battle got within two hundred yards of our breastworks, and as they did not get that near to us the artillery had it all to themselves.

## LIEUTENANT GEORGE W. BICKNELL
### 5TH MAINE INFANTRY, UPTON'S BRIGADE

*On May 13 Meade, attempting to turn the Rebel right, marched the VI Corps toward a ford on the Ny River. Warren's V Corps had a foothold south of the stream, and at dawn on May 14 Upton's brigade—reduced to some 800 men—crossed it and occupied high ground near the Myers farmhouse. But Brigadier General Ambrose Wright's Georgia Brigade checked the Yankees, as Bicknell recounted in his regimental history.*

By the time the line was formed, there was only one vidette of the enemy to be seen; and the brigade commander, desirous of ascertaining whether there was any considerable force of the enemy in that vicinity, directed the colonel of the Ninety-sixth Pennsylvania to send a man forward and reconnoiter, and gain the information desired. A bright little fellow, some thirteen years of age, a stray waif in the army, who had been a sort of a waiter around head-quarters, begged for the privilege of going, saying he "wasn't afraid, they couldn't hit him." Permission was granted, and away the little fellow galloped within shooting distance of the enemy, where he halted, and coolly surveyed the situation, until several shots admonished him of his dangerous position. Waving his little cap at them, he turned his horse, and reported that he saw "lots of them in the woods." The future history of that brave little fellow would be interesting, if it should continue as well as it commenced.

Nothing serious was apprehended, and General Meade and staff were at the extreme front, endeavoring to examine the position with their glasses, when suddenly a yell, and three lines of battle of the enemy arose from their concealment and pressed down upon our devoted lines, while a battery opened a sharp fire. It was observed that General Meade and staff found it necessary to hasten their steps somewhat to avoid being captured. Although our line was only a thin skirmish line, the brigade held their ground and poured in a rapid fire, until overwhelming numbers compelled them to beat a hasty retreat. The Fifth Maine was able, fortunately, to move directly across the river to the left, and not a man was lost, although necessity obliged a wide scattering, inasmuch as there were no supports. It was really a ludicrous and laughable retreat.

*Captain Andrew J. Stone of the 9th New Hampshire Infantry—part of the IX Corps—was wounded in a skirmish on May 18 and died in Fredericksburg two days later. Stone's regiment lost 184 men at Spotsylvania, most of them in the fight on May 12.*

*Federal soldiers who succumbed to their wounds in a Fredericksburg hospital await burial in a military cemetery as a photographer (background) prepares to record the grim toll of the fighting at Spotsylvania. This stereograph was one of eight images of the scene made by employees of Mathew Brady's gallery, most likely on May 19, 1864.*

# "Lee is *not* retreating: he is a brave and skilful soldier and he will fight while he has a division or a day's rations left."

## LIEUTENANT COLONEL THEODORE LYMAN
### Staff, Major General George G. Meade

*A wealthy Harvard-educated intellectual and a leading naturalist of his day, Lyman befriended then-Captain Meade during an 1856 scientific survey in Florida. In 1863 he accepted a position on the general's staff. Lyman's letters to his wife, Elizabeth, constitute an astute chronicle of the 1864 campaign.*

The great feature of this campaign is the extraordinary use made of earthworks. When we arrive on the ground, it takes of course a considerable time to put troops in position for attack, in a wooded country; then skirmishers must be thrown forward and an examination made for the point of attack, and to see if there be any impassable obstacles, such as streams or swamps. Meantime what does the enemy? Hastily forming a line of battle, they then collect rails from fences, stones, logs and all other materials, and pile them along the line; bayonets with a few picks and shovels, in the hands of men who work for their lives, soon suffice to cover this frame with earth and sods; and within one hour, there is a shelter against bullets, high enough to cover a man kneeling, and extending often for a mile or two. When our line advances, there is the line of the enemy, nothing showing but the bayonets, and the battle-flags stuck on the top of the work. It is a rule that, when the Rebels halt, the first day gives them a good rifle-pit; the sec-ond, a regular infantry parapet with artillery in position; and the third a parapet with an abattis in front and entrenched batteries behind. Sometimes they put this three days' work into the first twenty-four hours. Our men can, and do, do the same; but remember, our object is offense —to advance. You would be amazed to see how this country is intersected with field-works, extending for miles and miles in different directions and marking the different strategic lines taken up by the two armies, as they warily move about each other.

The newspapers would be comic in their comments, were not the whole thing so tragic. More absurd statements could not be. Lee is *not* retreating: he is a brave and skilful soldier and he will fight while he has a division or a day's rations left. These Rebels are not half-starved and ready to give up—a more sinewy, tawny, formidable-looking set of men could not be. In education they are certainly inferior to our native-born people; but they are usually very quick-witted within their own sphere of comprehension; and they know enough to handle weapons with terrible effect. Their great characteristic is their stoical manliness; they never beg, or whimper, or complain; but look you straight in the face, with as little animosity as if they had never heard a gun.

Now I will continue the history a little. But first I will remark that I had taken part in two great battles, and heard the bullets whistle both days, and yet I had *scarcely seen a Rebel* save killed, wounded, or prisoners! I remember how even line officers, who were at the battle of Chancellorsville, said: "Why, we never saw any Rebels where we were; only smoke and bushes, and lots of our men tumbling about"; and now I appreciate this most fully. The great art is to *conceal* men; for the moment they show, *bang, bang*, go a dozen cannon, the artillerists only too pleased to get a fair mark. Your typical "great white plain," with long lines advancing and manœuvring, led on by generals in cocked hats and by bands of music, exist not for us. Here it is, as I said: "Left face —prime—forward!"—and then *wrang, wr-r-rang*, for three or four hours, or for all day, and the poor, bleeding wounded streaming to the rear. That is a great battle in America.

*Confederate prisoners crowd the slopes of a ravine dubbed the "Punch Bowl," an improvised holding area near the Army of the Potomac's supply base at Belle Plain, on the Potomac River. Between May 13 and May 18 some 7,500 Rebels passed through Belle Plain en route to the Federal prison compound at Point Lookout, Maryland. Nearly half of them had been captured on May 10 and 12 during the Union assaults on the Mule Shoe.*

# "I Will Take No Backward Steps"

General Grant's repeated failure to shatter the Rebel line compelled him to give up at Spotsylvania and seek a more advantageous place to attack. Toward this end the Union commander, as he had done after the Wilderness battle, sought to use maneuver to draw Robert E. Lee from his stronghold.

But before the curtain finally fell on the fighting at Spotsylvania, the Rebels launched an offensive of their own. On May 19 the ever-aggressive Lee, suspecting that Grant had withdrawn troops from the Union right, determined to make a reconnaissance in force in that direction. He ordered Ewell to take his corps across the Ny River and strike in the direction of Fredericksburg with the objective of cutting the Yankees' line of communications.

About 5:00 that afternoon, Ewell was leading his troops toward the Fredericksburg road

*On May 21 Grant and Meade assembled their staffs in the yard of Massaponax Church to discuss the next phase of their offensive. Calmly puffing a cigar, Grant sits on the church pew beneath the trees at center in Timothy O'Sullivan's photograph. Meade, in slouch hat, is on the end of the pew at left.*

when he stumbled onto unexpectedly strong opposition—7,500 fresh Union troops, most of them pulled from the heavy artillery regiments defending Washington. As Ewell's vanguard surged across the fields of the Harris farm, they collided with the countercharging former artillerymen, new to their role as infantry.

A vicious fight ensued. The Federal line broke, but the green Union troops managed to rally and hold. Ewell's horse was shot from under him, and he fell hard to the ground, injured. By 6:00 p.m. reinforcements from two Union corps were arriving, and Ewell, far from the main body of Confederate troops, was forced to retreat. He had suffered some 900 casualties.

With that last spasm of bloodshed the fighting around Spotsylvania Court House came to an end. The toll taken by the recent battles had been devastating to the Federals. Grant's Army of the Potomac had suffered 18,399 casualties at Spotsylvania, on top of 17,666 in the Wilderness, for a total of 36,065 dead, wounded, or missing since May 5. About 4,000 more Union soldiers had been sent back to Washington hospitals to recover from illnesses, and another 14,000 had either deserted or returned home when their enlistments expired. As a result Grant could count only 56,124 effective fighting men on May 19—half the mighty force he had led into the Wilderness just two weeks earlier. Replacements available to fill the gaps in the Federal battle line amounted to only 12,000.

To make matters worse for Grant, the other Federal armies on the move in Virginia had met with dismal failure. Franz Sigel, whose mission had been to occupy the Shenandoah Valley, was instead routed at New Market by a small Confederate force under Major General John C. Breckinridge. With Sigel in retreat, Breckinridge could spare two brigades—2,500 men—to reinforce Lee.

The other Union force at work in the East, Benjamin Butler's Army of the James, had fared no better. Butler advanced so timidly southeast of Richmond that on May 16 Rebel general P. G. T. Beauregard had seized the initiative and attacked him. At the Battle of Drewry's Bluff, Beauregard inflicted 4,000 casualties on the Yankees and drove Butler back into Bermuda Hundred, a peninsula formed by the junction of the James and Appomattox Rivers.

Beauregard's Rebels then threw a line of earthworks across the peninsula's neck. Butler's army, Grant remarked later, had been "as completely shut off from further operations directly against Richmond as if it had been in a bottle strongly corked." Only a small force was needed to keep Butler bottled up, allowing Beauregard to send Lee an entire division of about 6,000 men.

These additions to Lee's command made up for some of the heavy losses—about 11,000 men in the Wilderness and 10,000 at Spotsylvania—he had suffered during the first weeks of May. An even worse blow for Lee had been the toll of commanders: A. P. Hill sick, Ewell faring poorly, Longstreet badly wounded. But the greatest loss was the death of Lee's cavalry chief, the colorful Jeb Stuart, who was wounded in a skirmish with Sheridan's cavalry at Yellow Tavern and who died on May 12.

On May 21, Grant resumed the chess game of maneuver with his formidable enemy. He intended to return to his plan of sidestepping past the Confederate right flank in the direction of Richmond. Perhaps this time he could catch Lee with his guard down.

Hancock was to lead the march. His II Corps would step out in the direction of Milford Station, marching just east of the Richmond, Fredericksburg & Potomac Railroad. Because Hancock would have a head start on the rest of the Army of the Potomac and would thus give the appearance of being on an independent mission, Lee might be tempted to lash out at the II Corps. If he bit, Grant would descend on Lee with his other three corps and crush the outnumbered Confederates.

But Lee was not to be decoyed. As soon as he detected the Federal movement, he dropped south, ignoring Hancock and keeping his army between the Federals and Richmond. Lee decided that the nearest spot where he could establish a strong position was behind the steeply banked North Anna River. Entrenching there, he could protect the direct route to the capital as well as the vital railroad town of Hanover Junction, where the Virginia Central met the Richmond, Fredericksburg & Potomac. It was at Hanover Junction that Lee was to pick up reinforcements, a total of 8,500 men.

Lee had ample time to execute his maneuver. Ewell's corps had only about 25 miles to march to reach the junction, while Hancock, who had to use inferior routes, had 34 miles to cover. Ewell moved out at noon on May 21, followed by Anderson's troops. Hill, sufficiently recovered from illness to resume command of his corps, was to remain in position through the night to make sure that the last of the Federals had departed Spotsylvania Court House. At

8:00 a.m. Lee told his staff, "Come, gentlemen," then mounted Traveller and rode south.

Grant was in the saddle as well. At Guiney Station, 10 miles south of Fredericksburg, he had his headquarters tent pitched at the Motley house, then rode over to the nearby Chandler farm to explain his presence. A woman there told him that Stonewall Jackson had died on the estate the year before. Grant said that he had known Jackson at West Point and in Mexico and that he had appreciated the general's abilities. Grant said he could "understand fully the appreciation your people have for him." The woman recounted Jackson's final hours and began to weep. Taking his leave, Grant issued orders that her property go unharmed.

Lee stopped during the night to rest for a couple of hours beside Polecat Creek, then resumed his ride to the North Anna. He arrived the next morning, May 22, just as Ewell's column got over the river and deployed to cover the railroad crossing at Hanover Junction. Later that day Anderson arrived, followed by Hill the next day, the troops spreading out along the river bluff to cover bridges and fords. Lee realized that his strong North Anna position offered obstacles to any Federal maneuver. Perhaps he could catch Grant's army awkwardly astride the river and deliver a crushing counterblow.

Nevertheless, for the time being Lee wanted his troops to rest and "refresh themselves" after 17 straight days of fighting and marching. Despite the commander's good wishes for his men, however, the Confederate commissary lacked the resources for providing the refreshment Lee had in mind. "We were allowed one pint of corn meal (not sifted) and one-fourth of a pound of bacon for one day's ration," wrote a hungry Rebel in his diary. He added that since "there was nothing in that country to steal, we were pretty badly off."

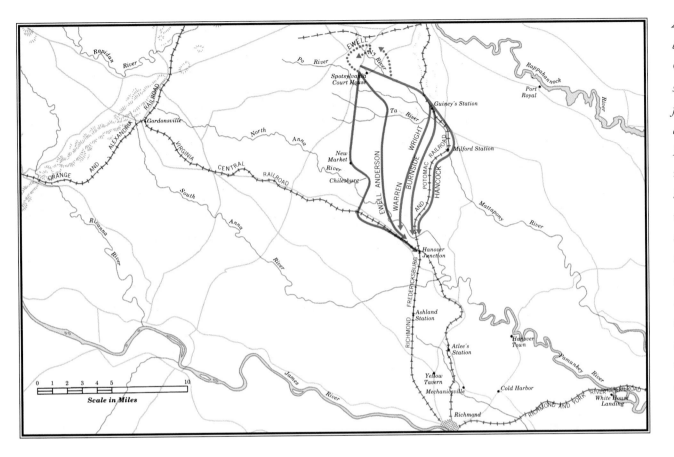

*After suffering another bloody repulse on May 18, Grant decided once again to sideslip around Lee's right flank. Before the Yankees could move, however, Ewell's Rebels attacked the northern end of Grant's line, although the outcome was inconclusive. The next evening the Union army began moving in stages toward the North Anna River. But once again Lee responded quickly, getting his army in motion and winning the race to the south side of the river.*

The better-supplied Federal army, meanwhile, was in a confident mood despite the exhaustion of the troops. The weather was fine, the roads were dry, and the men heading south once again. One of Hancock's officers wrote, "There was an idea that we were still advancing, that there was a plan that would be carried out successfully. When we reached the North Anna I think the general feeling was that we should roll on, like a wave, up to the very gates of Richmond."

As they marched into the town of Bowling Green, Hancock's infantrymen found slaves lining the road. The shops were closed and the townspeople were staring at the troops from porches or from behind shuttered windows. As some of the soldiers broke ranks to loot the shops, they were mocked by the more daring of the white onlookers: "Are you going to Richmond? You'll lay all your bones in the ground before you get sight of it."

When they reached the North Anna, the Yankees probed across the river in several spots and discovered that Lee, once again, had devised a seemingly impregnable defensive position, a wedge-shaped line anchored on a bluff that bristled with artillery and was protected by elaborate earthworks. On May 24 the Federals attacked Lee's redoubt in two separate places, and both attempts failed to win an inch of ground.

Grant, having seen two assaults so strongly opposed, concluded that a concentrated push would be folly. In a wire to Major General Henry Halleck, Grant reported: "To make an attack from either wing would cause a slaughter of our men that even success would not justify." Therefore, Grant intended to withdraw and proceed to sidle once again around Lee's right.

Despite the standoff, Grant felt optimistic. The fire, he believed, was fading from the Army of Northern Virginia. "Lee's army is really whipped," Grant wrote. "The prisoners we take now show it, and the action of his army shows it . . . . I may be mistaken, but I feel that our success over Lee's army is already assured."

Grant was mistaken. Ahead lay Cold Harbor and a fresh killing ground, where Robert E. Lee and his Rebels would inflict thousands more Union casualties on the road to Richmond.

# CORPORAL CHARLES J. HOUSE

## 1ST MAINE HEAVY ARTILLERY, TYLER'S BRIGADE

*The heavy artillery regiments stripped from the defenses of the nation's capital were well disciplined, but few of the men had combat experience. On May 19, Brigadier General Robert O. Tyler's brigade, assigned to the IX Corps, saw its first action against Ewell's corps on the Harris and Alsop farms northeast of Spotsylvania. House, a farmer from Brewer, Maine, escaped with slight wounds here and in June, and ended the war as a first lieutenant.*

The regiment embarked on a transport at the foot of 7th street during the forenoon of May 15, and landed at Belle Plain the same evening, where it remained until the morning of the 17th, when it took up the line of march, passed through Fredericksburg and arrived at Spottsylvania at 11 o'clock that evening. We had now literally

*Confederate dead, probably men of Ramseur's North Carolina Brigade, lie ready for burial in the yard of the Alsop farmhouse. This image was part of a series taken on May 20 by photographer Timothy O'Sullivan. During the battle, Ramseur's Tar Heels drove Tyler's artillerymen from the Alsop farm in fierce fighting. One of Tyler's men recalled that the Rebels "came crashing through us, firing as they came." Among the slain was Lieutenant Cyrus P. Jones of the 14th North Carolina (above), a shoemaker from Davidson County.*

arrived at the seat of war and were liable to be called into action at any time. Made up from good material, perhaps no better and certainly no worse than the average regiment from the old Pine Tree state, the schooling we had received while in the defences of Washington had made us thorough soldiers so far as drill and discipline were concerned but we lacked the practical knowledge of fighting the enemy or how best to protect ourselves when in range of the enemy's bullets. This we learned later on in the hard school of experience, that is, what few of us there were left after thirty days of such schooling.

All day the 19th, the troops from the right of our army were moving away to the left and the Fredericksburg Pike, over which our supply trains were moving, became uncovered and the enemy, always feeling for an opportunity, had advanced a force under General Ewell, which had cautiously moved along until late in the afternoon they struck the wagon train protected only by a light guard which was immediately swept away and our supplies were in their hands. Our regiment chanced to be nearest the point of attack and it was started at once on the double quick. About the time we started a heavy shower came on but on we rushed through rain and mud, and as we neared the train filed off to the right so as to bring ourselves into line, then made a dash for the wagons. The force of the enemy at that point was not a heavy one and they were brushed away without a halt on our part, some being captured but the larger part fell back to their main line. Advancing for half a mile through the thicket without meeting the enemy we emerged into a clearing, a field of perhaps ten acres, divided nearly equally by a small sluggish brook fringed by low trees and running from right to left. The ground sloped gently on our side of the brook but was steeper beyond up to the edge of the woods where the enemy were posted. Up this hill the force driven from the wagon train were rushing as we came out of the woods, but were soon out of sight.

The regiment moved two-thirds the way down the slope where they were brought to a halt, and firing commenced which lasted two hours and twenty minutes. During all this time the men stood, fought just as you see them in pictures, and were the coolest lot of men I ever saw under any circumstances. They loaded, took aim and fired, then would deliberately clear the smoke from their guns by half cocking, throwing off the old cap and blowing into the muzzle, always giving the gun time to cool a little before reloading. Men were falling, to be sure, but those who were able got away to the rear while those who were not, lay quietly along the line and the survivors were too much engaged with their work to notice much about them until the enemy retired and the firing ceased. . . .

Later on I accompanied a squad of men who were going on to the field to bring off the body of Lieutenant John F. Knowles of our company who had been killed. As we neared the point where we had stood in line I noticed eight or ten of our men laid out side by side, the beams of the moon struggling through the fleecy clouds, lighting their upturned faces all smeared with the smoke of battle, some showing gaping wounds and all ghastly and lifeless. Looking to the right where the color guard and Company M had stood, was a similar lot of dead carefully laid out, beyond this another and another until the woods were reached, and the same thing away to the left. It was a solemn moment as I gazed on the scene at that midnight hour, my first look upon a deserted battle field, and how forcibly those rows of dead men reminded me of the gavels of reaped grain among which I had worked on my native hills, but here the reaper was the angel of death.

## BRIGADIER GENERAL E. PORTER ALEXANDER
### COMMANDER, FIRST CORPS ARTILLERY

*Alexander relates here a rare incident in which Robert E. Lee's officers were amused at their revered commander's discomfiture. Alexander served with distinction at North Anna, Cold Harbor, and Petersburg. He pursued a postwar career in railroads and served as special envoy to Nicaragua. In 1907, he published an account of the war, "Military Memoirs of a Confederate." This account comes from a second memoir, "Fighting for the Confederacy," that remained unpublished for nearly a century.*

At about 2 P.M., Sunday [the] 22nd, we reached Hanover Junction & went into camp a little north of it, near a nice looking farm house . . . on a little knoll. Our march had been about 30 miles in about 18 hours. I saw a few chickens about the farm house & tried to buy them, but the owner thought Confederate money no temptation & said that he had but few & he wanted them for seed.

The next morning, Monday [the] 23d, we were lying quietly in camp when suddenly the fire of a battery was opened from the opposite bank of the North Anna about a mile away & shells began to land about promiscuously. The enemy had followed us up much more closely than we seemed to expect, & he announced himself as if he was in a hurry & meant business. I quickly ran Parker's rifle battery . . . up on the knoll by the farm house, & began to return the fire of the Federal battery. One of their shells struck the farm house, & the owner & his family . . .

*Men of Captain Albert F. Thomas' 2d Maine Light Artillery relax at their guns while another Federal battery bombards Confederate positions across the North Anna River in this sketch by Alfred Waud. Thomas' battery fired more than 300 rounds from its four 3-inch ordnance rifles during the two days that it occupied the riverbank.*

who were already somewhat scared up, swarmed out like bees & fled as fast as they could run—man, wife, & daughters. I just happened to see them in time & I shouted after, "I say, won't you sell me those chickens now?" He shouted back, "Yes, pay me next time you see me." So Willie Mason & Winthrop & Joe & I chased down the chickens & caught the last one of them, & Willie tied them on his saddle & took them to camp. . . .

I have another recollection of the evening & an amusing one. While we had been dueling with the enemy's guns Gen. Lee had had some of the engineers looking for a line of battle for our corps, & they did not agree whether we should form in front or in rear of a sort of flat swamp about a half mile back from the river. A little before sundown the gen. sent me to look over both lines & then make him a report at his headquarters near Hanover Junction. It was dusk when I got there, and a regular little council was held under a big, lone oak tree in a forty acre clearing. All around us troops were going into bivouac for the night.

Men loaded with bunches of canteens, which rattled as they walked, were wandering about inquiring for wells & springs & streams. Company cooks were kindling their fires & impatient mules were braying for their suppers. The air was still & it was one of those evenings when all sounds are distinct & far-reaching. Gen. Lee sat on a big root, his back against the tree, with some of his own staff around & some three or four engineers. . . . Those who wanted the line in front of the swamp were invited to explain why, & then those who preferred to have the swamp in front. Gen. Lee heard the arguments, which were all brief & to the point, for all night would be needed to distribute troops & artillery, & prepare for the assault at day break, which we fully expected. Then Gen. Lee decided that the line should have the swamp in front, & began giving details about the location of the troops.

Just then a teamster began to remonstrate with a mule, some hundred yards or more across the clearing. His remarks were as audible as if he had been under the tree with us. "Get around there you damned infernal long-eared son of a jackass," & a tremendous whack emphasized the injunction. Gen. Lee could stand anything better than having an animal maltreated. He hesitated a moment in his speech & gave that peculiar little shake of his head which he used when he was worried, & which we used to call snapping at his ear. But the misunderstanding between the man & the mule only seemed to widen. I won't try to repeat his lurid language, for I could not do it justice, & only a pile driver could describe the whacks which accompanied his volley of oaths. Gen. Lee stopped his discourse, snapped at his ear a time or two, & then shouted out in a tone which I thought would scare anybody, "What are you beating that mule for?" But the teamster evidently thought only that some one was guying him, for assuming a sort of Georgia cracker whine in his voice, he sung out, "Is this any of you-r-r mule?" It was an awful moment. Not one of us dared to crack a smile. The general snapped at his ear again a time or two, & then apparently determined to finish with us first, before making good his claim to the mule. I have no doubt that he did this as soon as we were gone and to the teamster's satisfaction, but I never heard any particulars.

## LIEUTENANT COLONEL HORACE PORTER

Staff, Lieutenant General Ulysses S. Grant

*Despite increasing Federal pressure on all fronts, the result of Grant's plan to coordinate the efforts of all the Union armies, many Southerners remained confident of a final victory for the Confederacy. Here Porter recalls an encounter that Grant and his staff had with two fiercely partisan Southern women when the Federal commander paused at their house overlooking the Mattapony River on May 22.*

When we reached this plantation, the escort and the junior staff-officers lounged about the grounds in the shade of the trees, while General Grant, accompanied by two or three of us who were riding with him, dismounted, and ascended the steps of the porch. A very gentle and prepossessing-looking lady standing in the doorway was soon joined by an older woman. . . . The ladies, seeing that the officer with whom they were conversing was evidently one of superior rank, became anxious to know who he was, and the older one stepped up to me, and in a whisper asked his name. Upon being told that he was General Grant, she seemed greatly surprised, and in a rather excited manner informed the other lady of the fact. The younger lady, whose name was Mrs. Tyler, said that she was the wife of a colonel in the Confederate army, who was serving with General Joe Johnston in the West; but she had not heard from him for some time, and she was very anxious to learn through General Grant what news he had from that quarter. The general said, "Sherman is advancing upon Rome, and ought to have reached that place by this time." Thereupon the older lady, who proved to be the mother-in-law of the younger one, said very sharply: "General Sherman will never capture that place. I know all about that country, and you have n't an army that will ever take it. We all know very well that Sherman is making no headway against General Johnston's army." . . .

General Grant replied in a quiet way: "General Sherman is certainly advancing rapidly in that direction; and while I do not wish to be the communicator of news which may be unpleasant to you, I have every reason to believe that Rome is by this time in his possession." The older lady assumed a bantering tone, and became somewhat excited and defiant in her manner; and the younger one joined with her in scouting the idea that Rome could ever be taken. Just then a courier rode up with despatches from Washington containing a telegram from Sherman. General Grant glanced over it, and then read it to the staff. It announced that Sherman had just captured Rome. The ladies had caught the purport of the communication, although it was not intended that they should hear it. The wife burst into tears, and the mother-in-law was much affected by the news, which was of course sad tidings to both of them.

The mother then began to talk with great rapidity and with no little asperity, saying: "I came from Richmond not long ago, where I lived in a house on the James River which overlooks Belle Isle; and I had the satisfaction of looking down every day on the Yankee prisoners. I saw thousands and thousands of them, and before this campaign is over I want to see the whole of the Yankee army in Southern prisons."

Just then Burnside rode into the yard, dismounted, and joined our party on the porch. He was a man of great gallantry and elegance of manner, and was always excessively polite to the gentler sex. He raised his hat, made a profound bow to the ladies, and, as he looked at his corps filing by on the road, said to the older one, who was standing near him, "I don't suppose, madam, that you ever saw so many Yankee soldiers before." She replied instantly: "Not at liberty, sir." This was such a good shot that every one was greatly amused, and General Grant joined heartily in the laugh that followed at Burnside's expense.

*Edwin Forbes called this sketch of a Federal column on the road to the North Anna "Washing Day," having shown a soldier drying his handkerchief and socks on his rifle barrel. The incessant fighting, punctuated by long, hard marches that characterized Grant's overland campaign in central Virginia, allowed little time for the amenities of life. "It is fight and run, run and fight," recalled a Federal surgeon. "Move to the left all the while—get whipped sometimes when we don't know it, and then turn in and whip the rebs the very worst way. So we go."*

## CAPTAIN ANDREW J. MCBRIDE

### 10TH GEORGIA INFANTRY, BRYAN'S BRIGADE

*Born in Fayetteville, Georgia, in 1836, McBride was a lawyer in Atlanta before being elected a captain in the 10th Georgia in 1861. He served gallantly, taking command of the regiment at Gettysburg when all the senior officers went down. Wounded slightly in the Wilderness, McBride fought on until another wound at Cold Harbor knocked him out of action for the rest of the war. He was promoted to lieutenant colonel in February 1865 while convalescing in Augusta, Georgia.*

Battle Field
May 29th 1864
The great battle is not yet over, there is only a lull—the first for twenty five days, the sullen roar of artillery even now reminds us that the last act of the bloody tragedy is yet to be enacted.—we all feel that Palida Moss is only temporarily satiated and even now hovers over the fair fields and blooming vales of Virginia ready to begin a carnival more cruel and more horrible than any he has yet held on the "dark and bloody ground" of the Old Dominion.—Aye we all feel, that yet another hecatomb of human bodies, slaughtered at the bidding of Abraham Lincoln, must rise to satiate the bloody Molock of the North. Alas! yes almost before the shriek of his wounded who perished in the flames of the burning wood in the Wilderness and at Spotsylvania have died upon our ears, almost before their blood has dried upon the earth, he is ready with an unparalleled cruelty to offer new victims—Oh what strange dreams must fill his brain in the deep "silent watches of the night"? or if perchance in the "visions of the night" the Ghosts of his murdered victims (whose charred and blackened bodies now lie scattered by thousands through the Wilderness and upon the heights of Spotsylvania) should pass in review his dream would indeed be more

terrible than the reality witnessed by Richard the third—There are many incidents of a thrilling interest which I would like to relate, but cannot now. Grant after three desperate efforts, on as many different roads has been forced to his Gunboats on the Pamunky and York rivers, he is now at a position which he could have reached without the loss of a single man, but what a fearful price has he paid for it? his loss cannot have been less than fifty thousand while ours will not greatly exceed

fifteen thousand—the great difference can be quickly and satisfactorily accounted for when it is remembered that we have fought most of the time, behind breastworks—but enough of these battles you will see better accounts of them in the papers. . . . I have been in command of the regt since the first day of the fight and have but little time to write if I can I will write to you before going into battle but I can hardly tell when that will be though it may be in a few hours.

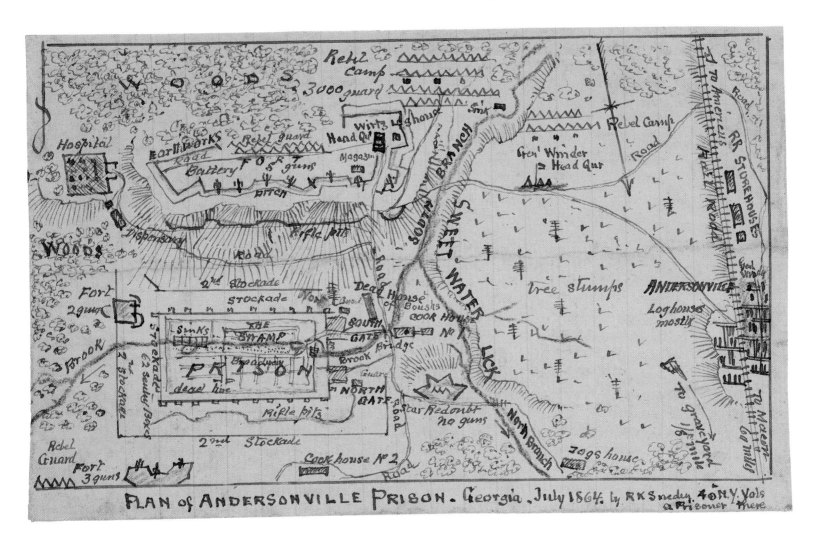

*Private Robert K. Sneden of the 40th New York Infantry drew this map of Andersonville prison in July 1864. Sneden had been detailed as a topographical draftsman when he was captured at Locust Grove, Virginia, on November 27, 1863. As one of the first prisoners sent to the new military prison at Andersonville, Sneden witnessed the influx of hundreds of prisoners of war taken in the Wilderness and at Spotsylvania. The prison, formally named Camp Sumter, was located northwest of Americus, Georgia. Overcrowding, poor sanitation, exposure, and inadequate rations led to a high mortality rate. Sneden survived the harsh conditions and was paroled in December 1864.*

# GLOSSARY

*abatis*—A defensive barrier of fallen trees with branches pointed toward the enemy.

*adjutant*—A staff officer assisting the commanding officer, usually with correspondence.

*battery*—The basic unit of artillery, consisting of four to six guns. Or an emplacement where artillery is mounted for attack or defense. A battery is generally open or lightly defended in the rear.

*bivouac*—A temporary encampment, or to camp out for the night.

*bounty*—A monetary incentive given to induce men to enlist. A bounty jumper was a soldier who took a bounty upon enlisting and then deserted.

*breastwork*—A temporary fortification, usually of earth and about chest high, over which a soldier could fire.

*brevet*—An honorary rank given for exceptional bravery or merit in time of war. It granted none of the authority or pay of the official rank.

*Bucktails*—Nickname for the 13th Pennsylvania Reserves and, later, other select Pennsylvania units. Recruits were required to bring in a deer's tail as proof of their prowess with a rifle. The men then wore the tails in their hats.

*caisson*—A cart with large chests for carrying artillery ammunition; connected to a horse-drawn limber when moved.

*canister*—A tin can containing lead or iron balls that scattered when fired from a cannon.

*cap*—Technically a percussion cap. A small, metal cover, infused with chemicals and placed on the hollow nipple of a rifle or revolver. When struck by the hammer the chemicals explode, igniting the powder charge in the breech.

*carbine*—A lightweight, short-barreled shoulder arm used especially by cavalry.

*change front*—To alter the direction troops face to deliver or defend against an attack.

*Coehorn*—A small mortar, light enough to be carried by four men.

*double-quick*—A trotting pace.

*double-shotted artillery*—Artillery charged with two projectiles rather than the normal one.

*echelon*—A staggered or stairsteplike formation of parallel units of troops.

*enfilade*—Gunfire that rakes an enemy line lengthwise, or the position allowing such firing.

*file closer*—A soldier marching in the rear of a line of battle to make sure that the formation stayed in order.

*flank*—The right or left end of a military formation. To flank is to attack or go around the enemy's position on one end or the other.

*forlorn hope*—A last-ditch, desperately difficult or dangerous assignment, or the body of soldiers given such a task.

*furlough*—A leave of absence from duty granted to a soldier.

*garrison*—A military post, especially a permanent one. Also, the act of manning such a post and the soldiers who serve there.

*grapeshot*—Iron balls (usually nine) bound together and fired from a cannon. Resembling a cluster of grapes, the balls broke apart and scattered on impact. Although references to grape or grapeshot are numerous in the literature, some experts claim that it was not used on Civil War battlefields.

*haversack*—A shoulder bag, usually strapped over the right shoulder to rest on the left hip, for carrying personal items and rations.

*howitzer*—A short-barreled artillery piece that fired its projectile in a relatively high trajectory.

*limber*—A two-wheeled, horse-drawn vehicle to which a gun carriage or a caisson was attached.

*Minié ball*—The standard bullet-shaped projectile fired from the rifled muskets of the time. Designed by French army officers Henri-Gustave Delvigne and Claude-Étienne Minié, the bullet had a hollow base that expanded, forcing its sides into the grooves, or rifling, of the musket's barrel. This caused the bullet to spiral in flight, giving it greater range and accuracy. Appears as minie, minnie, and minni.

*muster*—To assemble. To be mustered in is to be enlisted or enrolled in service. To be mustered out is to be discharged from service, usually on expiration of a set time.

*Napoleon*—A smoothbore, muzzleloading artillery piece developed under the direction of Napoleon III. It fired a 12-pound projectile (and therefore was sometimes called a 12-pounder). Napoleons were originally cast in bronze; when that material became scarce in the South, iron was used.

*oblique*—At an angle.

*orderly*—A soldier who was assigned to a superior officer for various duties, such as carrying messages.

*Palida Moss*—Misspelling of *pallida mors*, a Latin term meaning "pale death," from a saying by the Roman poet Horace: "Pale Death, with impartial step, knocks at the cottages of the poor and the palaces of kings."

*parapet*—A defensive elevation raised above a fort's main wall, or rampart.

*parole*—The pledge of a soldier released after being captured by the enemy that he would not take up arms again until he had been properly exchanged.

*picket*—One or more soldiers on guard to protect the larger unit from surprise attack.

*pioneer*—A construction engineer.

*provost guard*—A detail of soldiers acting as police under the supervision of an officer called a provost marshal.

*ration*—A specified allotment of food for one person (or animal) per day. The amounts and nature of rations varied by time and place throughout the war. *Rations* may also refer simply to any food provided by the army.

*redoubt*—An enclosed, defensive stronghold.

*rifle pit*—A hole or shallow trench dug in the ground from which soldiers could fire weapons and avoid enemy fire. Foxhole.

*salient*—Part of a fortress, line of defense, or trench system that juts out toward the enemy position.

*section of artillery*—Part of an artillery battery consisting of two guns, the soldiers who manned them, and their supporting horses and equipment.

*skirmisher*—A soldier sent in advance of the main body of troops to scout out and probe the enemy's position. Also, one who participated in a skirmish, a small fight usually incidental to the main action.

*small arms*—Any hand-held weapon, usually a firearm.

*solid shot*—A solid artillery projectile, oblong for rifled pieces and spherical for smoothbores.

*stack arms*—To set aside weapons, usually three or more in a pyramid, interlocking at the end of the barrel with the butts on the ground.

*Stars and Bars*—The first national flag of the Confederacy. It had two broad, horizontal red stripes separated by one white stripe, and a dark blue field in the canton with from seven to 13 white stars representing the states of the Confederacy.

*sutler*—A peddler with a permit to remain with troops in camp or in the field and sell food, drink, and other supplies.

*traverse*—A trench or other defensive barrier that runs obliquely to the enemy's guns to protect against enfilading fire.

*Zouaves*—Regiments, both Union and Confederate, that modeled themselves after the original Zouaves of French Colonial Algeria. Known for spectacular uniforms featuring bright colors—usually reds and blues—baggy trousers, gaiters, short and open jackets, and a turban or fez, they specialized in precision drill and loading and firing muskets from the prone position.

# ACKNOWLEDGMENTS

*The editors wish to thank the following for their valuable assistance in the preparation of this volume:*
Rickie Brunner, Alabama Department of Archives and History, Montgomery; Richard F. Carlile, Dayton; Jerry Cotten, University of North Carolina, Chapel Hill; Susan Greendike, Massachusetts State House Flag Project, Boston; Henry Groskinsky, New York; Steve Hill, Westwood, Mass.; Terri Hudgins, The Museum of the Confederacy, Richmond; Mary Ison and Staff, Library of Congress, Washington, D.C.; Maria Kirby-Smith, Camden, S.C.; Robert E. L. Krick, Richmond; Robert K. Krick, Fredericksburg, Va.; Paul Loane, Cherry Hill, N.J.; JoAnna M. McDonald, Capitol Preservation Committee, Harrisburg, Pa.; Howard Madaus, Cody, Wyo.; Sue Miller, *Civil War Times Illustrated*, Harrisburg, Pa.; Nelson Morgan, Hargrett Rare Book and Manuscript Library, University of Georgia, Athens; Roseanne O'Canas, High Impact Photography, Baltimore; Dorothy Olsen, Georgia State Capitol Museum, Atlanta; Ann Marie Price, Virginia Historical Society, Richmond; Teresa Roane, The Valentine Museum, Richmond; Paul Romaine; Gilder Lehrman Collection, New York; Larry Sherer, High Impact Photography, Baltimore; Kathy Shoemaker, Robert W. Woodruff Library, Emory University, Atlanta; Ann Sindelar, Western Reserve Historical Society, Cleveland; William Styple, Kearny, N.J.; Sandra M. Trenholm; Gilder Lehrman Collection, New York; William A. Turner, La Plata, Md.; David Wynn Vaughan, Atlanta; Frank Wood, Alexandria, Va.; Marie C. Woods, Sewanee, Tenn.; Mac Wyckoff, Fredericksburg, Va.

# PICTURE CREDITS

*The sources for the illustrations are listed below. Credits from left to right are separated by semicolons, from top to bottom by dashes.*
All calligraphy by Mary Lou O'Brian/Inkwell, Inc. Dust Jacket: Front, Massachusetts Commandery of the Military Order of the Loyal Legion and the U.S. Army Military Institute (MASS-MOLLUS/USAMHI), copied by A. Pierce Bounds; rear, The Museum of the Confederacy, Richmond. 6, 7: Map by Paul Salmon. 8: Special Collections (Orlando Poe Collection), U.S. Military Academy Library, copied by Henry Groskinsky. 11: Map by Peter McGinn. 14: *The Thomas J. Armstrong Papers, 1859–1868*, Manuscript Collection, William Madison Randall Library, University of North Carolina at Wilmington, photographed by Henry Mintz. 15: Department of Archives and Manuscripts, Auburn University, Auburn, Ala., photographed by Henry Mintz. 16: Courtesy Barry Jett, photographed by Andy Franck and Karen Jones of High Impact Photography; courtesy of Art Collection, Harvard Law School. 17: Library of Congress, neg. no. LC-B8171-7518. 18: William A. Turner Collection. 19: The Valentine

Museum, Richmond; Roger D. Hunt Collection at USAMHI, copied by A. Pierce Bounds. 20: Library of Congress, neg. no. LC-B8184-10602. 22: MASS-MOLUS/USAMHI, copied by A. Pierce Bounds. 25: Map by R. R. Donnelley & Sons Co., Cartographic Services. 26: Library of Congress, Forbes #127. 27: John W. Kuhl Collection at USAMHI, copied by A. Pierce Bounds; MASS-MOLLUS/USAMHI, copied by A. Pierce Bounds. 28: Library of Congress, Waud. #191. 29: From *Recollections of a Maryland Confederate Soldier and Staff Officer under Johnston, Jackson and Lee*, by McHenry Howard, Williams & Wilkins Co., Baltimore, 1914; Arthur Kent. 30, 31: Library of Congress, neg. no. LC-B811-702. 32: Rochester Historical Society—Library of Congress, Waud #909. 33: Civil War Library and Museum, MOLLUS, Philadelphia, copied by A. Pierce Bounds; Civil War Library and Museum, photographed by Larry Sherer, courtesy Russ Pritchard and George Juno. 34: Library of Congress, Forbes #218. 35: MASS-MOLLUS/USAMHI, copied by A. Pierce Bounds. 37: Map by William L. Hezlep. 38: Special Collections Department, Robert W. Woodruff Library, Emory University. 39: MASS-MOLLUS/USAMHI, copied by A. Pierce Bounds; Smithsonian Institution, National Museum of American History, Washington, D.C., photographed by Larry Sherer. 40: Map Division, Library of Congress, photographed by Larry Sherer. 41: MASS-MOLLUS/USAMHI, copied by A. Pierce Bounds. 42: Courtesy Paul Loane, photographed by Robert J. Laramie. 43: MASS-MOLLUS/ USAMHI, copied by A. Pierce Bounds. 44: From *One of Jackson's Foot Cavalry*, by John H. Worsham, The Neale Publishing Company, New York, 1912. 45: Maine State Archives, neg. no. 898, courtesy William B. Styple; William A. Turner Collection. 47: Roger D. Hunt Collection at USAMHI, copied by A. Pierce Bounds—The Museum of the Confederacy, Richmond, photographed by Katherine Wetzel. 48: The Valentine Museum, Richmond. 49: Robert Schell Ulrich. 50: USAMHI, copied by A. Pierce Bounds; MASS-MOLLUS/USAMHI, copied by A. Pierce Bounds. 51: Library of Congress, Forbes #213. 52: Courtesy Brian Boeue, photographed by Henry Mintz. 53: Cook Collection, The Valentine Museum, Richmond. 54: Roger D. Hunt Collection at USAMHI, copied by A. Pierce Bounds. 55: Courtesy Bob High, photographed by Henry Mintz—Homer Babcock Collection, photographed by Larry Sherer. 56: USAMHI, copied by A. Pierce Bounds; Richard K. Tibbals Collection at USAMHI, copied by A. Pierce Bounds. 57: From *With the Old Confeds: Actual Experiences of a Captain in the Line*, by Samuel D. Buck, H. E. Houck & Co., Baltimore, 1925, copied by Philip

Brandt George; William A. Turner Collection. 58: MASS-MOLLUS/USAMHI, copied by A. Pierce Bounds; Library of Congress, Waud #681. 59: Cook Collection, The Valentine Museum, Richmond; William A. Turner Collection. 61: Map by William L. Hezlep. 62: From *The Story of a Cannoneer under Stonewall Jackson*, by Edward A. Moore, The Neale Publishing Company, 1907, copied by Philip Brandt George; courtesy of Charles W. Proffit, photographed by Henry Mintz. 63: Courtesy of Thomas Panter, photographed by Henry Mintz. 64: North Carolina Museum of History, Raleigh; courtesy Theron E. Frary. 65: Library of Congress, Waud #157. 66: Texas State Library & Archives Commission. 67: The Gilder Lehrman Collection, on deposit at the Pierpont Morgan Library, photographed by Robert D. Rubic. 68: Courtesy Maria Gaillard Cortes and Mrs. Edmund Kirby-Smith III. 69: From *History of the One Hundred Fiftieth Regiment Pennsylvania Volunteers*, by Lt. Col. Thomas Chamberlin, F. McManus, Jr. & Co., Printers, Philadelphia, 1905; Alex Chamberlain Collection at USAMHI, copied by A. Pierce Bounds. 70: The Museum of the Confederacy, Richmond—Library of Congress, Waud #467a; courtesy Historical Times, Inc. 72: Courtesy Commonwealth of Massachusetts, photographed by Douglas Christian; Richard F. Carlile Collection. 73: From: *From Manassas to Appomattox: Memoirs of the Civil War in America*, by James Longstreet, J. B. Lippincott Co., Philadelphia, 1896. 74, 75: Confederate Museum, Charleston, South Carolina, photographed by Harold H. Norvell—courtesy Lewis Leigh, Jr., Leesburg, Va., photographed by Larry Sherer; MASS-MOLLUS/USAMHI, copied by A. Pierce Bounds. 76: Dr. Francis A. Lord Collection at USAMHI, copied by A. Pierce Bounds; Dr. K. Dietrick Collection at USAMHI, copied by A. Pierce Bounds. 77: Library of Congress, Waud #535. 78: Library of Congress, Waud #656. 79: Courtesy Paul Loane, photographed by Robert J. Laramie. 80: Library of Congress, Waud #695. 81: MASS-MOLLUS/ USAMHI, copied by A. Pierce Bounds; Albion Historical Society Collection at USAMHI, copied by A. Pierce Bounds. 82: Scott Hann Collection at USAMHI, copied by A. Pierce Bounds—New York Division of Military and Naval Affairs, Albany, photographed by Randall Perry (2). 83: Roger D. Hunt Collection at USAMHI, copied by A. Pierce Bounds. 84: MASS-MOLLUS/USAMHI, copied by A. Pierce Bounds. 87: Map by R. R. Donnelley & Sons Co., Cartographic Services. 88, 89: Library of Congress, Forbes #210. 90: Courtesy Kirk Denkler, copied by Evan H. Sheppard; The Valentine Museum, Richmond. 91: MASS-MOLLUS/ USAMHI, copied by A. Pierce Bounds. 92: Library of Congress, Forbes #180. 93: *Confed-*

*erate Veteran*, vol. 22 (June 1914); Cook Collection, The Valentine Museum, Richmond. 94: USAMHI, copied by A. Pierce Bounds; Cook Collection, The Valentine Museum, Richmond. 95: Library of Congress, Waud #403. 96: Gil Barrett Collection at USAMHI, copied by A. Pierce Bounds. 97: MASS-MOLLUS/USAMHI, photographed by A. Pierce Bounds; Roger D. Hunt Collection at USAMHI, copied by A. Pierce Bounds. 98: MASS-MOLLUS/USAMHI, photographed by A. Pierce Bounds; painting by Julian Scott, Drake House Museum/Plainfield Historical Society, photographed by Henry Groskinsky. 99: Courtesy Paul Loane, photographed by Robert J. Laramie. 100: Library of Congress, Forbes #217. 101: The Gilder Lehrman Collection, on deposit at the Pierpont Morgan Library, photographed by Robert D. Rubic. 103: Map by Walter W. Roberts. 104: Courtesy Thelma Haley Collection, from *The Rebel Yell & the Yankee Hurrah: The Civil War Journal of a Maine Volunteer*, edited by Ruth L. Silliker, Down East Books, Camden, 1985. 105: The Cincinnati Historical Society. 106: Courtesy Paul Loane, photographed by Robert J. Laramie. 107: David Wynn Vaughan. 108: Map Division, Library of Congress, photographed by Larry Sherer. 109: From *History of the 121st New York State Infantry*, by Isaac O. Best, published by Lieut. Jas. H. Smith, Chicago, 1921, copied by Philip Brandt George. 110: USAMHI, copied by A. Pierce Bounds. 111: Library of Congress, Waud #752—Mike Dove. 112: Civil War Library and Museum, MOLLUS, Philadelphia. 114: Library of Congress, Forbes #212. 115: The Museum of the Confederacy, Richmond. 117: Map by Walter W. Roberts. 118: Jane Fulcher Collection at USAMHI, copied by A. Pierce Bounds. 119: Library of Congress, neg. no. LC-B8184-5037. 120: Robert Diem Collection at USAMHI, copied by A. Pierce Bounds. 121: The Museum of the Confederacy, Richmond, photographed by Katherine Wetzel. 122: Painting by Thure de Thulstrup, Seventh Regiment Fund, Inc., New York. 123: Roger D. Hunt Collection at USAMHI, copied by A. Pierce Bounds. 124: Courtesy Paul Loane, photographed by Robert J. Laramie. 125: MASS-MOLLUS/USAMHI, copied by A. Pierce Bounds. 126: North Carolina Museum of History, Raleigh. 127: Joseph C. Knox, Jr. & Brooks Preik, Wilmington, N.C., copied by Henry Mintz—*Confederate Veteran*, vol. 22 (1914). 128: Library of Congress, Waud #713. 129: William A. Turner Collection. 130: Erick Davis Collection, copied by Jeremy Ross; The Museum of the Confederacy, Richmond; Frank & Marie-Thérèse Wood Print Collections, Alexandria, Va. 131: Erick F. Davis; Michael J. McAfee Collection. 132: MASS-MOLLUS/ USAMHI, copied by A. Pierce

# BIBLIOGRAPHY

## BOOKS

Abbott, Henry Livermore. *Fallen Leaves: The Civil War Letters of Major Henry Livermore Abbott.* Ed. by Robert Garth Scott. Kent, Ohio: Kent State University Press, 1991.

Abbott, Lemuel Abijah. *Personal Recollections and Civil War Diary, 1864.* Burlington, Vt.: Free Press Printing, 1908.

Alexander, Edward Porter. *Fighting for the Confederacy: The Personal Recollections of General Edward Porter Alexander.* Ed. by Gary W. Gallagher. Chapel Hill: University of North Carolina Press, 1989.

Best, Isaac O. *History of the 121st New York State Infantry.* Chicago: Jas. H. Smith, 1921.

Bicknell, George W. *History of the Fifth Regiment Maine Volunteers.* Portland, Maine: Hall L. Davis, 1871.

Black, John D. "Reminiscences of the Bloody Angle." In *Glimpses of the Nation's Struggle: Papers Read before the Minnesota Commandery of the Military Order of the Loyal Legion of the United States, 1892-1897,* Vol. 4. Wilmington, N.C.: Broadfoot, 1992 (reprint of 1898 edition).

Brockway, Charles B. "Across the Rapidan, 1864: Hard Fighting in the Wilderness." In *Campfire Sketches and Battlefield Echoes.* Comp. by W. C. King and W. P. Derby. Springfield, Mass.: King, Richardson, 1889.

Buck, Samuel D. *With the Old Confeds: Actual Experiences of a Captain in the Line.* Baltimore: H. E. Houck, 1925.

Caldwell, J. F. J. *The History of a Brigade of South Carolinians.* Dayton: Morningside Bookshop, 1984 (reprint of 1866 edition).

Casler, John O. *Four Years in the Stonewall Brigade.* Dayton: Press of Morningside Bookshop, 1982.

Chamberlin, Thomas. *History of the One Hundred and*

*Fiftieth Regiment, Pennsylvania Volunteers, Second Regiment, Bucktail Brigade.* Philadelphia: F. McManus, Jr., 1905.

Cogswell, Leander W. *A History of the Eleventh New Hampshire Regiment Volunteer Infantry in the Rebellion War, 1861-1865.* Concord, N.H.: Republican Press Association, 1891.

Coward, Asbury. *The South Carolinians: Colonel Asbury Coward's Memoirs.* Ed. and comp. by Natalie Jenkins Bond and Osmun Latrobe Coward. New York: Vantage Press, 1968.

Cudworth, Warren H. *History of the First Regiment: Massachusetts Infantry.* Boston: Walker, Fuller, 1866.

Dame, William Meade. *From the Rapidan to Richmond and the Spottsylvania Campaign.* Baltimore: Green-Lucas, 1920.

Dawson, Francis W. *Reminiscences of Confederate Service: 1861-1865.* Ed. by Bell I. Wiley. Baton Rouge: Louisiana State University Press, 1980.

Dickert, D. Augustus. *History of Kershaw's Brigade.* Wilmington, N.C.: Broadfoot, 1990 (reprint of 1899 edition).

Galloway, G. Norton. "Hand-to-Hand Fighting at Spotsylvania." In *Battles and Leaders of the Civil War,* Vol. 4. Ed. by Robert Underwood Johnson and Clarence Clough Buel. New York: Thomas Yoseloff, 1956.

Galwey, Thomas Francis. *The Valiant Hours: Narrative of "Captain Brevet," an Irish-American in the Army of the Potomac.* Ed. by W. S. Nye. Harrisburg, Pa.: Stackpole, 1961.

Gordon, John B. *Reminiscences of the Civil War.* New York: Charles Scribners Sons, 1904.

Haines, William P. *History of the Men of Co. F: With*

*Description of the Marches and Battles of the 12th New Jersey Vols.* Mickleton, N.J.: n.p., 1897.

Haley, John West. *The Rebel Yell & the Yankee Hurrah: The Civil War Journal of a Maine Volunteer.* Ed. by Ruth Silliker. Camden, Maine: Down East Books, 1985.

Heth, Henry. *The Memoirs of Henry Heth.* Ed. by James L. Morrison, Jr. Westport, Conn.: Greenwood Press, 1974.

Howard, McHenry. *Recollections of a Maryland Confederate Soldier and Staff Officer under Johnston, Jackson and Lee.* Dayton: Press of Morningside Bookshop, 1975.

Hunter, Alexander. *Johnny Reb and Billy Yank.* New York: Neale, 1905.

Hyde, Thomas W. *Following the Greek Cross: Or, Memories of the Sixth Army Corps.* Boston: Houghton, Mifflin, 1894.

Lyman, Theodore. *Meade's Headquarters 1863-1865: Letters of Colonel Theodore Lyman, from the Wilderness to Appomattox.* Ed. by George R. Agassiz. Boston: Atlantic Monthly Press, 1922.

McAllister, Robert. *The Civil War Letters of General Robert McAllister.* Ed. by James I. Robertson, Jr. New Brunswick, N.J.: Rutgers University Press, 1965.

McMahon, Martin T. "The Death of General John Sedgwick." In *Battles and Leaders of the Civil War,* Vol. 3. Ed. by Robert Underwood Johnson and Clarence Clough Buel. New York: Thomas Yoseloff, 1956.

Melcher, Holman S. "An Experience in the Battle of the Wilderness." In *War Papers: Read before the Commandery of the State of Maine, Military Order of the Loyal Legion of the United States,* Vol. 1. Wilmington, N.C.: Broadfoot, 1992 (reprint of 1898 edition).

Mixson, Frank M. *Reminiscences of a Private.* Columbia, S.C.: State, 1910.

Mulholland, St. Clair A. *The Story of the 116th Regiment, Pennsylvania Infantry.* Philadelphia: F. McManus, Jr., 1899.

Page, Charles D. *History of the Fourteenth Regiment, Connecticut Vol. Infantry.* Meriden, Conn.: Horton Printing, 1906.

Peirson, Charles Lawrence. "The Operations of the Army of the Potomac, May 7-11, 1864." In *Papers of the Military Historical Society of Massachusetts,* Vol. 4. Wilmington, N.C.: Broadfoot, 1989.

Porter, Horace. *Campaigning with Grant.* New York: Century, 1897.

Prentice, Sartell. "The Opening Hours in the Wilderness in 1864." In *Military Essays and Recollections: Papers Read before the Commandery of the State of Illinois, Military Order of the Loyal Legion of the United States.* Vol. 2. Wilmington, N.C.: Broadfoot, 1992 (reprint of 1894 edition).

Pyne, Henry R. *The History of the First New Jersey Cavalry.* Trenton: J. A. Beecher, 1871.

Rhea, Gordon C.:
*The Battle of the Wilderness: May 5-6, 1864.* Baton Rouge: Louisiana State University Press, 1994.
*The Battles for Spotsylvania Court House and the Road to Yellow Tavern: May 7-12, 1864.* Baton Rouge: Louisiana State University Press, 1997.

Seymour, William J. *The Civil War Memoirs of Captain William J. Seymour: Reminiscences of a Louisiana Tiger.* Ed. by Terry L. Jones. Baton Rouge: Louisiana State University Press, 1991.

Small, Abner R. *The Road to Richmond: The Civil War Memoirs of Major Abner R. Small of the Sixteenth Maine Volunteers.* Ed. by Harold Adams Small. Berkeley: University of California Press, 1939.

Smith, William W. "Account of Dr. William W. Smith." In *Southern Historical Society Papers,* Vol. 32. Ed. by R. A. Brock. Wilmington, N.C.: Broadfoot, 1991 (reprint of 1904 edition).

Sorrel, G. Moxley. *Recollections of a Confederate Staff Officer.* Dayton: Morningside Bookshop, 1978.

Stearns, Austin C. *Three Years with Company K.* Ed. by Arthur A. Kent. Rutherford, N.J.: Fairleigh Dickinson University Press, 1976.

Stevens, C. A. *Berdan's United States Sharpshooter in the Army of the Potomac: 1861-1865.* Dayton: Press of Morningside Bookshop, 1984.

Todd, William. *Seventy-Ninth Highlanders: New York Volunteers in the War of Rebellion, 1861-1865.* Albany, N.Y.: Press of Brandow, Barton, 1886.

Toney, Marcus B. *The Privations of a Private.* Nashville: Private printing, 1905.

Weygant, Charles H. *History of the One Hundred and Twenty-Fourth Regiment, N. Y. S. V.* Newburgh, N.Y.: Journal Printing House, 1877.

White, William S. *Contributions to a History of the Richmond Howitzer Battalion.* Richmond: Carlton McCarthy, 1883.

Wilkeson, Frank. *Recollections of a Private Soldier in the Army of the Potomac.* Freeport, N.Y.: Books for Libraries Press, 1887.

Worsham, John H. *One of Jackson's Foot Cavalry.* Ed. by James I. Robertson, Jr. Jackson, Tenn.: McCowat-Mercer Press, 1964.

Yeary, Mamie, comp. *Reminiscences of the Boys in Gray: 1861-1865.* Dayton: Morningside, 1986.

## PERIODICALS

Acheson, Alex W. "At Spottsylvania Court House." *Philadelphia Weekly Press,* Oct. 27, 1886.

Bradwell, Isaac G. "Second Day's Battle of the Wilderness, May 6, 1864." *Confederate Veteran,* January 1920, Vol. 28.

Campbell, Robert. "Texans Always Move Them." *The Land We Love,* October 1868, Vol. 5.

Coxe, John. "Last Struggles and Successes of Lee." *Confederate Veteran,* June 1914, Vol. 22.

Farley, Porter. "Reminiscences of the 140th New York Volunteer Infantry: Wilderness, May 5th, 1864." *Rochester Historical Society Publication,* 1944, Vol. 22.

House, Charles J. "How the First Maine Heavy Artillery Lost 1,179 Men in 30 Days." *Maine Bugle,* April 1895.

McCown, James L. "Memoirs of James L. McCown: Company K, 5th Virginia Infantry, Stonewall Brigade, April 2, 1864-August 4, 1864." *Rockbridge County* News (Lexington, Va.), Feb. 12-19, 1953.

Wynn, B. L. "Lee Watched Grant at Locust Grove." *Confederate Veteran,* February 1913, Vol. 21.

## OTHER SOURCES

Armstrong, Edward H. Letter, April 8, 1864. Thomas Armstrong Papers. Wilmington, N.C.: University of North Carolina, William Madison Randall Library, Manuscript Collection.

Bucknam, George. Memoirs. Carlisle Barracks, Pa.: U.S. Army Military History Institute.

Justice, Benjamin W. Letter, May 4, 9, 1864. Benjamin Wesley Justice Papers. Atlanta: Emory University.

Kent, William C. Letter, May 4, 1894, Memoirs. *Civil War Times Illustrated* Collection. Carlisle Barracks, Pa.: U.S. Army Military History Institute.

Linebarger, T. James. Diary, papers. Anne Linebarger Snuggs Papers. Chapel Hill: University of North Carolina, Southern Historical Collection.

McBride, Andrew J. Letter, May 29, 1864. Andrew J. McBride Papers. Durham, N.C.: Duke University.

McGill, J. W. Report, Sept. 9, 1864. James H. Lane Papers. Auburn, Ala.: Auburn University, Department of Archives.

Phillips, James E. Unpublished memoirs. James Eldred Phillips Papers. Richmond: Virginia Historical Society.

Scott, Alfred L. "The Scott Boys of Belair in the Civil War." Unpublished memoirs. Richmond: Virginia Historical Society.

Stamp, J. B. "Ten Months Experience in Northern Prisons." Unpublished manuscript. Auburn, Ala.: Auburn University, Department of Archives.

Venable, Charles S. Letter, May 11, 1864. Charles S. Venable Papers. Chapel Hill: University of North Carolina, Southern Historical Collection.

# INDEX

*Numerals in italics indicate an illustration of the subject mentioned.*

TIME® Time-Life Books is a
division of Time Life Inc.

**TIME LIFE INC.**
PRESIDENT and CEO: George Artandi

**TIME-LIFE BOOKS**
PRESIDENT: Stephen R. Frary
PUBLISHER/MANAGING EDITOR: Neil Kagan

**VOICES OF THE CIVIL WAR**

DIRECTOR OF MARKETING: Pamela R. Farrell

# THE WILDERNESS

EDITOR: Paul Mathless
*Deputy Editors:* Kirk Denkler (principal), Harris J. Andrews,
Philip Brandt George
*Art Director:* Ellen L. Pattisall
*Associate Editor/Research and Writing:* Annette Scarpitta
*Senior Copyeditors:* Judith Klein, Mary Beth Oelkers-Keegan
*Picture Coordinator:* Daryl Beard
*Editorial Assistant:* Christine Higgins

*Initial Series Design:* Studio A

*Special Contributors:* Brian C. Pohanka, Gordon C. Rhea,
Henry Woodhead (text); Connie Contreras, Charles F.
Cooney, Robert Lee Hodge, Susan V. Kelly, Beth Levin,
Henry Mintz, Dana B. Shoaf (research); Janet Dell Russell
Johnson (design and production), Roy Nanovic (index).

*Correspondent:* Christina Lieberman (New York).

*Director of Finance:* Christopher Hearing
*Directors of Book Production:* Marjann Caldwell,
Patricia Pascale
*Director of Publishing Technology:* Betsi McGrath
*Director of Photography and Research:* John Conrad Weiser
*Director of Editorial Administration:* Barbara Levitt
*Production Manager:* Marlene Zack
*Quality Assurance Manager:* James King
*Chief Librarian:* Louise D. Forstall

*Consultants*

J. Tracy Power is a historian at the South Carolina Department of Archives and History and the author of *Lee's Miser-
ables: Life in the Army of Northern Virginia from the Wilderness
to Appomattox.* His other publications include articles in *Civil
War History* and *Civil War Times Illustrated* and contributions
to the *Encyclopedia of the Confederacy.*

Gordon C. Rhea is the author of the award-winning books
*The Battle of the Wilderness, May 5-6, 1864,* and *The Battles for
Spotsylvania Court House and the Road to Yellow Tavern, May
7-12, 1864.* He regularly conducts battlefield tours and is a frequent speaker at Civil War symposia. Mr. Rhea is currently
completing a volume that will follow Lee and Grant to the
North Anna River.

First printing. Printed in U.S.A.
School and library distribution by Time-Life Education,
P.O. Box 85026, Richmond, Virginia 23285-5026.

TIME-LIFE is a trademark of Time Warner Inc. U.S.A.

Library of Congress Cataloging-in-Publication Data
The Wilderness / by the editors of Time-Life Books.
    p.  cm.—(Voices of the Civil War)
    Includes bibliographical references and index.
    ISBN 0-7835-4718-8
    1. Wilderness, Battles of the, Va., 1864.
    I. Time-Life Books. II. Series.
E476.52.W53  1998
973.7'36—dc21                                    98-13298
                                                      CIP

OTHER PUBLICATIONS:

HISTORY
*The Civil War*
*The American Indians*
*What Life Was Like*
*Lost Civilizations*
*The American Story*
*Mysteries of the Unknown*
*Time Frame*
*Cultural Atlas*

SCIENCE/NATURE
*Voyage Through the Universe*

DO IT YOURSELF
*The Time-Life Complete Gardener*
*Home Repair and Improvement*
*The Art of Woodworking*
*Fix It Yourself*

TIME-LIFE KIDS
*Library of First Questions and Answers*
*A Child's First Library of Learning*
*I Love Math*
*Nature Company Discoveries*
*Understanding Science & Nature*

COOKING
*Weight Watchers® Smart Choice Recipe Collection*
*Great Taste~Low Fat*
*Williams-Sonoma Kitchen Library*

For information on and a full description of any of the Time-
Life Books series listed above, please call 1-800-621-7026
or write:

Reader Information
Time-Life Customer Service
P.O. Box C-32068
Richmond, Virginia 23261-2068